MRS. CHIANG'S SZECHWAN COOKBOOK

MRS. CHIANG'S SZECHWAN COOKBOOK

ELLEN SCHRECKER

WITH JOHN SCHRECKER

HARPER & ROW, PUBLISHERS
NEW YORK
HAGERSTOWN
SAN FRANCISCO
LONDON

Designed by Dorothy Schmiderer

Drawings by Noel Malsberg

Library of Congress Cataloging in Publication Data

Chiang, Jung-feng.
  Mrs. Chiang's Szechwan cookbook.
  Includes index.
  1. Cookery, Chinese.   I. Schrecker, Ellen, joint
author.   II. Schrecker, John, joint author.   III. Title.   IV. Title:
Szechwan cookbook.
TX724.5.C5C554   641.5′951′38   74–1854
ISBN 0–06–013803–2

81 82 83 10 9 8 7 6 5

To our children

CONTENTS

ILLUSTRATIONS

ACKNOWLEDGMENTS

A cookbook is a collaborative venture, this one more than most. For, in addition to the usual type of advice and support, our friends and colleagues also tested our recipes for us. We could not have written this cookbook without either their criticism or their encouragement. Among those who helped us in this way were Carla Berg, Karen Brazell, Anne Thompson Lee, Anna Laura Rosow, Judy and Norman Stein, and Carol Thompson. We would particularly like to thank Kate and Wally Gilbert and Mary Wolf. They were our main testers, and their discriminating observations and comments have become an integral part of this book.

We would also like to thank Chuan Ju-hsiang, Betty Anne Clarke, Teruko Craig, Betsy Groban, Anita Gross, Signe Hammer, Jiang Tsoy-guay, Diana Kennedy, Fran McCullough, Alan Lelchuk, Andrew Nathan, Jonathan and Naomi Rubinstein, Eugene Wu, and Silas Wu. But, above all, we want to acknowledge the assistance of John Schrecker. He was our translator, goad, and guide. And, in many ways, this is his cookbook as much as ours.

A NOTE ON ROMANIZATION

Chinese is written in characters, not letters, and contains some sounds that are not used by English speakers. There is no perfect system for rendering Chinese words into phonetically accurate English. In this cookbook we have used the Pinyin system of romanization rather than the more common Wade-Giles one. Pinyin is the system that is presently used in the People's Republic of China, and it is somewhat better than the Wade-Giles, which forces you to pronounce *p* as *b* and *k* as *g*.

The values of the letters that differ from English are as follows:
a as the a in squash
ai as the ie in pie
ao as the ow in cow
e as the u in duck
i as the ea in pea
o as the o in coffee, but o in ong as the u in pudding
ou as the ough in dough
u as the oo in food
c as the ts in catsup
ch as it is in English
q as the ch in cheese
x as the sh in sherry
z as the dz in adze
zh as the j in jam

Actually, we haven't written every Chinese word in Pinyin. Proper names, in particular, have often been left in the old-fashioned romanization, simply because they will be more recognizable to American readers. Szechwan is, thus, Szechwan, not SiChuan. Similarly, Mrs. Chiang's name could have been rendered with greater accuracy as Jiang; we chose the Wade-Giles spelling in order to make it seem more obviously Chinese.

PREFACE

I met Chiang Jung-feng in 1969 in Taipei, in Taiwan, where my husband John and I had gone to pursue John's Chinese language studies and our love of Chinese food. She began as our cook and housekeeper; she soon became a friend and teacher and eventually co-author of this cookbook. Jung-feng was born and raised on a farm on the outskirts of Chengtu, the culinary heart of the province of Szechwan. The family was large and the land was rich; they grew or raised almost all their food and they ate well. Rice, wheat, vegetables in a variety unknown in America, pork, chicken, ducks, geese, pigeons, fresh-water fish and crayfish were the raw ingredients of an extraordinarily rich and varied peasant diet.

Mrs. Chiang's mother was a superb cook and her father a demanding connoisseur. As a girl in prerevolutionary China, Mrs. Chiang knew her relations with a future mother-in-law would largely depend on her ability as a cook, so she applied herself to learning with a singlemindedness no American girl of today would match. She married a soldier, with whom she traveled to Shanghai and then to Taiwan where, in the cosmopolitan city of Taipei, she began to experiment with new recipes and new ingredients. By the time we met her she had a repertoire of hundreds of magnificent dishes. She loved to cook and, like most people from Szechwan, loved to eat; Szechwanese are known in other provinces as *haochigui*, "good-eating devils."

We wanted Chiang Jung-feng to come back to America with us. I was finishing my Ph.D. and looking for a job, and we needed someone to look after the children as well as to cook. We all had doubts about whether Szechwan home cooking could be successfully transplanted to America: could the right ingredients be found? Mrs. Chiang was used to cooking over an open fire; could our American kitchen be adapted to her methods? But she was eager to come, and everyone's worries disappeared the moment she entered our kitchen. The ingredients were available, the kitchen was adequate, and soon all our favorite Szechwanese dishes miraculously appeared on our dinner table.

Exhilarated by her success, Mrs. Chiang devoted more and more time to cooking, re-creating the culinary delights of Szechwan in the middle of New Jersey. We were euphoric. My husband spent hours with her discussing food and planning elaborate menus, while I took to following her around the kitchen with a little blue notebook. Our friends began pestering us for recipes. Soon Mrs. Chiang and I began to think about compiling a cookbook, and this volume is the result. The recipes are hers, the writing is mine. My husband acted as translator and collaborator.

Our personal journey to a love of Chinese food is a story in itself, an odyssey that took us from the Cantonese restaurants of Philadelphia to a knowledge of what we came to call the *zhen wer*, the true taste of Chinese cooking. My husband majored in East Asian studies at the University of Pennsylvania, where he haunted the local Chinese restaurants. He could read Chinese and courted me in Chinese restaurants, where he would order dishes I had never heard of. He soon taught me all he knew; by the standards of Cantonese restaurant cooking in 1961, we were experts in Chinese food.

Then we went to Taiwan, where John was to take advanced language training. Our illusions quickly disappeared; we had not begun to experience real Chinese food. Its tastes and textures were always vivid, clear and bright; American Chinese food by contrast was muddy, bland and crude. Instead of smothering everything with a thick concoction heavily laden with cornstarch and monosodium glutamate, the chefs of Taipei usually relied on the cooking process itself to produce delicate, unobtrusive sauces.

Most of the dishes we ate in Taipei were not even available in America. We knew that regional cooking in China is highly individualized, but we had no idea what this meant until we went to Taiwan—the perfect place to sample the cuisines of China, since its people come from every province in China. The regional cooking of China is as varied as the national cooking of Europe. On Taiwan we discovered elaborate dishes like Hunanese ham with honey sauce and squab dumplings in broth, and experienced the delight of oily scallion cakes bought from street vendors. There were formal banquets, where exquisite *haute cuisine* with its ritualized presentation was set off by boisterous drinking games. There were hundreds of tiny shops and food stalls, each with its special type of dumpling, so tempting we often paused for a snack. In every restaurant we found waiters eager to discuss the menu and analyze the merits of a dish. In China, as in France, fine food is a serious concern to everyone from street vendors to first-class chefs, and virtually every citizen is a gourmet.

We had expert assistance in our explorations. Mr. Liang, one of John's language teachers, organized spectacular feasts at the best restaurants in Taipei. Our first housekeeper, Su-feng, came from Szechwan. She was an expert at the highly spiced yet subtle cuisine of her province, long considered one of the glories of China. As my spoken Chinese improved, I took to hanging around the kitchen before dinner, discussing the art of cooking and copying down her methods. I also attended a cooking school, and on Su-feng's day off I cooked what I had been taught.

When we came back from that first glorious year on Taiwan, our worst doubts about American Chinese restaurants were confirmed. They were not preparing real Chinese food. They were cavalier about altering recipes; we were now knowledgeable enough to be shocked when they served the famous Szechwan chicken with hot peppers and peanuts made with snow peas and cashews, or a simple Pekingese dish of lamb and scallions similarly touched up with snow peas and smothered in a thick brown sauce. In frustration, we spent hours reminiscing with friends who had been to East Asia, analyzing how the "true taste," or *zhen wer*, differed from what we were getting, and why it was not being produced.

I took to the kitchen and found I could turn out a few authentic dishes using only what was available at the local Chinese grocery and the supermarket. When our small circle of experienced China hands declared that I had indeed reproduced the *zhen wer*, we decided that restaurants had simply grown careless.

In 1969 John got an academic leave and we were finally able to return to Taipei. Thanks to Su-feng we were in love with Szechwan home cooking. The kitchen gods must have been with us, for we had the good fortune to find Mrs. Chiang; this book is the result of that happy chance. She brought to our collaboration her thorough mastery of Chinese cooking; we brought our long interest in Chinese food and our kitchen. The result is that Mrs. Chiang's recipes have all been tested in an American kitchen, using locally available ingredients. This is neither a translation of a Chinese cookbook nor an adaptation of Chinese cooking for American tastes. We have undertaken to provide recipes that will allow the American cook to produce the *zhen wer*, the true taste of Chinese food.

This does not mean the recipes are difficult; on the contrary, most are easy to follow once a few basic techniques have been mastered. What it does mean is that we have followed certain basic principles we think are essential.

First, we decided to limit the book to Szechwan cooking. Because each major provincial cooking style is highly individualized, the best way to learn the techniques, tastes and, most important, the spirit of Chinese cuisine is to approach it on a regional basis. Mrs. Chiang's background, the excellence of Szechwanese food and its increasing popularity in America made our choice obvious.

We eliminated any dish that can't be made properly in America. This is primarily a question of ingredients. The basic ingredients of a surprising number of dishes can be found in the supermarket. Chinese spices and pastes, most of which are either dried or in cans, can be found in Chinese grocery stores or ordered by mail. As the recipes show, substitution of an American for a Chinese ingredient is sometimes possible; more often an ingredient can be omitted if it can't be found. But in the end there are some dishes that simply cannot be made here. Bamboo shoots, for instance, are an important part of some dishes, both for texture and flavor. But fresh bamboo shoots can't be found in America and those in cans are flaccid and have a strong metallic taste. Mrs. Chiang feels there is no point in attempting a dish in which bamboo shoots are a crucial ingredient, because it is impossible to achieve the *zhen wer* with canned ones.

With some exceptions, we have restricted the recipes to everyday dishes rather than *haute cuisine*, which is difficult to prepare and frequently uses ingredients that are exotic even in China. Chinese home cooks themselves seldom attempt it, and it is almost impossible to reproduce in an American kitchen. This does not mean we have left out the "best" recipes. In China everyday cooking and *haute cuisine* are equally celebrated. *Haute cuisine* is banquet food, reserved for weddings and formal occasions. It is not ordinarily offered even in the "best" restaurants.

Good cooking depends on the right preparation. To help the American cook avoid the errors that commonly distort Chinese food in this country, we have provided the information we think will help in the exploration of an unfamiliar cooking territory. An introductory essay discusses the nature of Chinese cuisine, describing the various regional cuisines in terms of both banquet and everyday cooking. There is a section on ingredients and a list of stores where they can be bought or ordered. There are sections on kitchen equipment, cooking methods and menu planning. Read these sections carefully before you begin cooking; a knowledge of menu planning, for instance, will help you avoid the common mistake of including too many hot dishes in one meal. Finally, in each recipe we have tried to show what makes that particular dish distinctive and exactly what problems may be encountered in cooking it.

The recipes are limited in number, but they include a wide and representative sampling of different types of dishes and tastes. Our goal is to allow the American cook to learn about and re-create the true taste of Chinese food. With care, attention to detail and practice it can be done. The *zhen wer* will not disappoint you.

ELLEN SCHRECKER

PART I
THE FOOD
OF CHINA

1 - THE SPIRIT OF CHINESE CUISINE

An appreciation of Szechwan home cooking demands some understanding of the overall spirit of Chinese cooking. China has one of the two great cuisines of the world; France, of course, has the other. Debate over which is better is pointless, since the two cuisines are incomparable. There is no Chinese counterpart to the wines and cheeses of France, nor are there any French equivalents for China's savory pastries and stir-fried dishes. Yet the conditions that led to the development of sophisticated gastronomic traditions in the two countries are remarkably similar. Both nations enjoy the rich, varied agriculture and long coastline needed to supply a wide range of raw ingredients; historically both have also had the cultivated leisure class necessary to exploit these resources. In each country, chefs and connoisseurs alike were willing to innovate, to invent new dishes and incorporate new foods into the cuisine. But what ultimately distinguishes a cuisine is the quality of everyday food, and in both France and China popular concern for good food runs deep. A truffled galantine of pheasant or a whole chicken stuffed with bird's nest is a gastronomic wonder, but it is the constant availability of, say, an excellent pâté in the French countryside or a spicy dish of Szechwanese noodles in a small market town that sustains a tradition of fine food.

The history of Chinese cooking is a mystery that remains largely unstudied. The best English book on the subject, Hsiang Ju and Tsuifeng Lin's *Chinese Gastronomy*, describes the food brilliantly but says little about its history. Even Mrs. Chiang doesn't know why the people of Szechwan eat hot peppers. Still, certain things are clear. Confucian China's rational, this-worldly outlook on life provided a social climate in which a great cuisine could develop. Food was a source of pleasure as well as a necessity, and its proper preparation was a matter of concern. Confucius taught that cooking, like all other human affairs, had to follow established principles: "The rice could never be white enough and the minced meat could never be chopped finely enough. When it was not cooked right, he would not eat."*

Everyone in China, from peasant to gentleman scholar, was and is a gourmet. Mrs. Chiang's family talked constantly about food, and her fondest memories of childhood involve food. The Chinese understand that good cooking is an art that can be practiced by people at all levels of society; the elemental good taste that is basic to a true appreciation of fine food manifests itself as strongly in a peasant household as at a court banquet. In China, only an ignorant snob would deny that a cheap bowl of noodles or plate of dumplings could taste as good in its own way as an expensive dish of bird's nests.

If this is surprising, it helps to remember that for centuries Chinese peasants were more prosperous than their Western counterparts. The endemic famine and poverty we associate with prerevolutionary China were a recent phenomenon, the product of political dislocations and a rising population, so the reestablishment of a decent standard of living since the revolution is in some ways testimony to the basic Chinese tradition.

Szechwan is a special province of gourmets; isolated deep in the heart of China, it is a prosperous province whose rich agriculture was undisturbed by the political upheavals of the coast. As a girl, Mrs. Chiang heard about floods and famines elsewhere in China, but they

* Hsiang Ju Lin and Tsuifeng Lin, *Chinese Gastronomy* (Hastings House, New York, 1969, p. 35).

never disturbed her family's placid life in the fertile countryside outside of Chengtu.

"Our life revolved around my mother's kitchen," she recalls. "She cooked all our meals on a big, wood-burning brick stove that practically filled the kitchen. My brothers and sisters and I would run in and snatch a piece of fruit or a bit of salted vegetable to eat on the way to school. We spent rainy days around the stove, making lollipops or frying glutinous rice until it popped like popcorn.

"By the time I was ten, I was allowed to help my mother in the kitchen. I loved it. I washed pots, chopped vegetables, and kept the fire going. Sometimes when my mother was very busy I got to cook a dish. But mainly I watched, listened, and learned. There was a lot to learn. My mother made nearly everything we ate, including condiments. I learned to make soy sauce and bean curd, hot pepper paste and wine."

Mrs. Chiang's mother spent nearly all day in the kitchen because she cared so much about good cooking. She was a great natural cook; even rice was cooked with finesse. When she made it for company, she parboiled it and then steamed it gently over a pot of vegetables, infusing each with the essence of the other:

"Even when there was no company she cooked with great care. My father was very demanding. If he didn't like the dinner, he would stomp out of the house and go to a restaurant. My mother had to cook well."

Not only did Mrs. Chiang's mother cook well; she taught her daughter the recipes that provide the bulk of this cookbook. Even more important, she transmitted her deep understanding of food and her respect for its natural qualities. Mrs. Chiang has an amazingly sensitive palate. She can taste a dish at a restaurant, analyze its ingredients, describe how it was cooked, and say what should be done to improve it. Such refinement can only come from years of eating, cooking, and talking about good food.

For an American to appreciate Chinese food with even a fraction of Mrs. Chiang's sophistication requires an understanding of some of the fundamental principles of Chinese gastronomy. The ordinary American cooking vocabulary is not adequate to convey the spirit of Chinese cuisine; to discuss Chinese food in American terms reveals only its most superficial elements—its cooking methods and its condiments. It does not convey the spirit of the cuisine or explain what it is that China's cooks and gourmets are mutually trying to achieve.

Nor are recipes enough. It is essential to know how the food is eaten, what goes into a meal, what dishes accompany each other. Out of context, food may seem unbalanced, strange, or dull. Rice, for example, is never eaten plain in Szechwan, but how is an American cook to know that? An American may prepare several Szechwan dishes, serve the rice separately—and, finding the food too spicy and the rice uninteresting, wonder how sixty million people can eat the stuff day in and day out.

The author of a French cookbook has no such problem, because American and French cooking have a common tradition. The ingredients are the same; there is nothing exotic about a stick of butter or a pint of cream. And Americans are familiar with the way French food is eaten. We have experienced, or can imagine from films and books, nursing a croissant and café au lait in a Paris café, or eating a sumptuous meal at a three-star restaurant. We can envision the elegant setting, the dishes we might be served, can recall or imagine the taste of rich sauce and fine wine. Whether these experiences are literary or real, they are in the possession of every American who opens a French cookbook.

With authentic Chinese cuisine, however, an American is at a loss. There is no shared culture, and neither real nor vicarious experience helps us know what it is like to buy a bowl of steaming noodles from a street vendor or eat at a famous Peking Duck restaurant in Peking. China is foreign, and the Chinese food available in this country is deracinated.

Language is perhaps the most serious problem. French is *the* language of Western cooking; terms like *soufflé* and *meringue* need no translation. But with Chinese we are at a loss; the name of every dish must be explained. We are faced with a highly developed cuisine that possesses its own specialized vocabulary, as intricate and refined as the vocabulary of French cuisine and considerably more precise in describing food than English can be. We have, for example, only one word, *hot*, to describe both temperature and spiciness. The Chinese have two, *re* for heat, *la* for pepperiness. The criteria for analyzing Chinese food are complex, and a precise, almost scientific vocabulary has evolved to express them.

In the following pages we shall briefly describe some of the most important characteristics of Chinese food. For Americans, food is largely a matter of taste, although smell is sometimes important too. A Chinese gourmet is far more sensual. Each dish is considered not only in terms of its taste and fragrance, but equally in terms of its texture, appearance, and nutrition. Each aspect is analyzed with astonishing sensitivity and great clarity.

TASTE AND FRAGRANCE

Taste, the most important element in food, is the most carefully described. The Chinese know, as we have learned, that the aroma of something is intimately connected to its flavor. They consider that aroma an integral part of the flavor, and the Chinese word for it, *wer*, means both "taste" and "odor." Fragrance comes through the taste buds as well as the nostrils. A sensitive Chinese gourmet like Mrs. Chiang will bite into a crisp-fried shrimp ball and describe it as fragrant, or *xiang*. This is a taste. Cooked garlic is *xiang*. Szechwan peppercorns, incredibly so. There is also the taste that comes from the natural flavor of an ingredient, a sweet, fresh taste that the Chinese call *xien*. One thinks of the fresh, delicately rich and sweet flavor of shrimp and lobster, the delicate flavor of fish; these are *xien*. Richness is a taste called *nong*, characteristically found in heavy, complicated meat dishes. The concentrated, meaty essence of a long-simmered beef stew is *nong*, as is the almost unbearably rich and luxurious flavor of a fresh ham that Mrs. Chiang has cooked in a dark and sweet anise-flavored sauce. What we consider tastes in America—salty, sweet, bitter, sour, and hot—are all present in the food of China, but they are parts of the more complicated flavors, elements to be manipulated to produce special effects. Mrs. Chiang uses sugar to make her Red-Cooked Pork richer and more *nong*; she also uses it to make shrimps sweeter and more *xien*. She adds salt to enhance the fragrance, or *xiang*, of one of her crisp Oily Scallion Cakes.

The essence of a taste, whether it is fragrant, fresh, or rich—*xiang*, *xien*, or *nong*—comes from the natural flavors of ingredients. Every effect created by a Chinese cook is achieved by recognizing that basic flavor and then working either to accentuate it or combine it with other complementary or contrasting flavors. Mrs. Chiang knows which spices and condiments to use to bring out the fresh flavor of a fish and which to use to mask its undesirable fishy taste. She knows which spices and condiments make a fresh vegetable taste fresh and sweeter, more *xien*, than it would be if it were cooked without any seasonings. She knows that long, slow cooking with soy sauce will heighten the naturally rich, deep flavor of beef. But, above all, she knows how to combine flavors and ingredients to achieve unusual and intricate effects, combinations that often reveal the original flavor of something more sharply than if it was simply left alone. These combinations of flavors can be convoluted and complex. A dish can be, as Pork in the Style of Fish is, hot, sweet, sour, rich, fresh, savory, and fragrant, all at the same time. This juxtaposition of flavors is particularly highly developed in the cuisine of Szechwan but it is an important element in all Chinese food. Sweet and sour dishes illustrate in a very popular way just how brilliantly a combination of apparently opposing tastes can succeed, such combinations often emphasizing otherwise neglected elements in the natural flavor of a particular ingredient. Thus, Mrs. Chiang's combination of eggs and crabmeat (Crab and Egg, page 213) brings to the fore the surprisingly rich flavor common to both ingredients, as well as their sweetness, or *xien*.

TEXTURE

Chinese food is meant to be felt as well as tasted. It is this emphasis on the tactile quality of the cuisine which is one of its chief differences from Western food. Except for inconsequential things like potato chips, what foods do we have that are important primarily for their textures? Interesting textures, and interesting combinations of textures especially, play a vital role in China's cuisine at every level. Some of the most famous and most luxurious foods are texture foods. The crisp skin of Peking Duck is eaten separately so that its special texture can be thoroughly appreciated. The most famous texture food of all is bird's nest, which is not really a nest, but the gelatinous saliva secreted by a species of South Pacific swift to hold its nest together. It has no taste, but its slightly crunchy, yet elusive, resiliency provides a strange, almost unearthly, sensation. Bird's nest is a rich man's food, a banquet dish far too expensive for most people to indulge in except on special occasions. But there are plenty of more common texture foods, and Mrs. Chiang uses them often: cellophane noodles, with their rubbery resilience; tree ears, a common fungus with a slippery, gelatinous texture; and crisp, crunchy fresh water chestnuts. All of these are essentially tasteless, yet all of them are employed to add some kind of an interesting feel to the food.

Mrs. Chiang emphasizes the textures of ordinary foods as well, doing this mainly by contrasting them with other ingredients. She sets off the crispness of green peppers against the fibrous texture of shredded pork. A crunchy combination of raw carrots, cucumbers, and cellophane noodles would be served inside a soft pancake. The custardlike smoothness of fresh bean curd needs no foil to be appreciated; combining it, as Mrs. Chiang does, with water chestnuts, tree-ears, and ground pork in Pock-Marked Ma's Bean Curd, or *mapo doufu,* exaggerates its texture brilliantly.

Mrs. Chiang also uses various cooking methods to obtain special effects. Deep-fat frying, of course, produces crispness. So, too, does very quick stir-frying, especially of vegetables. There is an element of textural interest in almost every dish Mrs. Chiang makes. She respects the feel of her ingredients and uses it to achieve certain specific effects. These are not subtle. After all, Americans, who rarely think about the texture of their food, always notice the crispness of Chinese vegetables.

PHYSICAL APPEARANCE

The physical appearance of the food is another important element in the cuisine of China. In its most elaborate form, this concern can manifest itself in something as ornate as a platter of cold sliced meats arranged in the shape of a peacock. Such productions usually require a professional hand and belong in the realm of *haute cuisine,* but home cooks like Mrs. Chiang are no less concerned about the appearance of each dish they serve their families. Color and shape are the main elements Mrs. Chiang manipulates to make her food look good. As with taste and texture, she searches for interesting combinations and contrasts. There are some foods and combinations of ingredients she considers to be particularly pretty, liking, for example, the juxtaposition of pink and yellow in her recipe for Crab and Egg. Mrs. Chiang occasionally adds a colorful ingredient like carrots to a stir-fried dish with the express purpose of making it more interesting to look at, a practice thoroughly in keeping with Chinese traditions. The standard

Chinese guide for professional chefs describes the color of every finished dish as well as its taste and texture.

Shape is as important as color. Uniformity, rather than contrast, is the rule here. Mrs. Chiang tries to make all the important ingredients in a dish the same size and shape. If she shreds the pork, she shreds the cabbage, too. Chunks go with chunks, cubes with cubes. No matter how much their tastes, textures, and colors may differ, the physical size and shape of the main ingredients must be identical.

NUTRITION

Another element in the Chinese appreciation of food, though only indirectly a sensual one, is that of nutrition. This is something that Americans can readily understand, for it is becoming our national obsession, too. Mrs. Chiang grew up in a family that knew that a proper diet was essential for good health. Though her mother had probably never heard of vitamins, she was as concerned about providing her children with a balanced diet as any American housewife is today. Somehow, she even knew that liver and spinach were particularly nutritious. And she always served plenty of fresh vegetables, fresh eggs, and freshly killed poultry along with the rice that was the family's staple. It was a good diet, and it produced a healthy family. Mrs. Chiang doesn't remember anybody getting really sick. The family never bought medicine. When somebody had a cold, her mother would feed the invalid a special homemade preparation of sweet wine and ginger. It was probably more of a treat than a treatment.

Like many Chinese, Mrs. Chiang's mother believed that some foods were particularly effective in combating specific diseases or in strengthening certain parts of the body. She treated rashes, insect bites, and other skin ailments with garlic, which she simply rubbed over the affected area. Occasionally, she substituted a paste made from the leaves of a bitter melon vine for the garlic. She extracted oil from orange peels and used it medicinally, too. Then there were the special foods. Animal hearts were good for your heart, liver for your liver. Snake meat was very special; it was supposed to cure blindness, especially if it came from a poisonous species. There was a snake store near our first house in Taipei. Its proprietor displayed his venomous wares in wire cages in front of the shop, and whenever a customer, who was usually an elderly gentleman with very thick glasses, arrived, the proprietor would put on a terrific show of snaring and decapitating a snake. Then he would retire to the rear of the store to turn the dead serpent into a bowl of very expensive, but presumably efficacious, soup.

Even discounting such specific benefits, it is clear that the diet of a Szechwanese peasant family like Mrs. Chiang's is nutritionally superior to the average present-day American one. It is better balanced, with a greater emphasis on vegetables and simple starches. The vegetables themselves are more nutritious, for Chinese cooking methods preserve vitamins better than American ones. In addition, refined sugar and cholesterol-producing saturated fats, the scourges of the American dinner table, rarely appear in the food of Szechwan. Nor do very many calories. Eating normal amounts of Chinese food in the Chinese manner is a delicious way to lose weight. But you must eat it the way Mrs. Chiang does, with what seems to Americans to be an inordinate amount of rice. The rice is necessary to provide bulk; it is filling, not fattening. And, in an era of rising food prices and worldwide scarcities, a Chinese diet presents all sorts of economic and moral advantages.

2 - BANQUET FOOD, HOME COOKING, AND THE REGIONAL CUISINES

There are two useful ways to look at Chinese food. One can examine the cooking styles and specialties of regional cuisines, or one can compare banquet food, *dacai* (literally, "big dishes"), with everyday food, *xiaocai* (or "small dishes"). Actually there is not much difference between these two approaches, for most Chinese food is *xiaocai*. To describe it, therefore, is to describe regional cooking. *Haute cuisine* is more nearly a national style; most banquet dishes transcend provincial boundaries.

BANQUET FOOD (*dacai*)

Dacai is the luxurious cuisine demanded by special occasions, such as weddings or formal dinner parties. It is not more delicious than *xiaocai*; it simply has a different function. Banquet food customarily requires the most expensive ingredients and makes extravagant use of ordinary food. Enormous quantities are obligatory. When Mrs. Chiang was young, Szechwan country banquets featured whole ducks, whole fresh hams, and soups made out of whole chickens: these were literally *dacai*. The more sophisticated dinners of the wealthy included luxury items like shark's fins and bird's nests. The food emphasized texture and was subtle and delicate.

In the cities, formal banquets are held in a restaurant or catered at home by professional cooks, since *dacai* are not part of the repertoire of the home cook. Many of the dishes require elaborate preparation and special skills; even in restaurants *dacai* must be ordered ahead.

On our second stay in Taiwan we organized an eating club to explore the *dacai* of our favorite restaurants, since twelve people was the minimum for which a chef would mobilize his skills to produce a banquet. In addition to the exotic food, we soon discovered the pleasures of Chinese banquet rituals, which govern every aspect of the meal. The seating, around a large, round table, is done according to an elaborate system of rank and status. One never drinks except in response to someone else's toast, and drinking games—paper, scissors, stone or odds and evens—help keep the wine flowing. The rituals are all formalized, but the result is anything but stiff. A Chinese banquet is livelier than most casual American gatherings, and the food is infinitely better.

The ritual of food service is, of course, carefully observed. First come a selection of four cold hors d'oeuvres, delicate morsels like thousand-year-old eggs, smoked fish, and thinly sliced cold meats arranged, if the chef is ambitious, in beautiful patterns. If the banquet is Hunanese, there are sweet fried nuts.

Then come the serious dishes, one at a time. Shark's fins or bird's nests are presented early on to show the quality of the banquet, which is graded and priced by the fanciest dish offered. Most expensive is a bird's nest meal, followed by shark's fins and sea cucumber, or bêche-de-mer. Peking Duck is not technically a banquet dish; if it appears, you know you are getting the cheapest banquet in the house.

If the restaurant has particularly good stir-fried dishes, they come next. Szechwan banquets invariably include a platter of large prawns in a sweet red sauce, *ganshao mingxia*. Whole ducks or chickens are commonly included, as are whole squabs, tiny ones cooked so perfectly that the skin is brown and crisp while the rich flesh remains tender and moist. A large piece of meat, such as a fresh ham, or *tipan*, is also *dacai*; we had a Cantonese banquet in Taipei featuring a whole suckling pig. Its crisp skin was served separately, like the skin of Peking Duck.

At strategic points during the meal, waiters pass around hot towels or whisk away the greasy, bone-filled plates and replace them with clean ones. Soups are served at regular intervals; mild and delicate, they refresh the palate for more feasting. There is always a vegetable dish, something amusing like baby ears of corn and tree ears, or a seasonal delicacy like *doumiao*, the tender green shoots of a young bean plant. Toward the end of the meal a whole fish usually appears, followed by a final soup, perhaps a sweet one with lotus seeds or delicate white fungi. A starch is served at the end, a symbolic gesture to ensure that no one leaves the table hungry. Fresh fruit, the only suitable dessert, ends the banquet.

REGIONAL FOOD

Although every banquet we went to featured the same kind of delicate and luxurious *dacai*, the food was always identified with a particular region. Every Chinese restaurant on Taiwan specializes in the food of a particular province, usually the head chef's home province. To be sure, many banquet dishes are prepared the same way in every restaurant, no matter what its provenance, but just as many are regional specialties. A Pekingese restaurant would serve Peking Duck at a banquet, a Shanghai restaurant would serve a Shanghai dish like a fresh ham, or *tipan*. Frequently, everyday dishes in the cuisine of one province are *dacai* in another. Mrs. Chiang told us that shrimps were always banquet food in Szechwan because they were so exotic there, but in a coastal area like Canton they are everyday ingredients. Because they are *haute cuisine*, the *dacai* of a particular province tend to be closer in taste and appearance to the banquet dishes of the other areas than to the earthier style of that region's own everyday food. Szechwanese *dacai*, for example, are never hot.

When we turn to the everyday food of China, we find the regional differences much more pronounced, but even here there are many national dishes. Shrimp balls, fried rice, steamed fish, most clear soups, sweet and sour dishes, and won tons are made and eaten in every part of China. Each province may give a local touch to the preparation of these foods—as Mrs. Chiang adds a few hot pepper flakes to her Won Ton Soup—but the dishes themselves aren't regional. Some dishes originated in one part of China and spread to others. There is a type of red-cooked, or *hongshao*, dish in which the main ingredients simmer for hours in a sweet and rich soy sauce-based stock. Recipes for it appear in most Chinese cookbooks, and Mrs. Chiang makes several things this way, but it is really a dish from Shanghai. Similarly, *jiaoz*, the savory pork dumplings of Peking, can be found all over China.

The Chinese love to classify, but, when confronted with the task of analyzing their own cuisine and identifying the major regional styles and important subgroups, they have never been able to agree completely on a standard system. The reason is clear. The gastronomic wealth of China is so immense it doesn't fall into neat little categories. The major regional cuisines are those that cover the broadest range of dishes; but each province, and often each prefecture, has its own local specialties. One standard Chinese cookbook lists eight major schools of cooking, another five, and a third three. As far as I can figure out, the ruling principle seems to be to ensure that one's own provincial cuisine reaches the majors. Szechwan always does.

The most convenient system is to divide China geographically into four important culinary regions: north (Peking), south (Canton), east (Shanghai), and west (Szechwan). When viewed from this perspective, many of the more difficult to classify cuisines turn out to belong to border provinces open to gastronomic influences from several sides. Fukien, which sometimes ranks as a major school of cooking, lies on the coast between Shanghai and Canton. Hunan, in the heart of China, is next to Szechwan and down the river from Shanghai. Hunanese food is hot like Szechwan's and rich like Shanghai's.

North

Northern China is wheat-growing country. Its inhabitants eat magnificent noodles and breads instead of rice. There are several famous noodle restaurants in Taipei, all run by northerners. The menus of these restaurants are so extensive that you cannot simply order a plain dish of fried noodles, or *chaomian*; you must first specify what shape noodle you want fried. Knife-cut, fish-shaped, and cat's ear are among the most popular varieties. One of our favorite Peking-ese dishes is something called *chaobing*, which is like *chaomian* but is made out of leftover pancakes cut into thin strips and fried as if they were noodles. This is real working-class food, and a large plate of *chaobing* with a few shreds of pork and some vegetables couldn't, at least at the time we first tasted it, have cost more than twenty cents.

The breads of northern China are as varied and splendid as the noodles. Many of them are made specifically to accompany certain dishes; plain crêpes, or *baobing*, go with Peking Duck, while sesame seed biscuits, or *shaobing*, go with Mongolian barbecued lamb. We are particularly fond of oil strips with biscuits, or *youtiao shaobing*, crullerlike pieces of deep-fried dough stuffed into warm sesame seed biscuits like hot dogs into rolls. They rank next to croissants as one of the world's great breakfast foods. They are never made at home; you buy them from street vendors, as we did, every day.

Most people associate the northern school of cooking with Peking. Actually, however, the indigenous food of Peking comes from the nearby province of Shantung, and many Pekingese restaurateurs are natives of Shantung. Pekingese food is robust and straightforward. The liberal use of garlic and scallions imparts a lovely, faintly smoky flavor to even the most ordinary dishes. Northern cooks also produce what we consider to be the best sweet and sour dishes in China. Lamb, which is rarely eaten elsewhere in China, is a Pekingese specialty. It was introduced to the Chinese capital by the neighboring Mongolian tribes, and many of the ways in which it is prepared reflect its ethnic origins. The most famous of these is the so-called Mongolian barbecue, which the Chinese eat when they want to go out "for Chinese food." Mongolian barbecues are casual affairs where each diner selects his own mixture of raw lamb and condiments to be cooked before his eyes on a domelike iron grill. Pekingese cooks have more Chinese ways of preparing lamb; one of the best is *congbao yanzron*, literally "exploded lamb with scallions," a subtle, smoky-tasting dish that comes with a plate of sesame seed biscuits, or *shaobing*, into which you stuff the lamb.

The most famous, though not necessarily the most delicious, Peking-ese specialty, is, of course, roast duck. The great Peking duck restau-rants of Taipei and Peking breed their own birds. In these restaurants the duck reaches your table in several courses. First the skin, golden and crackling, to be eaten with hoisin sauce and raw scallions inside a thin flour crêpe, or *boabing*; then the tender duck meat; and, finally, a rich soup made from the bird's bones and feet. A friend who recently returned from China described a meal at a Peking Duck restaurant in Peking where the duck was served in seven different ways.

South

The southern province of Kwangtung, which includes the city of Canton, has a semitropical climate, a rich agriculture, and a long coastline. All this lushness has produced a cuisine typified by variety. Seafood dishes abound, but rare, exotic ingredients are its really distinguishing feature. Cantonese chefs excel in the preparation of shark's fins, turtle, snake, and pigeon. Nothing is highly spiced, textures are emphasized, and the natural flavors of the ingredients dominate most dishes. Quick stir-frying is the preferred cooking method. The light and subtle dishes that characterize the regional cuisine are quite different from most of the dark, heavy glop that passes for Cantonese food in this country.

The savory pastries of Canton are particularly delightful, lighter and more delicate than those of other provinces. Whole meals are built around them—the famous Cantonese *yim cha*, or tea lunches. We went to some impressive ones in Hong Kong, a city that is, after all, populated by Cantonese. They are held in huge restaurants the size of ballrooms, where waiters circulate among the patrons carrying large trays covered with little plates of dumplings and other delicacies. There is no menu; you simply lift whatever you want off a tray. The waiter tallies up your bill at the end of the meal by counting the plates on your table. Tea lunches are as frustrating as they are delicious. We couldn't bear the leaving of a single type of pastry untasted, and would spend the entire meal trying to catch the eye of every waiter in the room.

East

The fertile countryside of the Yangtze delta on the east coast of China has been compared by one author to the lush French province of Burgundy. It is a heavily populated area, rich in agriculture, in fresh- and salt-water fish and shellfish, and in the sophisticated palates of its gourmets. Characteristically, its cooking is rich, too. This is the food associated with Shanghai, dark, opulent meat dishes whose heavy sauces contain a touch of sweetness. The area's chefs achieve their effects with unusual combinations of ingredients. The most luscious steamed pastries we ever ate were made by a native of Yangchow, a gastronomic center north of Shanghai, who filled them with a mixture of ground pork and crabmeat. Eels are another regional specialty; one of our favorite Shanghai restaurants in Taipei served them very fresh and covered with a rich, yet slightly peppery, sauce. The main tourist attraction of the Yangtze delta, the West Lake, is as famous for its food as for its beauty. Even on Taiwan, a West Lake sour fish would be worthy of every star in Michelin's book. It combines the freshest possible fish, which has to remain alive until the minute before it is to be cooked, with an ethereally delicate sweet and sour sauce.

West (The Food of Szechwan)

Szechwan is a special place, so it is hardly surprising that its food is special, too. The province lies deep in the interior of China, protected by mountain ranges and by the almost impassable Yangtze gorges. It was the final redoubt to which Chiang Kai-shek moved the seat of his beleagured government during the darkest days of World War II. Yet, despite its isolation, Szechwan is one of the most prosperous and heavily populated parts of China. Almost anything grows there. The rich, red soil of the central plain around Chengtu, where Mrs. Chiang grew up, can produce three crops a year. Since the third century B.C., when the first Chinese settlers arrived, the legendary wealth of Szechwan has drawn successive waves of immigrants. They straggled through the treacherous mountain passes and battled the river rapids to reach the bamboo-covered hillsides and well-irrigated lowlands of the fertile province.

This constant influx of people from other parts of China has meant that, although Szechwan has always been a frontier province, its culture is unmistakably Chinese. Its dialect is but a minute deviation from the standard Mandarin spoken all over North China, and its food, though distinctive, occasionally hints at other cuisines. Some of the red-cooked dishes Mrs. Chiang prepares have the richness and sweet taste of Shanghai. Her recipe for Pork Shreds with Hoisin Sauce, or *jiangbao rousi*, suggests Peking in its combination of condiments, the same ones—scallions and hoisin sauce—that accompany Peking Duck. But most Szechwanese dishes are ebulliently and deliciously Szechwanese.

Szechwanese food can be dangerous. Once you become addicted to it, as we are, all other food, Chinese or Western, seems pallid and bland. Szechwanese dishes are more interesting, their tastes more lively and varied. A multiplicity of flavors is even more typical of Szechwanese cooking than hotness; Mrs. Chiang says this is what really differentiates Szechwanese food from that of the rest of China. The flavors are more complicated and their combinations more dramatic; each dish is an intricately constructed mosaic of tastes and aftertastes. Powerful and subtle at the same time, the food of Szechwan overwhelms the palate with a brilliant interplay of spices and condiments; Szechwanese cooks use more quantity and a greater variety of seasonings than do those of any other province. Even Mrs. Chiang's versions of the dishes of other regions, or of national dishes (take, for example, her Fried Noodles, or *chaomian*), are seasoned more imaginatively, and contain more ginger, garlic, and scallions, than the versions produced in other provinces. The taste of the finished dish is correspondingly more exciting. Mrs. Chiang's Pork Dumplings, or *jiaoz*, are not spicy, but they make all other *jiaoz* seem dull. Her Shrimp Balls are similarly more fragrant and interesting.

Of course, Szechwanese food is hot, too. Mrs. Chiang uses hot peppers mainly to bring out the complicated flavors of the food. These peppers are powerful—so potent, in fact, that Mrs. Chiang has to open the windows when she cooks with them because the fumes from their cooking make her cough. Eating them makes many people sweat. Yet, when they are added to food, especially to food that is already highly spiced, they seem to stimulate the palate. The first thing you encounter when you take a bite of an authentically peppery Szechwanese dish is a flash of hotness. It passes quickly, and you soon become aware of all the other ingredients in the dish: the sharp freshness of ginger, the nutlike richness of sesame oil, the saltiness of soy sauce, the tang of vinegar, the savory aroma of garlic, the mild bitterness of scallions. One after another they assault you in a clear, bright panorama of flavors. You taste tastes you've never experienced before with a sensitivity and discrimination you never thought you possessed. It takes a while, but once acclimated to the hotness of Szechwanese food, you will find that your own perceptions of tastes have become extraordinarily acute and your enjoyment of them correspondingly increased.

In addition to hot peppers and all of the regular Chinese spices, Szechwanese cooks have their own special spice—*huajiao*, or Szechwan pepper. Mrs. Chiang uses it a lot. *Huajiao* is not hot the way other pepper is; it possesses a distinctive kind of aromatic hotness that the Chinese call *ma*. When you taste some Szechwan pepper, you will experience two unfamiliar sensations. One is a mild numbness on your tongue and the other is an amazing fragrance, totally unlike anything you have ever known. The aromatic flavor of *huajiao* defies description, but it is an important part of many of Mrs. Chiang's most magnificent dishes and gives them a fragrance and character that proclaim with unmistakable clarity, "This is Szechwanese."

Peppery and complex though the flavors of Szechwan may be, they are not chaotic. Mrs. Chiang's recipes are anything but random collections of condiments. This cannot be stressed strongly enough. The recent popularity of the cuisine in America has led many Chinese restaurants to serve a bastardized Szechwanese type of food that is not really Szechwanese at all, just hot. Real Szechwanese food belongs to a sophisticated culinary tradition whose practitioners have developed and codified the most auspicious combinations of ingredients and tastes and established definite rules for the composition of every dish. A gifted cook like Mrs. Chiang may add a few personal touches to a specific dish, but she will always preserve the essential structure of the recipe.

Take, for example, something prepared in the style of fish, or *yuxiang*, a type of dish that is instantaneously recognized as Szechwanese all over China. A Pekingese *yuxiang* dish would be as unthinkable as French spaghetti. Mrs. Chiang explains that the people of Szechwan developed *yuxiang* dishes to compensate for their province's lack of seafood. A dish in the style of fish doesn't taste like fish; it's not supposed to. It merely adapts a method used for cooking fish to other ingredients. When she makes something in the style of fish, Mrs. Chiang uses all the techniques she learned from her mother for enhancing the *xien*, or fresh flavor of a fish. This produces food of incredible intricacy and richness. Mrs. Chiang's *yuxiang* dishes are hot, or *la*; they are also aromatically so, or *ma*. They are fragrant, or *xiang*, as well as sweet and sour and rich. They are texturally exciting, too, for Mrs. Chiang makes them with gelatinous tree ears and crunchy water chestnuts.

One taste is worth a thousand words. Though I could describe all the famous specialties of Mrs. Chiang's home province, the best way to appreciate the brilliance of Szechwan's food is to eat it. This cookbook contains recipes for all the classic dishes of Szechwan. It includes such famous things as Hot and Sour Soup, Pock-Marked Ma's Bean Curd, Double-Cooked Pork, Bon Bon Chicken, Ants Climb a Tree, and Fragrant, Crispy Duck as well as dozens of other equally delicious, though less celebrated, dishes. The food these recipes produces is authentic Szechwanese home cooking; it isn't restaurant food. For that reason, some of these dishes may differ from the kinds of things that are produced in the so-called Szechwanese restaurants of this country. And, though Mrs. Chiang's version of a dish is not the definitive recipe for that dish—there is no single standard version of any Szechwanese dish—chances are that it is far closer to what the ordinary people of Szechwan eat every day than anything else you can get in this country. We also think it is better.

PART II

PREPARING THE FOOD OF CHINA

3 - INGREDIENTS

Mrs. Chiang has been cooking authentic Szechwanese food in the United States for over four years. Clearly, obtaining the proper ingredients for making Chinese food here is not a serious problem. What difficulties there are arise from two very different sources: first, finding the necessary Chinese ingredients, and second, and no less important, getting the ordinary fresh produce needed for making Chinese food. There are no substitutes for fresh vegetables, fish, or meat. You can't, for example, stir-fry a package of frozen spinach, and, while there's nothing very exotic about string beans, if they're out of season and not on the supermarket shelf, you can't make the famous Szechwanese dish of Dry-Fried String Beans (page 259) no matter how extensive your supply of Oriental bean pastes and spices may be. The open-air markets of Taiwan were colorful and exciting, but most of what they sold can be found in any supermarket in America. Garlic, scallions, cabbage, green peppers, spinach, pork, chicken, fish, and shrimps are as essential for making real Szechwanese food as any specifically Chinese spices and condiments.

The Chinese ingredients Szechwanese food requires should not be a problem. With five or six standard items, you should be able to make over half of the recipes in this cookbook. Nor are those ingredients hard to get. As more and more Americans are becoming interested in Chinese cooking, things like soy sauce that once required a special trip to Chinatown can now be found on a supermarket shelf. And most of those which can't are dried, bottled, or canned so you can buy them by mail or purchase a several months' supply whenever you go to a Chinese market. Ginger is the only absolutely essential Chinese ingredient used by Mrs. Chiang that has to be fresh. Many ordinary supermarkets and grocery stores are beginning to stock it regularly, and, in any case, it will keep for weeks in the refrigerator.

Once you know what to look for, you will be amazed at the variety of non-Chinese places that stock Chinese ingredients. Gourmet shops, supermarkets, and other kinds of specialized retailers might carry things like soy sauce and dried mushrooms. When we lived in central New Jersey, we used to be able to purchase fresh bean curd and noodles, as well as bottled and dried ingredients, at a local Oriental gift shop. With a little detective work, you may uncover other similarly unorthodox sources of Chinese ingredients. Even Chinese restaurants are a possibility.

None of this ingenuity is necessary if you live near a large city with its own Chinese section, for the most efficient way to obtain everything you need for serious Chinese cooking is to patronize a Chinese market. There, under one roof, are all the staples you might be able to purchase outside of Chinatown, as well as all of those you couldn't possibly find anywhere else. Even the most sophisticated gourmet shop has yet to carry ancient eggs, Szechwanese preserved vegetables, or tiny dried shrimps. In addition, a Chinese market will provide you with fresh Chinese vegetables and such otherwise difficult-to-obtain cuts of meat as fresh bacon and pork kidneys.

There is also no better way to appreciate the culture behind China's cuisine than to go shopping in Chinatown. Enter one of its tiny markets and you are in a foreign country. The floor space is taken up with huge tins of olive-green pickled vegetables, silvery dried fish, and creamy white blocks of bean curd. Strings of scarlet sausages and golden roast ducks hang from hooks in the ceiling. Gaily decorated canisters of tea line the walls, along with intriguing cellophane packets of rare spices, bottles of strange dark sauces, and cans of preserved loquats, litchees, and other mythical fruits. Even if a store has all the physical accouterments of an ordinary supermarket (and many Chinese markets are quite modern), the contents of its shelves are still Asian. Fill your shopping cart with peanuts from Szechwan, hoisin sauce from Hong Kong, dried noodles from Taiwan or Shanghai, canned fruits from Canton. The labels are romantic in themselves, covered with Chinese characters and pictures of cloud-covered mountains and Oriental deities. Even the sounds of a Chinese market are exotic. No Muzak here, but the clashing cacophony of a Peking opera and the shopkeeper conversing with his customers in the musical tones of Cantonese.

There are economic as well as cultural benefits to be gained from shopping in Chinatown. Items considered gourmet luxuries in other parts of town are staples here, and priced accordingly. In addition, there are real economies of scale. Gallon containers of soy sauce will provide you with substantial savings, as will similarly large cans of peanut oil and twenty-five-pound bags of rice. The quality is better, too. The ginger is more tender, the garlic heads are larger, and the noodles are fresher and more delicate. A Chinese market will also sell all the non-Oriental items you need for Chinese cooking, since its proprietor usually stocks a full line of groceries, fresh fish, vegetables, and meats. You may also be able to pick up some ready-made Chinese delicacies to stretch your menu. Roast ducks and spareribs are common items. If there is a Chinese pastry shop nearby, you may be able to buy some steamed breads or savory pastries to take out. Many a busy Chinese housewife does this when she wants to give her family an extra treat without a lot of extra work. Occasionally you may not be able to get everything you want at any one store or even anywhere in Chinatown. Since many Chinese ingredients are imported or grown only in a few places in the United States, it often happens that a particular item will be unavailable, out of season, or out of stock. Even in Taiwan, fresh water chestnuts, for example, were sometimes impossible to find.

I have appended a list of Chinese grocery stores to this section. It is meant primarily as a guide to sources of mail-order supplies, but many of the stores are regular retail outlets that carry a wide variety of Chinese ingredients. Actually, any Chinese market will probably sell everything you need. Take this book with you the first few times you shop in Chinatown, so that you can point to the characters for the items you want if you can't find them right away. Though there are many regional dialects, the written language is the same all over China, and the characters for soy sauce mean "soy sauce" no matter how they may be pronounced.

Because the whole question of Chinese ingredients seems to present such a challenge to many American cooks, and because we believe that making real Chinese food in America depends on using the proper ingredients, we have tried to make the following list as comprehensive as possible. We describe all the special Chinese items called for in our recipes, and discuss the other essential, though not necessarily Oriental, ingredients as well. In each case we consider the question of substitutions. This is, in our opinion, the most serious problem confronting anyone who wants to create authentic Chinese food in the United States. All too often other authors, in an attempt to simplify the preparation of Chinese food for American cooks, specify the use of ingredients that, though easy to obtain, completely alter the character of the food. Nothing can distort the true taste of a dish, its *zhen wer*, as much as the use of the wrong ingredients. Since many of the most exotic and hard-to-get ingredients are primarily texture foods anyhow, omitting them will have little effect on the final flavor of the dish. Substitutions will! If a feasible substitute for a particular item exists, we have, of course, mentioned it. Otherwise, we have been quite dogmatic in our opposition to any substitutions. If in doubt, *don't*.

The following list of ingredients is alphabetical according to the way the ingredient is ordinarily spoken of—that is, Chinese noodles, not noodles, Chinese; and dried tree ears, not tree ears, dried.

豆腐

BEAN CURD (*doufu*)

For a discussion of this ingredient, see pages 219-220.

豆芽

BEAN SPROUTS (*douya*)

For a discussion of this ingredient, see page 236.

粉絲

CELLOPHANE NOODLES (fensi)

These noodles are fun. Also known as "bean thread noodles," "Chinese vermicelli," and "transparent noodles," they are, indeed, transparent. When soaked in water they have a strangely resilient, almost bouncy, texture that Mrs. Chiang uses to add a special feel to many of her best dishes, especially soups and salads. Cellophane noodles owe their unusual properties to the fact that, unlike their more mundane wheat- and rice-flour cousins, they are made from ground mung beans. They were one of the few things that Mrs. Chiang's mother didn't make at home.

Cellophane noodles are always sold dried. They are whitish, thread-like, brittle and slightly translucent. They usually come in 1-pound boxes or bags that contain several smaller cellophane-wrapped packages of noodles inside. Both Chinese and Japanese food stores sell them. They have to be soaked before they can be used, but this is a simple process, for it takes only 5 minutes, even in cold water, for them to soften, expand, and become transparent.

白菜

CHINESE CABBAGE (baicai)

Chinese cabbage, or baicai, was one of the most common vegetables in Szechwan. Mrs. Chiang's family cultivated several different varieties, some for pickling and some for eating fresh. Although few of these particular cabbages are available in this country, several similar types are grown here, and they are not hard to get. The kind Americans know as celery cabbage is often available in supermarkets. It is about the size and shape of a head of romaine lettuce, with very thick white stems and narrow, crisp leaves. Other types of Chinese cabbages are sold in Chinese markets; these generally have larger leaves than celery cabbages do. Since all these varieties taste about the same, any kind of Chinese cabbage can be used for these recipes. Regular round American cabbage, baoxingcai in Chinese, has a much stronger taste and should not be substituted for Chinese cabbage, as it will change the taste of the finished dish. There are several dishes that do use it, however, as it is a Chinese vegetable, too. Cantonese speakers know Chinese cabbage as *bak choy*.

麵

CHINESE NOODLES (*mian*)

For a discussion of this ingredient, see page 278.

荳 沙

CHINESE RED BEANS (*dousha*)

These tiny round beans, considerably smaller than ordinary peas, are sold in plastic bags in Chinese food stores.

黃 酒

CHINESE RICE WINE (*huangjiu*)

The basic Chinese wine comes from rice, not grapes. Mrs. Chiang's family made its own wine, which was used for cooking and informal drinking. It was mild and sweet. For special occasions, the family would buy a better grade of wine. There were many varieties available, for each region, and sometimes each town or village, produced its own type of wine. Most of them were what is called "yellow wine," or *huangjiu*, a name encompassing as many different varieties as red wine does in the West. The most famous yellow wine came from Shaoshing, a town not far from Shanghai. Today wines made in the Shaoshing way are given the Shaoshing name whether or not they come from there, just as some California wines are called Burgundies and Chablis. We tasted real Shaoshing wine once; it was mellow and as smooth as water. Like its distant Japanese cousin, sake, Chinese rice wine is served warm and sipped from tiny cups. It tastes like warm sherry.

Like the French, the Chinese use wine in their cooking. Fish cookery in particular depends on wine to eliminate the "fishy" taste and bring out the delicate flavor of fresh fish and shellfish. Both yellow wine and Shaoshing are acceptable; Mrs. Chiang generally uses the most ordinary kind of yellow wine because it's cheaper. You, however, may have trouble finding either variety. Liquor stores in the Chinese sections of large cities carry imported Chinese wines, and we have occasionally succeeded in persuading liquor dealers elsewhere to order some specially for us. You don't have to, though, for a satisfactory substitute exists—sherry. After experimenting with sake and a host of other Oriental spirits, Mrs. Chiang discovered that plain, ordinary cooking sherry was a fine substitute. Why this should be the case, since Chinese wine is made from rice and sherry from grapes, we have no idea. But it works, one of the few Western items that can be substituted for a Chinese ingredient without seriously damaging the *zhen wer*. (By cooking sherry we mean any low-priced brand from the liquor store.)

冬 菇

DRIED BLACK MUSHROOMS (*donggu*)

These large, charcoal-brown, slightly leathery mushrooms have a tantalizing smoky flavor. They are a luxury in China, where they are prized both for their taste and their texture. They grew wild in Szechwan, and Mrs. Chiang remembers foraging for them in the fields around her childhood home. In this country, they come dried. You can find them in Chinese and Japanese food stores in cellophane bags of various sizes. They are expensive, but a small package goes a long way; dried mushrooms last forever. Neither dried European mushrooms nor fresh white ones are satisfactory substitutes; there are none. If you can't get dried black mushrooms, just omit them. They are nice, but not essential.

In most cases, dried mushrooms must be soaked before they can be used. Put them in a small bowl and cover them with boiling water. Soak them until they are soft, about 20 to 30 minutes. Then rinse them off, remove the tough center stems, and use the caps as specified in the recipe. Sometimes Mrs. Chiang reserves the liquid in which the mushrooms have soaked, sometimes she doesn't; it depends on the recipe.

紫 菜

DRIED KELP (*zicai*)

This is a form of seaweed that you can usually buy in either a Japanese or Chinese food store. It comes dried, in long strips, folded up and packaged in cellophane.

金 針

DRIED LILY BUDS (*jinzhen*)

Although there is nothing flowery about their taste, smell, or appearance, these pale golden stalks do indeed come from a member of the lily family. Often called "tiger lily buds" or "golden needles," they are added to dishes more for their crunchy texture than for their slightly musty flavor. They are available at Chinese grocery stores, where they are sold dried, usually in the form of a pressed block. They should keep indefinitely in an airtight container. Like all dried ingredients, they have to be soaked before they can be used in cooking.

乾 辣 椒

DRIED RED PEPPERS (*gan lajiao*)

In Szechwan, as in many countries with a spicy cuisine, the hotness of hot food comes from chili peppers. Except in those dishes which call for green peppers, where hot fresh green peppers can be used, these little finger-length red peppers provide all the heat for Mrs. Chiang's recipes, either in the form of hot pepper flakes in oil, hot pepper paste, or plain dried red peppers.

In Taiwan and Szechwan chili peppers were fresh, and each housewife dried her own. In this country they come dried, and are available in cellophane bags in Chinese grocery stores, as well as in Italian and Spanish markets. They will keep forever in an airtight container. If you can't get whole dried red peppers, you can substitute 1 teaspoon dried red pepper flakes (the kind you sprinkle over pizza) for 5 whole red peppers.

Red chili peppers are red hot. To make them less so, scrape out and discard the seeds, which are the hottest part of the pepper. You can also, of course, cut down on the number of peppers specified by the recipe. Don't omit them all, for the hotness is an essential element in many Szechwanese dishes.

豆豉

DRIED, SALTED BLACK BEANS (*douchi*)

These dried, salted black beans impart such a delightfully pungent, sour, and salty taste to dishes that, even though they are not Szechwanese in origin, Mrs. Chiang likes to cook with them. They are small, about the size of a pea, black, and partially dried. They come in plastic bags or tins and are available at Chinese markets. If you keep them in an airtight container, they should last indefinitely.

紫菜

DRIED SEAWEED (*zicai*)

Dried seaweed, dark greenish-black in color, is pressed into flat sheets about 8 by 10 inches after it is dried, and sold in cellophane-wrapped packages. Because it is very popular in Japan, it can be purchased in stores that sell Japanese foodstuffs, as well as in Chinatown.

紅棗

DRIED RED DATES (*hongzao*)

These can be obtained in Chinese markets. They are little wrinkled brown objects, about the size of hazelnuts, and come in cellophane bags.

蝦米

DRIED SHRIMPS (*xiami*)

These tiny dried and salted crustaceans add an unusual tangy note to those dishes in which they are used. They have no substitute. You can buy them in Chinese markets, where they are sold by the ounce in little cellophane bags. They are, alas, not cheap. Japanese dried shrimp are less useful, since they contain more shell than anything else.

Most of Mrs. Chiang's recipes call for dried shrimps to be soaked before they can be used. Put them in a small bowl and cover them with boiling water. Let them soak for at least an hour, then rinse and drain them. Be careful to remove any little hard pieces of shell remaining on them. You can, if you want, dig out the dark intestinal vein running down their backs. This is primarily a matter of appearance, not taste or hygiene. Mrs. Chiang removes the vein only when she wants to leave the shrimps whole and is therefore concerned about what they look like.

木 耳

DRIED TREE EARS (*muer*)

Tree ears, also known as "wood ears," "cloud ears," or "Judas's ears," are an edible fungus. They are used more commonly in Szechwanese cooking than in the cuisine of other provinces because they are more abundant there. One source claims that this is because the soil of Szechwan is so fertile; Mrs. Chiang says that it is because the climate is so damp. As a child she used to gather these fungi from the trees that grew along the canal near her home. But her mother used so many tree ears in her cooking that she always kept a package of dried, store-bought ones in the house in case the children couldn't find enough wild ones.

Tree ears have practically no taste; they are prized for their rubbery, gelatinous texture. If you can't find any or are dubious about consuming such an obviously fungoid foodstuff, you can omit them from a dish without damaging its flavor. They were expensive in Taiwan and were not always used, even in good Szechwanese restaurants.

In the dried form in which they come in America, tree ears look like wrinkled, blackish-gray cornflakes. They are usually sold by the ounce in small cellophane packages and will last forever. They range in color from black to medium brown, and some varieties are thicker than others. Chinese markets occasionally stock several grades of tree ears; Mrs. Chiang prefers the thinner, darker, and usually more expensive variety.

Tree ears have to be soaked before they can be used. Measure out the requisite amount of dried tree ears and put them in a small heat-proof bowl, cover them with boiling water, and let them soak for 15 or 20 minutes. Then rinse them off under running water and pick over them carefully to remove all the impurities, like tiny pieces of wood, that might still be embedded in them.

花生米

FRESH PEANUTS (*huashengmi*)

Fresh peanuts are an important ingredient in several of Mrs. Chiang's best dishes. Chinese markets and health food stores sell them shelled, by the pound. The Chinese ones usually retain their papery reddish-brown skin, the health food ones don't. Since some Chinese recipes call for the skins, you should probably buy the Chinese variety and remove the skins when you have to. The simplest way to do this is to put the peanuts in a bowl and cover them with boiling water. Wait about 5 minutes, then drain the peanuts. The skins will almost slip off by themselves. Because fresh peanuts are usually treated as if they were legumes, roasted peanuts are rarely an adequate substitute.

薑

GINGER (*jiang*)

It is impossible to make Szechwanese food without fresh ginger. Its characteristically pungent and sharp flavor is a crucial component of the crisp, bright spiciness that is the hallmark of the province's cuisine. And it is hard to think of any of Mrs. Chiang's recipes that don't call for at least one shred of it. Her family grew it, and, whenever her mother wanted some for cooking, she would dispatch one of the children to dig up a nice, fresh root.

Ginger is a root vegetable. Its skin is similar in color and texture to that of a potato, its flesh whitish and hard. Some ginger can be very fibrous and stringy; younger roots, on the other hand, are quite tender and have a pale, shiny skin. Fresh ginger, usually sold by the pound in individual gnarled pieces, each one roughly 4 inches long by 1 inch in diameter, is becoming increasingly easy to find in the United States. A few years ago you could only get it in a Chinese or Japanese grocery store, but now you can sometimes find it in supermarkets.

Since we have never been unable to get fresh ginger when we wanted it, we have not taken special precautions to preserve it. Like most root vegetables, it lasts a long time. We keep it in the vegetable bin of the refrigerator, lopping off a section or two whenever we need some. The cut ends dry out and, in a few weeks, so does the rest of the root. If your supply is uncertain, seal the ginger in plastic wrap before you refrigerate it. If your supply is very uncertain, there are a number of more drastic measures you can take to preserve your ginger. One is to peel it and store it in a jar of sherry in the refrigerator. Another is to bury it in a jar of damp sand and store it in the refrigerator. According to one authority, you can even plant it in the garden. The lengths to which some Chinese cooks go to guarantee their supply of fresh ginger testifies to its indispensability.

Mrs. Chiang has never found any decent substitutes. Neither powdered nor crystallized ginger will do. A canned variety exists. It can be used in an emergency, but it's not very satisfactory.

糯 米

GLUTINOUS RICE (*nuomi*)

This is a special kind of rice with round white grains that become translucent and very, very sticky when they are cooked. Unlike regular rice, it is never eaten plain but made into pastries and steamed dishes. Glutinous rice was an important holiday food in Szechwan. For the Qingming festival, when the family went to visit the ancestral tombs, Mrs. Chiang's mother made several types of sweet and savory dumplings, using a flour made out of ground glutinous rice. She also made little packages out of glutinous rice that contained bits of pork and vegetables, which she then wrapped in lotus or banana leaves and steamed. Weddings always required glutinous rice in its most glorious form, as the main ingredient in Eight Treasure Rice, or *babaofan*.

Both Chinese and Japanese food stores carry glutinous rice, usually in 5-pound sacks marked strangely, "Sweet Rice." Like the other kind of rice, it will keep indefinitely if stored in an airtight container.

海 鮮 醬

HOISIN SAUCE (*haixian jiang*)

One of the most important ingredients in many classic Szechwanese dishes, including the famous Double-Cooked Pork, is a thick, brown paste made out of sweetened wheat flour called *tianmian jiang*, or "sweet wheat paste." Other provincial cuisines also use *tianmian jiang*; it is, for example, the sweet sauce that traditionally accompanies Peking Duck. Yet, *tianmian jiang* is hard to buy in America. We scoured several Chinatowns for it; our entreaties, even in our most carefully pronounced Chinese and accompanied by very clearly written characters, produced only noncomprehension and no sweet wheat paste. Then we discovered hoisin sauce. The name and characters for it were different, but the stuff was the same. There, masquerading under the Cantonese title of "hoisin sauce," with characters that meant "sea-fresh sauce," was the thick, dark, sweet paste we knew as *tianmian jiang*. Usually, even if an ingredient has a different name in Cantonese, the written characters for it will be the same as the ones used by Mandarin speakers. Why hoisin sauce is different remains a mystery. But then, hoisin sauce seems to be a generally mysterious sauce in America. Other authors have variously described its main ingredient as being soy beans, plums, "vegetables," and even pumpkins. Apparently, wheat flour isn't exotic enough.

Hoisin sauce is available in Chinese markets in 1-pound tins. After you open the can, transfer its contents to a covered glass jar and store it in the refrigerator. It will keep for months.

辣 椒 油

HOT PEPPER FLAKES IN OIL (*lajiao you*)

This is the condiment Mrs. Chiang uses most often to add hotness when she cooks. It is a simple, but powerful, combination of hot red pepper flakes and peanut oil. You can buy commercially prepared hot oil, but it is not really satisfactory, and in any case the home-made version takes all of 3 minutes to prepare. Not only is it easy to make, but it keeps for weeks in a closed container in the refrigerator. The pepper flakes are the kind of crushed chili peppers that you sprinkle over a pizza. They are available in bottles on the spice shelf of every supermarket, or you can make your own by crushing whole dried red peppers. Here is the recipe.

¼ cup peanut oil	Heat the peanut oil in a small frying pan or saucepan over a high flame until it has just begun to smoke, then remove the oil from the flame and let it cool off for 5 seconds.
¼ cup hot pepper flakes	Add the hot pepper flakes to the hot oil; they will cause it to foam up. When the foaming subsides, add the salt. Stir well.
½ teaspoon salt	The hot pepper flakes in oil are now ready to use. You can transfer them to another container for storage. Just make sure you stir them up thoroughly every time you use them, so you add both flakes and oil to your dish.

辣 椒 醬

HOT PEPPER PASTE (*lajiao jiang*)

Thick, highly flavored pastes comprise a whole class of Chinese condiments. Tomato paste is the closest Western analog, both in use and in composition. The most commonly used Chinese pastes are made out of several kinds of beans, flour, sesame seeds, and hot peppers. The latter, hot pepper paste, or *lajiao jiang*, is a coarse paste made out of mashed red peppers. Its consistency is somewhere between that of chili sauce and relish. Mrs. Chiang adds it to dishes when she wants to give them a more complicated flavor and texture than can be obtained by using other, simpler, heating agents, like red pepper flakes in oil.

Back in Szechwan, Mrs. Chiang's mother made her own hot pepper paste; here in America, we buy it. Chinese grocery stores sell the stuff in jars imported from Taiwan under a variety of labels; the most common one is "hot chili paste with garlic." Once you open a jar of hot pepper paste, keep it tightly closed in the refrigerator. It should last several months, though with a gradual loss of potency. There is a closely related Szechwanese condiment called "hot bean paste," or *ladouban jiang*, which can be substituted for regular hot pepper paste if necessary. Using hot bean paste will alter the composition of the dish, but the essential taste will remain the same.

韭 菜

JIUCAI (*jiucai*)

This is a grasslike Chinese vegetable with a mild onion flavor that can sometimes be found in Chinese markets. Scallions are an acceptable substitute.

MONOSODIUM GLUTAMATE (*and why we don't use it*)

Contrary to popular belief, this crystalline white substance does not enhance the natural flavors of ingredients. It just adds its own, a pleasant sweet and salty one. MSG tastes good, which is why most bad Chinese restaurants use so much of it. With a lot of monosodium glutamate in your sauce, you don't need to add very much else. It is the ingredient that gives so much Chinese restaurant food its typically "Chinese restaurant taste." It is also the ingredient that gives those who are susceptible that tight feeling around the temples known as the "Chinese restaurant syndrome."

Although MSG was commercially available in Szechwan, few home cooks used it. Like here, it was a staple of big restaurants. Mrs. Chiang's mother never cooked with it, and neither does Mrs. Chiang. She relies instead on such things as garlic, ginger, scallions, sugar, soy sauce, sesame oil, Szechwanese and hot peppers, star anise, rice wine, and rice vinegar to set off the natural flavors of the ingredients she uses. The resulting food is often highly spiced and full of teasingly complicated flavors, but it tastes like real food and it won't make your temples throb.

花 生 油

PEANUT OIL (*huasheng you*)

Mrs. Chiang's family made its own cooking oil. They grew a plant especially for its oil-bearing seeds, which they took to a special press in the neighborhood to have the oil extracted. The family used this oil both for cooking and for light. Kerosene, which they would have preferred to burn in the small earthenware and porcelain oil lamps that lit the family's house, was too expensive for everyday use. The oil was light and fresh, perfect for cooking. It is, of course, unavailable in this country.

Because Mrs. Chiang feels that the wrong kind of cooking oil can ruin a dish, all her recipes specify peanut oil. It may cost more, but it makes a difference where it really counts, in the final taste of a dish. Other light vegetable oils, though usable in an emergency, have a stronger taste and impart a mildly un-Chinese flavor to most stir-fried dishes. Sesame oil is not a cooking oil, but a condiment. Because it is unknown in the West, many people mistakenly assume that the classiest Chinese dishes were fried in sesame oil. Actually, lard is the aristocrat of Chinese cooking fats, and a truly elegant household would have done much of its cooking in lard. Cholesterol aside, Mrs. Chiang considers lard too rich for her kind of food and much prefers peanut oil for everyday use.

You can get peanut oil at your local supermarket. But if you plan to cook a lot of Chinese food, buy your peanut oil in a Chinese market, where it comes in gallon cans.

螺 絲

PERIWINKLES (*luosi*)

For a discussion of this ingredient, see page 215.

油菜

RAPE (*youcai*)

For a discussion of this ingredient, see page 255.

飯

RICE (*fan*)

For a discussion of this ingredient, see pages 279-280.

糯 米

RICE, GLUTINOUS. *See* GLUTINOUS RICE

米 粉

RICE STICK NOODLES (*mifen*)

For a discussion of this ingredient, see page 287.

醋

RICE WINE VINEGAR (*cu*)

There are several kinds of Oriental vinegars available in Chinese grocery stores. Mrs. Chiang prefers the lighter Japanese style to the darker Chinese, and she uses it for all her cooking. It is pale and fairly mild. It, of course, will keep indefinitely without refrigeration. If you can't find any Japanese-type rice wine vinegar, substitute a light cider vinegar. Don't use a red wine vinegar or one flavored with herbs or spices.

葱

SCALLIONS (cong)

A Szechwanese cook without scallions would be as helpless as a French chef without onions or shallots. There are few of Mrs. Chiang's recipes that don't require them, and they have no substitute. Onions, literally "foreign scallions" in Chinese, may be botanically related, but they are much too sweet when they are cooked. Even though they were available on Taiwan, no onions ever crossed Mrs. Chiang's cleaver.

When you prepare scallions, break off the hairy roots, leaving the white part intact. Peel off the outer layer of skin, then rinse the scallions, and cut or chop them into the size pieces specified in the recipe. Mrs. Chiang uses both the white and the green parts of a scallion in most of her dishes.

麻 油

SESAME OIL (ma you)

This rich, golden brown oil is made from sesame seeds. Its nutlike flavor and appetizing aroma are totally unlike those of any other edible oil. Mrs. Chiang uses it regularly to enrich the overall flavor of a dish, but she never uses it for frying. It is a condiment, not a cooking oil. Its cost alone would make such a use absolutely prohibitive, and its flavor would overpower that of every other ingredient in the dish.

Sesame oil is not hard to find. Some gourmet shops carry it, as do both Chinese and Japanese food stores. It comes in bottles of various sizes and can even be purchased in half-gallon cans, which, if you do a lot of Oriental cooking, represent real savings. Sesame oil needs no refrigeration and will keep just about indefinitely. Use only Chinese or Japanese sesame oil; the pale yellow kind purveyed by health food suppliers is too highly refined for Chinese cooking and has very little taste.

芝蔴醬

SESAME PASTE (*zhima jiang*)

This thick, rich paste made from sesame seeds is similar in color and texture to peanut butter. It is imported, and can be found in bottles in Chinese markets. It will keep fairly well even after it is opened, and does not need refrigeration. It will, however, separate if it stands for any length of time, with the oil rising to the top and the thicker part of the paste settling to the bottom. Make sure to stir it up thoroughly before you use it.

Middle Eastern sesame paste, or *tahini*, is only a moderately good substitute. It is thinner, milder, and less aromatic than the Chinese variety. Use it only if you have no other alternative.

雪豆

SNOW PEAS (*xuedou*)

The snow peas used in the recipes in this book *must* be fresh; frozen ones will be limp, soggy, and uninteresting. You will usually be able to get fresh snow peas in a Chinese or Japanese market; if not, substitute green peppers, string beans, or any similarly crisp green vegetable for them.

醬 油

SOY SAUCE (*jiangyou*)

Soy sauce was such an important condiment in the large and busy peasant household where Mrs. Chiang grew up that the family made its own. The pungent brown liquid was aged in huge earthenware vats, large enough, Mrs. Chiang recalls, for a small girl to hide in. Both light and dark soy sauces were produced, as well as a rather unusual sweet variety. Although Mrs. Chiang feels that few ingredients available today either on Taiwan or in the United States are as good as those she remembers from Szechwan, she is more than satisfied with the soy sauce. She finds Kikkoman soy sauce particularly good—full-bodied, tasty, and uniform in quality.

There is a difference between light and dark soy sauces, but it is not a difference that matters for Szechwanese home cooking. It is a question of color, not taste or texture. Mrs. Chiang, then, uses Kikkoman soy sauce in all her cooking. Actually, the only variable that makes a significant difference in soy sauces is their saltiness. This is the factor that absolutely rules out the use of the kind made in America; it is too salty, and the taste is wrong. It also rules out the use of the *tamari* type of soy sauce sold in health food stores; it is too bland.

Luckily, good soy sauce is easy to find. Supermarkets and gourmet stores often stock Kikkoman in several different-sized bottles. But if you do a lot of Chinese cooking, you may want to purchase this most important of all Oriental ingredients in larger amounts. Both Chinese and Japanese grocery stores usually sell soy sauce by the gallon. It needs no refrigeration and will keep indefinitely.

春捲皮

SPRING ROLL SKINS (*chunjuan pi*)

For a discussion of this ingredient, see pages 313-314.

八角

STAR ANISE (*bajiao*)

Mrs. Chiang uses these flowerlike "stars" to add a pleasant licorice flavor to some of her most delicious slow-cooked meat dishes. Her mother used the spice more frequently, for the family grew its own star anise. Mrs. Chiang remembers picking the fragrant eight-pointed stars from a small tree in back of the house and setting them out to dry in the sun. In this country star anise is sold, dried, at Chinese grocery stores. Each dark brown star measures about an inch across, but few of them survive the trip to the retailers' shelves intact. Because of this, the star anise available here usually comes in fragments of various sizes that are packaged in little cellophane bags. Keep it in an airtight container and it should last indefinitely. If you are desperate for a substitute, add a few anise seeds or a drop of anise extract, but don't add too much. The flavor of star anise should be distinctive, not over-powering.

花 椒

SZECHWAN PEPPER (*huajiao*)

Szechwan pepper, or *huajiao*, is the regional spice of Szechwan. It is what gives Mrs. Chiang's peppery, hot Szechwanese specialties their particular, tingling fragrance. In addition to its unique aroma, Szech-wan pepper possesses an unusual quality, which the Chinese call *ma*. It is the slight numbness on your tongue this spice produces when you eat it. Mrs. Chiang's family grew their own *huajiao*. She claims that when you tasted the spice fresh, the numbing sensation it caused was more than slight. As a child, she would pick fresh peppercorns off a little tree near the house and let them dry in the hot summer sun. But her mother used so much Szechwan pepper in her cooking that the family often had to buy some to supplement their supply.

Szechwan pepper is not hot, as chili peppers are hot. Its flavor, though spicy, is far more complicated and aromatic. Since it is often used in conjunction with regular hot peppers, its numbing qualities tend to be confused with the genuinely mouth-burning qualities of ordinary red peppers. As far as we know, no other cuisine, Chinese or Western, uses Szechwan pepper. Its characteristic fragrance in a dish tells you that it is Szechwanese even before you taste it.

Except for their color, Szechwan peppercorns look pretty much like regular black ones. They are small, hard, dark brown, and wrinkled. They are sold in Chinese markets, usually in small cellophane packets. They will keep for a long time in an airtight container, but Mrs. Chiang cautions against buying too much at one time, for they lose some of their potency with age.

Mrs. Chiang uses Szechwan pepper in two ways—whole and ground roasted. She adds whole peppercorns to dishes that have to simmer for hours, like Fresh Ham (page 89) or Red-Cooked Pork (page 92). She also uses them for making pickles and marinating poultry. Most of the time, she uses her Szechwan pepper ground and roasted. She adds it to a dish while it is cooking or sprinkles it over one just before she serves it. Here is how to prepare it:

2 *to 3 tablespoons whole Szechwan peppercorns*	Put the Szechwan peppercorns in a small, flat frying pan over a low flame. Shake the frying pan gently for several minutes, until the peppercorns become fragrant and turn dark brown. Don't let them burn.
	Let the peppercorns cool, then pulverize them. If you have a blender, use it. If you don't, you can crush the peppercorns in the traditional way with a mortar and pestle or, as Mrs. Chiang used to do before she discovered the blender, with a rolling pin.

Since ground roasted Szechwan pepper loses its freshness and aroma fairly fast, don't prepare more than a few tablespoonfuls at a time. Keep the ground roasted Szechwan pepper in a tightly sealed container, of course.

四 川 榨 菜

SZECHWAN PRESERVED VEGETABLE (*sichuan zhacai*)

Mrs. Chiang's mother pickled many of the vegetables the family grew, then during the winter months she would serve them as a side dish with rice at almost every meal. She also used them as an ingredient in other dishes, especially soups. The family liked the sharp and sour taste of a few pickles in their otherwise bland soups. Mrs. Chiang says that many of the vegetables her mother pickled are not grown outside of Szechwan. But, because pickles can be canned without losing any of their potency, the imported kinds most Chinese grocery stores stock are quite acceptable. They usually come in cans labeled "Szechwan preserved vegetable." The vegetable is never identified, but it is probably the heart of an indigenous species of cabbage. The pickles themselves are olive green knobs about the size of a Ping-Pong ball. They are usually covered with a paste of finely ground red pepper, which should be rinsed off before the pickles are used in cooking. After you open a can of Szechwan preserved vegetables, transfer the unused pickles to an airtight jar or plastic bag and store them in the refrigerator. Since they are pickles, they will last a long time.

荸荠

WATER CHESTNUTS (*biji*)

Water chestnuts were not grown on Taiwan at the time of our first visit there. But such were the pressures of gastronomy that, despite the rigid embargo on things from the Chinese mainland, there was always a loophole through which these crunchy vegetables could get to the island.

Water chestnuts are a texture food, and are prized for their crispness. Fresh ones have a sweet and mild taste as well. Canned ones, unfortunately, have a slightly metallic "canned" taste, which detracts from the overall flavor of any dish in which they are used. You cannot substitute canned water chestnuts for fresh ones. If you can't get fresh water chestnuts (and they are sometimes difficult or impossible to find, even in Chinatown), omit them from the recipe. The taste will not be affected, only the texture. There are of course, some recipes in which the texture of fresh water chestnuts is crucial, like Shrimp Balls (page 210); those you can't make.

Fresh water chestnuts are round, blackish bulbs about the size of an ordinary chestnut. When they are available, they can be found in the produce department of a Chinese market, where they are sold by weight. Prepare them by cutting off the dark outer skin and chopping the hard white meat inside into whatever sized pieces the recipe requires. Unpeeled water chestnuts will keep for a week or two in the refrigerator.

餛 飩 皮

WON TON SKINS (*huntun pi*)

These are usually available by the package in Chinese grocery stores. They vary greatly in quality, the thinner and fresher the better, but one rarely has many options.

SOURCES OF CHINESE INGREDIENTS

This list of Chinese grocery stores is anything but complete; nor is it a list of the "best" or "most convenient" markets. It is intended primarily for those readers who will have to order ingredients by mail. The retailers who fill mail orders are marked by an asterisk (*). Any Chinese grocery store, whether listed here or not, should be able to supply all of the ingredients for the recipes in this book. It should also be able to supply you with any special cooking equipment you may need.

*Tuck Cheong Company
617 H Street, N.W.
Washington, D.C. 20001

Wang's Company
800 Seventh Street, N.W.
Washington, D.C. 20001

*Wing Sing Chong Co., Inc.
921-931 Clay Street
San Francisco, Calif. 94108

*Kam Shing Company
2246 Wentworth Avenue
Chicago, Ill. 60616

Eastern Market
46 Beach Street
Boston, Mass. 02111

Oriental Food Mart
909 Race Street
Philadelphia, Pa. 19107

Kam Man Food Products
200 Canal Street
New York, N.Y. 10013

*Oriental Country Store
12 Mott Street
New York, N.Y. 10013

United Supermarket
84 Mulberry Street
New York, N.Y. 10013

*Wing Fat Co., Inc.
35 Mott Street
New York, N.Y. 10013

4 - EQUIPMENT

Our first kitchen in Taiwan was a semiopen shed with a sink in it attached to the back of the house. There was no stove, no refrigerator, none of the special equipment I had always assumed was necessary for cooking, let alone for producing Chinese food. Our cook did all her cooking over a primitive, yet highly effective, mechanism, the size and shape of a bucket, which burned coal dust briquettes. We ate very well. When we returned to Taipei seven years later, we lived more sumptuously. The kitchen was a regular room inside the house, and it contained a sink. It also had a stove of sorts, two small burners that were connected to a large tank of bottled gas by a rubber tube. The rest of the equipment was on the same level; a few pans, a large chopping block, and a cleaver. This was all Mrs. Chiang needed to turn out a wide range of Szechwanese dishes.

In America the preparation of Chinese food does not require special equipment either. Every essential cooking procedure and technique can be duplicated using regular Western-style pots and pans. There are even some American gadgets that are more efficient for the preparation of Chinese food than the traditional implements. For example, Mrs. Chiang quickly discovered the advantages of an electric blender over a rolling pin for grinding roasted Szechwan peppercorns, that essential Szechwanese spice.

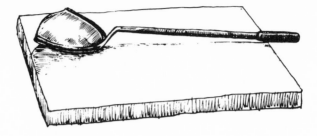

Cooking shovel

The pleasures of cooking Chinese food are increased, however, when a few basic Chinese utensils are used. The four important items are a wok, the traditional round-bottomed Chinese pan; a wok cover; a cooking shovel; and a cleaver. These tools were developed specifically for Chinese cooking, and they do make it easier. They also help give a sense of the spirit of Chinese cooking. But they are not indispensable; there is no point in buying them until you have experimented with a few recipes and are sure you want to continue cooking and eating Chinese food.

A few years ago a wok could be purchased only in Chinatown; today imported woks and sometimes even real Chinese cleavers and cooking shovels can be found in gourmet cookware and department stores. One American manufacturer has produced a reasonably attractive and efficient set of enamel pans that doubles as wok and steamer. But Chinatown remains the least expensive and most dependable source of real Oriental cooking equipment. Both traditional grocery stores and gift shops sell kitchen utensils, although they are often not on display; the proprietor can usually fetch anything you need from a back room. And cooking equipment can be ordered from most of the stores listed as filling mail orders.

A NOTE ON STOVES

The common Chinese technique of frying tiny pieces of food in extremely hot oil requires that the cook have complete control over the amount of heat she is using. Often a recipe specifies that you begin to cook something over a very high flame and then reduce the heat quickly as you add new ingredients. A gas stove is fine for this kind of cooking; the flame can be raised and lowered instantaneously, and the exact amount of heat can be carefully observed and regulated.

Electric stoves, on the other hand, require special tricks, but can produce excellent results when properly used. When Mrs. Chiang first came to America, we lived in a house with an electric range. It seemed to take forever for the burners to heat up and just as long for them to cool off. The split-second temperature adjustments that Chinese cooking required seemed impossible to obtain. Yet Mrs. Chiang overcame this handicap and managed to produce completely authentic Chinese food on that electric stove. She used two burners, one at high heat and one at a lower temperature. She would switch the pan from burner to burner to get the rapid temperature changes that the cooking required. In this case, as in so many others, a little ingenuity proved to be more important than any special equipment.

THE TOOLS

Szechwan home cooking requires only a few basic items; in the following pages we describe the four that Mrs. Chiang uses every day. In addition, we describe some utensils that, while not essential, are unique and often aesthetically satisfying. The list is not exhaustive; it serves only as an introduction to the equipment for cooking and eating that Mrs. Chiang and I consider most useful for the home cook.

The Cleaver

Chinese cooking involves a great deal of chopping, and for this there is no more efficient implement than the Chinese cleaver. Any good sharp chef's knife can be used, but there is no point in depriving yourself of the best tool for the job. Mrs. Chiang uses a heavy steel cleaver for all her chopping, and under her tutelage I have learned to prefer a cleaver even for Western cooking. It is far superior to an ordinary kitchen knife because it is heavier; it is more work to lift, but gravity takes care of most of the work of chopping. This gives you more control, since you can use your energy to guide the cleaver rather than to force it to cut. The blade of the cleaver is about 7 inches long and

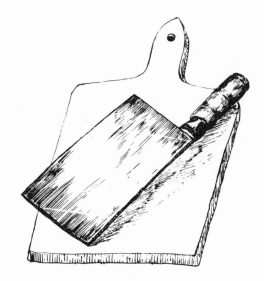

Chinese cleaver

3 inches wide. The round wooden handle is itself rather hefty. Although there are now some stainless steel cleavers on the market, most Chinese ones are made of regular carbon steel. The blade may darken and even rust a little. Don't panic—just try to keep your cleaver clean, dry, and sharp. You will need a good sharpening steel, which is not difficult to use, and you will need to remember to wash and dry the cleaver, by hand, immediately after using it. Do not put it in the dishwasher.

The Chopping Block

The indispensable counterpart of a cleaver is a good, solid chopping block. Mrs. Chiang's mother did all her chopping on a traditional Chinese chopping block, a 3-inch-thick section of log with the bark still on it. A less exotic American chopping block or board is perfectly adequate, as long as it has a large surface and is heavy enough to withstand the blows of a Chinese cleaver.

The Wok and Its Accessories

The wok is the archetypal Chinese utensil. ("Wok" is actually the Cantonese pronunciation for the name of this particular cooking vessel. People from Szechwan, like all other speakers, call it a *guo* and the standard English translation for the word is "pan." However, since the term "wok" has already become so ubiquitous in the United States, there is little point in sacrificing clarity for the sake of linguistic purity. In this cookbook, at least, a *guo* is a wok is a pan.) Although practically any of Mrs. Chiang's recipes can be made in a regular flat frying pan, there is no question about the advantages of a wok. Its round bottom and sloping sides allow the cook to fry any amount of ingredients in hot oil while continually scooping them up and stirring them around—the uniquely Chinese cooking technique known as "stir-frying." At the same time, the wok can be used to cook a dish that has to be simmered slowly for hours. It can also be easily converted into an effective steamer.

Many woks come with a circular ring stand designed to adapt them to American stoves. It is supposed to hold the pan steady so it doesn't roll around. The ring stand does, indeed, keep the wok from wobbling, but holds it much too far away from the flame for cooking. For a Chinese cook, the advantages of being able to get the pan really hot far outweigh those of a wobble-free cooking vessel. Anyhow, it is almost impossible for a fully-loaded wok to tip over.

When selecting a wok, be sure to get a big one. It can do anything a small one can, because its shape allows you to cook small amounts of food at the bottom. With larger amounts, you avoid the frustration of spills during vigorous stir-frying. Mrs. Chiang uses a wok about 14 inches in diameter. It looks huge on our kitchen stove, but she says it would have been considered small in Szechwan:

"We had four different-sized woks, each one designed to fit a space in our big brick stove. The smallest was for soup and the largest, which was truly immense, could cook enough fried noodles to feed all the field workers during the harvest."

Like cleavers, most woks are made of regular steel and can get slightly rusty (so be sure to wash your wok carefully, by hand, and dry promptly and thoroughly). They invariably turn black inside and out after a little use. There are stainless steel or aluminum woks on sale in sets practically everywhere. These woks are fairly small, 11 or 12 inches in diameter, and do not provide the best heat distribution; so do get a regular steel wok. And remember to season your wok before you use it. Brush the inside surface with cooking oil and heat the wok, over a low flame, until the wok is hot; then cool, wash, and dry.

A Steamer

Many specialty stores and Chinese groceries stock intriguing items such as bamboo scoops or oddly shaped strainers; they might be fun to experiment with, but are not essential for Szechwan home cooking. A steamer is another matter; these are both hard to find and expensive.

Luckily, a steamer is easy to improvise; the principle is simply to suspend a plate of ingredients over boiling water inside a covered container. There must be room for the steam to circulate freely around the food, and the lid must fit securely, to keep steam from escaping. Any large covered pot will do; a rack can be improvised from a large tin can with holes punched in the end, or you can buy an inexpensive metal vegetable steamer rack in any housewares store.

Mrs. Chiang converts our wok to an efficient steamer by fitting the metal ring stand inside the wok above an inch or two of water. The plate of ingredients rests on this ring and the wok cover holds in the steam. (The sloping sides of the wok make this possible; in a straight-sided pot you need a rack with legs.) The removable burner ring from the top of a gas stove works equally well. A more effective steamer would be hard to devise, especially since the sloping sides of the wok make it easy to remove the plate from the steamer without scalding your fingers.

Wok and ring stand

An Electric Rice Cooker

If you eat Chinese food every day, as we do, you might consider buying an electric rice cooker. It is an inexpensive appliance, about the size of a large saucepan, which does for rice what an automatic coffee maker does for coffee. It cooks the rice and then turns itself off automatically—and the rice is always perfect. Cooking rice requires more self-confidence than skill, and this gadget is the salvation of anyone who abhors undercooked rice yet is terrified of scorching it. Electric rice cookers are rapidly becoming standard items all over the Orient, and are usually available in Chinese and Japanese stores in this country. You might even recognize the brand names.

TABLEWARE

You don't need special tableware to eat Chinese food, but there is a certain anticlimax to spending time preparing an authentic Chinese meal and then eating it with knives and forks. All you really need to set an authentic Oriental table are chopsticks and rice bowls. Both are inexpensive, attractive, and useful.

Mrs. Chiang recalls, "Tableware was one of the few things we bought; we made practically everything else we used. Most of the time we ate with plain bamboo chopsticks, but when my mother's relatives came for a visit she brought out silver chopsticks, and two pairs of ivory ones that were kept for my grandparents."

Chopsticks

Once you have mastered them, chopsticks are amazingly versatile. They are standard kitchen equipment. Mrs. Chiang uses them constantly for stirring, and for such tasks as removing fried shrimp balls from a wok full of hot oil. They do not conduct heat, nor do they impart any taste of their own to the food as a metal spoon would. Chinese cooks and gourmets are highly sensitive to such slight nuances of flavor, and have always preferred nonmetallic implements for cooking and eating. Plain wooden chopsticks are the best kind to buy. The more elaborate lacquered or plastic ones are somewhat harder to use because they are slightly slippery. Ivory chopsticks, the most elegant of all, are correspondingly even more difficult to manipulate.

I must confess to grave doubts about the usefulness of any written instructions for the use of chopsticks. It is a skill that requires practice and a certain feeling for the proper method that even the most detailed primer cannot convey. Mrs. Chiang explained to us that nobody ever formally "teaches" Chinese children how to use chopsticks:

"We were given chopsticks as soon as we were old enough to sit up by ourselves. We were encouraged to experiment with them, and we learned by imitating our elders. My parents believed that if a child stuck out his fingers while eating his mother would die, and I remember being slapped when I didn't hold my chopsticks properly. That was the only instruction; by the time I was five I had mastered the chopsticks."

We tried this method, without the slapping of course, on our own children, and were pleasantly surprised to find that our oldest son had become remarkably proficient at the age of five and a half. If you can't grow up in a Chinese family, the best way to learn how to use chopsticks is to corner an experienced user and imitate everything he does. Lacking all other guides, here are some instructions. If you follow them carefully and practice, you should be adept within a short time.

Before you begin, make sure that you hold the chopstick by the square end and eat with the round. Then take up one chopstick and place it between the middle of your thumb and the tip of the ring finger of your right hand (left hand, obviously, if you are left-handed). The ring finger should hit the chopstick just below the point where it becomes round. The top part should be wedged firmly in the fleshy part of your hand between the thumb and index finger. When you press the middle of your thumb and your ring finger against the chopstick, it should be rigid. This chopstick is not supposed to move when you are eating.

Now hold the other chopstick like a pencil—that is, between the tip of your index finger, the middle joint of your third finger, and the tip of your thumb. The tip of the second chopstick should intersect with the tip of the first at about a 30-degree angle. Hold the upper chopstick gently and move it up and down slightly by applying pressure with your third finger. The bottom chopstick should not move.

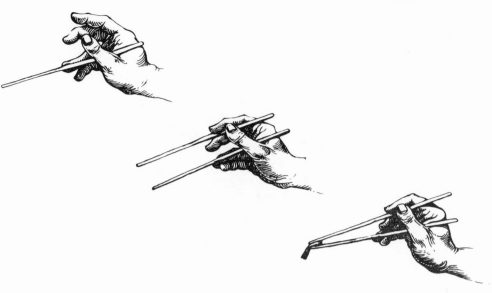

How to hold chopsticks

Before you try to pick anything up with the chopsticks, *make sure that the round tips are even with each other.* This is the only real trick involved in using chopsticks. Even if you are holding them correctly, you will not be able to manipulate them effectively or pick anything up unless the ends are the same length. Even them up by tapping the tips gently on the table or your plate.

Rice Bowls

These small porcelain bowls are a useful and attractive acquisition if you plan to serve Chinese food often. They hold about ¾ cup of cooked rice and can be used for a variety of other purposes, Chinese or Western. Any gift shop specializing in Orientalia is sure to have a selection.

Porcelain Spoons

If you plan to set a truly elegant table, you might even get some traditional Chinese porcelain spoons for eating soup. Their main advantage is that they don't impart a metallic taste to the food. This is of course, a highly delicate refinement and not a particularly essen-

Rice bowl and porcelain spoon

tial one. We Westerners have been eating with metal spoons for years without noticing their aftertaste. But then, few of our soups are as delicate and subtly seasoned as Mrs. Chiang's are.

ONE FINAL NOTE

It is important to keep in mind that, although all the various Chinese implements I have just described may add a certain psychological zest to the preparation and consumption of Chinese food, they have absolutely no effect on its taste. You don't even need a wok to be a good Chinese cook. As long as you use the proper ingredients and follow the recipes, you will achieve the true taste, or *zhen wer*, even if you cook in an ordinary frying pan and eat off paper plates. The casual substitution or omission of ingredients is a travesty, the use of a knife and fork is not.

5 - METHODS

There is nothing technically difficult about cooking Chinese food, but for some reason most Americans hesitate before a wok, as though fearing some mysterious Oriental challenge. But, with the proper ingredients and minimal attention to details, it is probably harder to ruin a Chinese meal than a Western one. Cooking procedures are simpler and less vulnerable to accident; there are no sauces to curdle, no soufflés to fall. Mrs. Chiang's most elaborate dishes, like Smoked Chicken or Eight Treasure Rice, are produced with a series of simple steps.

There is only one trick to Chinese cooking—organization. Preparing food for cooking is as crucial as the cooking process itself, and usually more time consuming. The main process is chopping, for everything that goes into a wok must be diced, sliced, minced, slivered, or shredded. Small pieces of food cook quickly, a definite advantage in a land like China, where fuel is scarce. And there are no knives at a Chinese dinner table, so all the food that reaches it must be precut into bite-sized pieces or else simmered so long that it falls apart at the slightest touch of a chopstick.

There is an aesthetic aspect to this method of preparing food, for all the important ingredients in a dish should be the same size and shape. If the main ingredient is pork shreds, all the other ingredients are shredded. Szechwanese food demands even more work with the cleaver than do other regional cuisines, because its complicated seasonings include large amounts of finely chopped garlic, ginger, and scallions. Food preparation is so crucial to authentic Szechwan cooking that we have divided the recipes (with two or three exceptions) into two parts, preparation and cooking.

The planning and pacing of food preparation distinguishes an experienced Chinese cook from a novice. Mrs. Chiang does almost all her chopping before she puts a single drop of oil in the wok. The reader will find the process an easy one if certain elementary rules are followed before cooking is begun. First, read through the recipe; much trouble can be avoided by knowing beforehand what has to be done. Next, assemble all your ingredients and chop them before starting to cook. Once you begin cooking, especially if you are making a quick stir-fried dish, you will not have time to mince a scallion or even measure out a spoonful of cornstarch and mix it with water.

The following section contains detailed descriptions of those Chinese kitchen techniques necessary for authentic Szechwanese home cooking. They are divided, like the recipes, into two sections: preparation, which is essentially chopping; and cooking. They are the cooking methods that Mrs. Chiang learned in her mother's kitchen, and, like all physical skills, they are easier to pick up in the flesh than on paper. The best way to learn how to cook Chinese is to watch an experienced Chinese cook. Fifteen minutes in the kitchen with Mrs. Chiang would be a far better introduction to the technical side of Szechwanese home cooking than pages of the most carefully written instructions. Fortunately, the specific techniques are neither difficult to master nor, in the long run, all that important. It makes no difference in the taste of the finished dish whether you mince fresh ginger with a narrow-bladed kitchen knife or chop it with a Chinese cleaver. Yet, because Chinese cooking methods are specifically designed for preparing Chinese food, they do make it easier and more accurate. And, that, of course, is the best reason for learning them.

PREPARATION

The main activity here is chopping, to which Mrs. Chiang devotes most of her time. She also does things like soaking dried vegetables, but no instructions are necessary for that kind of preparation.

Chopping

Mrs. Chiang's mother owned a narrow-bladed knife, but she used it rarely. All of her serious chopping was done with a cleaver. Different ingredients call for somewhat different chopping techniques, all of which I will describe, but the basic way of holding the cleaver and the material to be chopped remains the same.

Grasp the wooden handle of the cleaver firmly with your right hand (the reverse, obviously, if you are left handed). There is no special grip; whatever feels most secure and comfortable is correct. Use your left hand to feed the ingredients into the blade of the cleaver. Mrs. Chiang holds down the food she is about to cut with her fingernails and curls her fingers forward so that her knuckles, not her fingertips, come in contact with the broad side of the cleaver as it moves up and down. This enables her to control the cutting process with precision but no risk.

Three different types of food must be chopped: hard vegetables like ginger or water chestnuts, soft or leafy ones like scallions or Chinese cabbage, and meat.

Before chopping a hard vegetable like ginger, peel it. Then, pressing it down against the chopping block with the fingernails of your left hand, push it slowly toward the cleaver and cut it vertically into slices, ¼ to ⅛ inch thick. Use the cleaver with a slightly rocking motion. You do not have to exert much force on it; the weight of the cleaver will power it through. If you have to shred or chop the vegetable further, stack the slices one on top of the other and cut through them vertically into shreds, feeding the pile of slices slowly into the cleaver. If the recipe calls for even smaller pieces, stack the shreds in a pile and repeat the process. You may have to chop something like ginger into even tinier pieces. In that case, get your left hand out of the way and chop at your ingredients with small, even strokes of the cleaver until they reach the desired size. At no point should you have to use force: the weight of the cleaver alone is sufficient.

Soft and leafy vegetables like Chinese cabbage rarely have to be finely minced. For most of them, use your cleaver with a light back-and-forth sawing motion to cut the vegetables into chunks or shreds. Scallions have to be more finely chopped. Grasp them with the finger-nails of the left hand and feed them into the cleaver the way you would a hard vegetable. Cut them crosswise as fine as you can and then chop at them steadily until the pieces reach the desired size.

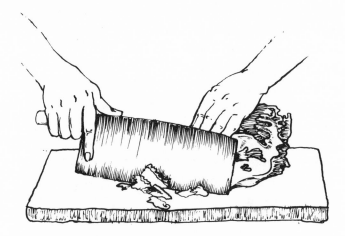

Chopping vegetables

Garlic is neither a soft nor a hard vegetable, but it is so commonly used in Szechwanese cooking that the best way to chop it should be described. Before peeling each clove, smash it with the flat side of your cleaver. The skin will zip right off and the garlic itself will be easier to chop because it won't skid all over the chopping block. Garlic cloves are generally too small to be cut into regular shaped pieces. Just chop at them steadily with gentle strokes of your cleaver until the pieces are the requisite size.

To make meat easier to cut, put it in the freezer first for about 10 or 15 minutes, until it becomes stiff but not frozen. When slicing lean pork or beef into shreds, press down on the meat with the palm of your left hand and cut it horizontally into several thin slices. Then stack the slices one on top of the other, grasp the pile with the fingernails of your left hand, and cut the meat into shreds as you feed it cautiously into the cleaver. There are no tricks involved in cutting meat into larger pieces. Use a slow, deliberate sawing motion. The only time Mrs. Chiang swings her cleaver with any vehemence is when she is hacking through bones.

Mrs. Chiang uses a cleaver for other culinary operations besides cutting. She likes to use the broad, flat side of the cleaver for smashing ingredients that don't have to be finely chopped, like ginger when it goes into a long-simmered dish or garlic cloves before she peels them. The cleaver is also useful for transferring ingredients directly from the chopping block to the wok. Mrs. Chiang cups her hand and uses it to scrape the chopped ingredients right onto the flat cleaver blade. The dull edge of the cleaver is an excellent tool for pounding and tenderizing meat, and even the handle has a function. Mrs. Chiang uses it with a small, deep bowl as a mortar and pestle to mash things like chopped garlic and ginger into a paste.

COOKING

Mrs. Chiang can produce hundreds of different Szechwanese dishes, each one more delicious than the last. Yet, for most of them, and for most of the recipes in this book, she uses only four different cooking methods: stir-frying, deep-fat frying, simmering, and steaming. These will be described below. Special techniques, like smoking, which are used in only one recipe will be explained fully in that recipe. Other cooking procedures, like boiling noodles, are so universal they need no explanation.

Stir-Frying

Stir-frying is the quintessential Chinese cooking technique, the rapid frying of diced, sliced, or shredded ingredients in a little oil over a high flame. Stir-frying looks more complicated than it is, mainly because everything happens so fast. With a high flame, pork shreds will cook in 2 minutes. Vegetables take only a little longer, and it is rare for any stir-fried dish to need more than 10 or 15 minutes on the top of the stove. If you were to telescope all the operations involved in cooking a simple American meal of meat, potatoes, and vegetables into a similarly short time span, you would probably find yourself working at an even dizzier pace.

If you have a wok, the traditional round-bottomed Chinese pan, use it. It is *the* pan for stir-frying; its sloping sides make it particularly easy to scoop ingredients up and around into the hot oil in the middle of the pan. A regular flat-bottomed frying pan will also work. It can be used in much the same way as a wok, although, since a larger surface of the pan is in direct contact with the flame, you may have to add more oil than the recipe calls for and you will probably have to be more careful about burning things. The following instructions are for a wok, but can be easily adapted to a flat frying pan.

The first step in stir-frying is to heat the wok. One reason for doing this, according to Mrs. Chiang, is to make sure that there are no drops of water clinging to the surface of the wok that would make the oil sputter as it gets hot. (In the best of all possible worlds, woks are always clean and dry. But all too often woks have a tendency to rust slightly when not in use, and you may have to wash yours out right before you use it.) Fifteen seconds over a high flame should be enough time to heat the wok before you add the oil.

You will have to wait a while, usually several minutes, for the oil to become hot enough for cooking. How long you wait depends on so many variables—the amount of oil, the conductivity of your pan, the heat of your stove—that you cannot rely on the times listed in the recipe. Determining when the oil is at the proper temperature for cooking is quite important. Too cold, and your ingredients will lie soggily in the bottom of the wok, absorbing oil instead of cooking in it. Too hot, and your ingredients, especially delicate ones like chopped ginger, will burn. A lifetime of experience has enabled Mrs. Chiang to grasp the perfect moment. It comes at the point when some little wisps of smoke first appear and a few tiny bubbles start to form. Mrs. Chiang suggests that the best way for a beginner to tell if the oil is right is to drop a tiny piece of chopped ginger or garlic or a sliver of scallion into the pan. If whatever you put in turns brown immediately, the oil is too hot. If it sinks to the bottom of the pan and just lies there, the oil is too cold. The ginger or garlic or scallion should float on the surface of the oil, sputtering and hissing.

The essence of stir-frying is to make sure that everything in the wok comes into contact with the hot oil in the bottom of it. The method depends on the amount of ingredients in the wok. If there are only a few things, like some chopped garlic and ginger, stir-frying consists of simply stirring them around in the hot oil so they don't burn. No special technique is required here. With more ingredients, the scooping motion commonly associated with stir-frying comes into play. According to Mrs. Chiang, it really involves two separate motions. The first is to dig under the ingredients with your cooking shovel or spoon and scoop them off the sides and into the middle of the pan. The second is to stir the stuff around in the center of the pan to make sure that it gets evenly cooked there.

Mrs. Chiang does not always hover over her wok and stir continuously. Unless she is cooking something that burns easily, like chopped ginger and garlic, she lets the contents of the wok cook quietly for several seconds before she redistributes them. A frenetic rhythm is less important than seeing that everything in the pan cooks evenly and quickly and without burning. I am constantly amazed by how calmly Mrs. Chiang stir-fries a wokful of spattering, sputtering ingredients. She makes it look easy, and it is.

Deep-Fat Frying

Where would the cuisine of Szechwan be without the crispness of Fragrant, Crispy Duck or the crunchiness of a fried shrimp ball? These are textures that come only from deep-fat frying. Fortunately, frying Szechwanese food in deep fat is just like frying anything else that way. Mrs. Chiang uses a wok; because of its shape she needs less oil than with a straight-sided pot. But any pot you normally use for deep-fat frying is acceptable. The Chinese have invented various types of wire and bamboo strainers for lifting food out of hot oil; they are available in Chinatown and at some gourmet stores. An ordinary slotted spoon works well, too. Mrs. Chiang uses chopsticks. They don't conduct heat, and, if you can manipulate them, they let you handle ingredients with precision and deftness.

Since each dish requires a different amount of oil and each stove has its own idiosyncrasies, there is little point in giving any specific instructions here for the amount of oil or its proper temperature. The recipes do that.

Like any thrifty housewife, Mrs. Chiang recycles the oil she uses for deep-fat frying. She lets the oil cool and the sediment settle to the bottom of the pan. Then she strains the oil gently into a large glass jar; a piece of cheesecloth inside a strainer works beautifully. She is careful to use the oil in which she has fried fish only for frying fish and that in which she fried sweet things for other sweet things. She keeps the oil in the refrigerator between uses.

Simmering

Mrs. Chiang makes some gloriously rich and savory stews, with large chunks of meat so tender they fall apart at the touch of a chopstick. They are among the easiest of her recipes to prepare, for they require little in the way of time-consuming preparations, and the basic cooking process, boiling the ingredients in a covered pot over a low flame, is as straightforward as it sounds. Mrs. Chiang has gotten considerable mileage out of our large spaghetti pot. She uses it for making such delicacies as Fresh Ham, or *tipan*, or for boiling all the many ingredients of a *liangban pinpan*, Mixed Cold Plate, together in the same rich, anise-flavored sauce. There are some slow-cooked dishes like Lions' Heads, or *shiz tou*, and Anise Chicken, or *hongshao bajiao ji*, which have to be partially stir-fried before they are stewed. This is because some of their ingredients, like Chinese cabbage or garlic, need to be fried first to release their flavors and to ensure that the long cooking that is necessary to make the meat tender does not turn the vegetables into an insipid mush. Although you can do the initial stir-frying of such a dish in a wok and then transfer everything into a large, covered pot for the final slow cooking, you don't have to. As long as you can cover your wok, you can simmer in it as well. And since simmered dishes can be prepared in advance and reheated just before serving, they are especially well suited for entertaining.

Steaming

Mrs. Chiang often steams food Western cooks bake or roast. Meat, fish, poultry, desserts, and even breads are all steamed, which allows them to cook undisturbed in their natural juices. Steaming produces particularly light and elegant dishes, in which are emphasized the freshness and delicate flavor of the original ingredients. Steamed breads and pastries are moister and softer than baked ones. Yet steamed dishes are remarkably easy to make. All you do is steam them. And for that all you need is a steamer, an implement that requires no technical skill to use. You can buy an authentic Chinese steamer or you can make your own (see page 54).

No matter what kind of a steamer you buy or make, the instructions for its use are the same. First, fill the bottom of the steamer with water and put it over a high flame. When the water is boiling, place the plateful of ingredients to be steamed on a rack or pedestal over the water. If you are steaming breads or pastries in a traditional bamboo steamer, put a piece of cloth on the bottom of each steamer tray to keep the pastries from sticking to the bamboo. Cover the steamer and let it do its work. The only thing you will have to do while the steaming is in process is to check the water level occasionally. Whenever the water seems low, add a little more. Some people like to keep a kettle of boiling water nearby for refilling the steamer.

Steam is hot stuff, so be careful not to scald yourself when you remove something from the steamer. Mrs. Chiang always waits a few minutes for the steamer to cool off before she unloads it.

6 - MENU PLANNING

Mrs. Chiang's arrival in America completely altered our life style. We began to give dinner parties, dozens of them, for her food was so good we felt obliged to feed all our friends. As we discussed these dinner parties ahead of time with Mrs. Chiang, we began to learn how much menu planning contributes to the enjoyment of Chinese food. We came to appreciate how cleverly a well-designed meal accentuates the special character of each dish while at the same time blending all the dishes together into one carefully constructed and harmonious whole. We also discovered that knowing how to plan a Chinese dinner not only helped us prepare interesting and appropriate meals at home, but also made it easy for us to order them in Chinese restaurants.

In this section we are going to discuss only the most basic principles of menu planning. To help you apply them to actual meals, we have appended some lists to this section. They classify the recipes in this cookbook into several useful categories, the most important being taste and ease of preparation. Once you learn the elementary rules of menu planning, using these lists will make arranging a real Chinese meal as easy as choosing from column A and column B.

The essence of Chinese menu planning is variety, which has three basic sources—the main ingredients of a dish, its taste, and its texture and appearance. Planning a two-dish family meal is much easier than designing an elaborate multicourse banquet, but the necessity for variety remains the same. Not only should each dish be different from the one before, but the dinner itself should be a variegated whole, encompassing as many different ingredients, tastes, textures, colors, and shapes as possible.

First, every meal should present a balanced mixture of kinds of foods. A meal consisting only of meat dishes, even if each one comes from a different category, would be disastrous. Mrs. Chiang's family ate much less meat and many more vegetables than we do. She recalls, "Except at New Year's, we never ate meat, fish, and poultry in the same meal or even on the same day; it would be too heavy! For lunch we would usually have two vegetable dishes, with sometimes an egg dish. For dinner we had four dishes, and only one would be meat or poultry. The others were always vegetables, pickles or bean curd. I am like my mother; I believe each meal should have a vegetable dish, or at least a dish with vegetables as well as meat."

A sophisticated balance of flavors is vital; the aim is to present as many different tastes as possible without repeating any. The more courses you add, the more difficult this is to do. There are four major taste groups: red-cooked and hot, anise-flavored, sesame-paste-flavored, and mild and gingery. They are all listed at the end of this section, and fully half the recipes in the book belong to one of them. This does not limit you to four or five dishes per meal, for there are dozens of other tastes that don't belong to any specific category. They range from the sweet taste of plain fried fish to pungent, salty black beans, from the subtle flavor of smoked chicken to the savory hotness of dry-fried beef.

When Mrs. Chiang plans a meal, she arranges the sequence of dishes to emphasize diversity. A delicate dish of Shrimp with Ginger and Wine is followed by spicy Pock-Marked Ma's Bean Curd, a rich Anise Chicken with a plain sautéed vegetable. Such contrasts bring out the unique qualities of each dish in the most vivid possible way. Occasionally, she serves dishes with similar tastes but very different main ingredients, like Shrimp with Ginger and Wine along with Sautéed Rape. But then she positions them at opposite ends of the meal.

These rules apply to all Chinese food. Szechwan cuisine adds a local complication: hotness. Gastronomic sense decrees that you do not precede a mild dish by an especially fiery one, for palates numbed by hot peppers can't fully appreciate delicate flavors. Mrs. Chiang usually follows a really hot dish with something assertive, though not necessarily peppery. Then she serves a mild dish.

The final element of a well-planned meal, the texture and physical appearance of its dishes, is quintessentially Chinese. Variety and contrast in the color of sauces and ingredients, the size and shape of pieces of food, and the texture—hard or soft, crunchy or gelatinous—are important. Mrs. Chiang enjoys planning a meal that includes crisp things like Shrimp Balls, soft things like bean curd, large hunks of meat and slivers, bright green vegetables, and pale pink shrimps. A meal that consists only of shredded food is as unconscionable as one in which everything is covered with a dark brown sauce.

Planning a meal is like playing chess: every time you choose a dish you have to assess its effect on the rest of the meal and how it will limit your available options. Suppose you are preparing a dinner party for ten people. You should probably count on serving about seven dishes and a soup. You might want to preface the meal with a light appetizer like nuts. If you serve Anise Boiled Peanuts, you will be unable to serve any other anise-flavored dish later, so you opt for Sweet Fried Nuts with pecans. Then, for the first regular dish, you choose Cold Kidneys in Sesame Sauce. You could serve Bon Bon Chicken instead—the sauce is the same—but then you eliminate other chicken dishes from the menu. Next you might want a simple dish of Sautéed Rape, its bright green color and fresh, natural taste a nice contrast to the complex flavors of the kidneys. Anise Chicken would be a logical next course (selecting it ruling out other anise-flavored dishes as well as other chicken ones). Though you could serve a different chicken dish like *gongbao jiding*, or Grand Duke's Chicken with Peanuts, doing so would prevent you from serving Double-Cooked Pork later in the meal, since they both have the same color sauce and the same sized chunks of meat and green peppers. Follow the chicken with a delicate shrimp dish, perhaps Shrimp with Ginger and Wine or some Shrimp Balls, which have the requisite mildness as well as a nice, crisp texture. A hot red-cooked dish is appropriate now. Double-Cooked Pork would be excellent. An equally delicious classic, Pork in the Style of Fish, would eliminate anything else in a similar style like Pock-Marked Ma's Bean Curd or a fish. A vegetable dish should follow, something light like Sautéed Spinach to balance the rich, heavy pork. The final dish before the soup should be a spectacular one, a whole fish, perhaps, or vibrant Pock-Marked Ma's Bean Curd. If you serve the latter, you will have to serve rice as well, for the spicy sauce demands a bland accompaniment. Soup would then be your final course, a delicate one like Seaweed Soup or Winter Melon Soup. Bean Curd Soup, though subtle and delicious, can't come after a *mapo doufu;* it's also made of bean curd. If you serve a fish, and don't serve rice, you can end the meal with a traditional starchy course after the soup, some Oily Scallion Cakes or a plate of Fried Noodles. Here is what your meal looks like:

Sweet Nuts (pecans)
Cold Kidneys in Sesame Sauce
Sautéed Rape
Anise Chicken
Shrimps with Ginger and Wine or Shrimp Balls
Double-Cooked Pork
Sautéed Spinach
Pock-Marked Ma's Bean Curd or Red-Cooked Fish
Rice
Seaweed Soup or Winter Melon Soup
Fried Noodles or Oily Scallion Cakes

The dinner is a balanced one, containing a wide variety of tastes and ingredients, as well as the two most famous Szechwanese specialties, Double-Cooked Pork and Pock-Marked Ma's Bean Curd. These dishes are not the only ones you could have chosen; at any point you could have substituted any one of a number of other dishes. The only consideration in selecting a specific dish is how it relates to the rest of the meal.

Another way to organize a meal is to plan it around a special dish; Fresh Ham, or *tipan*, for example, or Fragrant, Crispy Duck. If you do this, you should orchestrate the rest of the meal to lead up to that dish. This is not very difficult, because something like *tipan* is such a large dish that you will not need as many courses to round out the menu.

One serious consideration I have not yet dealt with is convenience. The preparation of a traditional Chinese dinner of many courses requires the services of at least one full-time cook. Many dishes cannot be made in advance but must be rapidly stir-fried over a high flame and served right away. This means that the cook, if he or she is moderately conscientious, must stay in the kitchen throughout the course of the meal. We have been to dinner parties at the homes of Chinese friends where we never caught more than a passing glimpse of the hostess until after we had finished eating. Menu planning for people who are willing to sacrifice the pleasure of their guests' company is not difficult. For others, it presents more of a challenge, though not an insuperable one. It simply requires you to consider the convenience of each dish, as well as its ingredients, taste, and physical appearance.

Fortunately, Mrs. Chiang's repertoire contains a large number of cold dishes and dishes that can be prepared in advance and reheated just before serving. These include some of the most spectacular items in this cookbook, like Smoked Chicken and Fresh Ham. Many dishes, like Pork Dumplings or Spring Rolls, can be partially made ahead of time and then simply boiled or fried at the last minute, a much less complicated procedure than the production of a stir-fried dish from scratch. Steamed dishes also require little last-minute effort. (All of these dishes are listed at the end of this section.) Even stir-fried dishes, if you do all your chopping ahead of time, should not take more than a few minutes in front of the stove. The easiest and often the cheapest way to feed a large crowd is to serve only one thing, a huge batch of Fried Noodles (page 283), or a mountain of Spring Rolls (page 313). This is what Mrs. Chiang's mother did when she had a houseful of people and didn't want to spend either time or money in feeding them. (These one-dish meal items have also been listed.)

How the meal is served is part of menu planning, too. Small family meals are always informal, but the more courses you prepare, the more attention you will have to pay to the order of serving. If you are only going to serve a few dishes, they can all be placed on the table at one time. For a larger dinner, it is probably easier to offer each course separately. Cold dishes should come first, soups and starches last. In between, the courses should be organized to emphasize as much diversity as possible. Rice is eaten throughout the meal.

When Mrs. Chiang's mother prepared an elaborate meal for visiting relatives, she would serve the courses one at a time. For regular family dinners, however, she put everything on the table at once. The members of the family sat on wooden benches around a large square table in the middle of the kitchen. Nobody ate individual portions of food off separate plates the way we do in the West. Only the rice was served separately, in small porcelain bowls. Each person used his chopsticks to help himself to some food from the communal dishes in the middle of the table. He would put the food on top of his rice and then eat it along with a mouthful of rice. Most of the children ate one or two bowls of rice, the adults more. Even though there were usually at least nine or ten people at the table, mealtimes were surprisingly quiet. Eating, not talking, was the rule. Mrs. Chiang remembers being sent away from the table, supperless, when she and her sister giggled too loudly.

As for beverages:

"We drank tea with every meal; we bought it because it was very cheap. We never drank milk. Wine was for special occasions, but my father liked to drink. He would invite his friends over for drinking and cards, and they would drink rice wine or *gaoliang*, a strong brew made from distilled millet. They would eat cold sliced meats or nuts, but that wasn't considered a regular meal."

THE LISTS: AN AID TO MENU PLANNING

These lists include only those recipes that fall into one or another of the categories we feel are most useful in menu planning: reddish brown, anise-flavored, sesame paste-flavored, mild and gingery, and other (dishes with distinct flavors that don't fall into another category). A recipe that is not listed is likely to be a simple stir-fried dish, or a bread, pastry, or soup. There are two sets of lists, the first classifying dishes mainly by their taste, the second by ease of preparation.

A glance at the first set of lists reveals that they are quite lopsided. There are five categories, but one of them, reddish-brown dishes, is disproportionately larger than all the others. It is based on color as well as flavor, and includes more than one taste. Most of the dishes in this category are hot and spicy. Those that aren't are also covered with thick, reddish-brown sauces and cannot decently be accommodated on the same menu with the hotter dishes unless you are planning a very large meal. Anise-flavored dishes also have dark brown sauces, but the sauces are much thinner and have such a distinctive taste that they deserve a separate category. If you plan to serve them at a meal with any of the other reddish-brown dishes, make sure that something of a lighter hue comes in between.

Hotness is not a class by itself, but it is important. We have indicated it on the lists with a fiery sign, ✿ . In some dishes hotness can be optional; we have noted that as well.

The second set of lists contains easy-to-prepare items, including most of the non-stir-fried dishes in the book. It also includes a list of dishes that can form the basis of an entire meal all by themselves. Many of these dishes are actually more complicated to prepare than most stir-fried dishes, but, since they can be made in advance, they are convenient for entertaining.

TASTE AND COLOR

These categories are general, but they are the most important ones for menu planning.

Reddish-Brown

All the dishes in this list are covered with a reddish-brown sauce. That may be all they have in common, but it should be enough to keep you from offering too many of them at any one meal.

Red-cooked or *hongshao* (All of these dishes are covered with rich and spicy sauce, full of garlic, ginger, and scallions):

✿ Red-Cooked Beef with Noodles (page 292)
✿ Red-Cooked Brains (page 152)
✿ Liver and Snow Peas (page 155)
✿ Red-Cooked Fish (page 190)
✿ Fish with Meat Sauce (page 193)
✿ Red-Cooked Fish Slices (page 200)
✿ Red-Cooked Shrimp (page 206)
✿ Red-Cooked Bean Curd (page 224)
✿ Spicy Chinese Cabbage (page 239)
✿ Eggplant with Chopped Meat (page 253)
✿ Noodles with Meat Sauce (page 294)

In the style of fish, or *yuxiang*:

✤ Pork in the Style of Fish (page 103)
✤ Pock-Marked Ma's Bean Curd (page 220)
✤ Eggplant in the Style of Fish (page 250)

Explosively fried with hoisin sauce, or *jiangbao*:

Pork Shreds with Hoisin Sauce (page 106)
Chicken with Hoisin Sauce (page 174)

Other (These dishes also have dark sauces, but somehow don't belong in any of the above categories):

✤ Double-Cooked Pork (page 94)
✤ Grand Duke's Chicken with Peanuts (page 171)
Snails (page 215)
✤ Ants Climb a Tree (page 290)
Soybeans (✤ optional) (page 338)

Anise-Flavored

Fresh Ham (page 89)
Red-Cooked Pork (page 92)
Mixed Cold Plate (anise liver, tongue, and duck) (page 98)
✤ Red-Cooked Beef with Noodles (page 292)
✤ Anise Chicken (page 167)
Anise Boiled Peanuts (page 336)

Sesame Sauce

✤ Kidneys in Sesame Sauce (page 147)
✤ Bon Bon Chicken (page 163)
✤ Cold Eggplant with Sesame Sauce (page 248)
✤ Don Don Noodles (page 299)

Mild and Gingery

(Many plain stir-fried vegetables can also be mild and gingery if you omit the optional red peppers):

Meat-filled Omelets (page 130)
Stuffed Cucumbers (page 133)
Pearl Balls (page 135)
Steamed Fish (page 197)
Shrimp with Ginger and Wine (page 208)
Crab and Egg (page 213)
Batter-Fried Bean Curd with Shrimp (page 226)
Sautéed Rape (page 255)
Pork Chop Noodles (page 296)
Pork Dumplings (page 306)

Other

(This category contains only those dishes which have unique flavors that are particularly useful for menu planning. It omits the plain stir-fried combinations of meats and vegetables, plain vegetables, soups, and breads or odd tidbits that one hesitates to actually call dishes):

Black Beans, Green Peppers and Pork Shreds
(❀ optional) (page 108)
❀ Pork, Cucumber, and Cellophane Noodle Salad (page 118)
Deep-Fried Pork Chops (page 123)
Sweet and Sour Spareribs (page 125)
Lions' Heads (page 127)
Lotus Root Balls (page 137)
❀ Dry-Fried Beef (page 139)
Smoked Chicken (page 161)
❀ Chengtu Chicken (page 175)
Fragrant, Crispy Duck (page 183)
Deep-Fried Smelts (page 198)
Shrimp in Red Sauce (page 203)
Shrimp Balls (page 210)
Two Sides Yellow (❀ optional) (page 229)
❀ Asparagus Salad (page 234)
Chinese Cabbage and Dried Shrimp (page 240)
❀ Cucumber, Carrot, and Cellophane Noodle Salad (page 245)
Spinach Salad (❀ optional) (page 258)
Dry-Fried String Beans (page 259)
Fried Rice (page 281)

Fried Noodles (page 283)
Fried Rice Stick Noodles (page 287)
Dumpling Knots (page 302)
Spring Rolls (page 313)
Won Tons (❋ optional) (page 319)

EASY-TO-PREPARE DISHES

These are all the dishes—noodles, breads, and so on—that can be made entirely or partially in advance or else can provide an entire meal in themselves. I have not included many soups in this category, but they are also very easy to prepare ahead of time.

Cold Dishes

(Not only can these be prepared in advance, they have to be):

Mixed Cold Plate (which includes anise-flavored liver, tongue, and duck) (page 98)
❋ Pork, Cucumber, and Cellophane Noodle Salad (page 118)
❋ Kidneys in Sesame Sauce (page 147)
Smoked Chicken (page 160)
❋ Bon Bon Chicken (page 163)
❋ Asparagus Salad (page 234)
Cucumber Salad (page 243)
❋ Cucumber, Carrot, and Cellophane Noodle Salad (page 245)
❋ Cold Eggplant with Sesame Sauce (page 248)
Spinach Salad (❋ optional) (page 258)
❋ Don Don Noodles (page 299)
Anise Boiled Peanuts (page 336)
Soybeans (page 338)
Pickled Vegetables (page 340)

Dishes That Can Be Entirely Made in Advance and Reheated Just Before Serving

(Most soups are in this category):

Fresh Ham (page 89)
Red-Cooked Pork (page 92)

Sweet and Sour Spareribs (page 125)
Lions' Heads (page 127)
Dry-Fried Beef (page 139)
❀ Red-Cooked Beef with Noodles (page 292)
❀ Anise Chicken (page 167)
Fragrant, Crispy Duck (page 183)
Deep-Fried Smelts (page 198)
❀ Eggplant with Chopped Meat (page 253)
Dry-Fried String Beans (page 259)
❀ Noodles with Meat Sauce (page 294)
Dumpling Knots (page 302)

Dishes That Can Be Made Almost Entirely in Advance:

(All of these dishes require preparation in advance, with only a simple final step like boiling, steaming, or deep-fat frying before they are eaten):

Steamed dishes:

Stuffed Cucumbers (page 133)
Pearl Balls (page 135)
Steamed Fish (page 197)
Flower Rolls (page 331)
Eight Treasure Rice (page 344)

Boiled dishes:

Pork Dumplings (page 306)
Won Tons (❀ optional) (page 319)

Fried dishes:

Deep-Fried Pork Chops (page 123)
Lotus Root Balls (page 137)
Shrimp Balls (page 210)
Spring Rolls (page 313)
Oily Scallion Cakes (page 326)
Sweet Fried Nuts (page 337)

One-Dish Meals

(These are mainly noodle-type dishes or heavy soups that do not require the accompaniment of rice to provide a full meal):

7 - A GUIDE TO THE RECIPES

We have tried to make our recipes as clear and detailed as possible. However, authentic Chinese food, and especially authentic Szechwanese food, is still a relative novelty to most American cooks, so some general discussion is in order. This section contains information about measurements, timing, the number of servings in a dish, and some characteristics of Chinese food and Szechwanese food in particular.

The recipes in this book are for the food a Szechwanese housewife prepared for her family in pre-revolutionary China. Mrs. Chiang learned the recipes at home in Szechwan, by watching her mother cook. I watched Mrs. Chiang prepare them in America, took notes on everything she did and wrote up the notes in the form of recipes. They produce completely authentic Chinese food, for we have not altered them in any way to conform to American ideas of what Chinese food should be. It is the food that we in America would call *home cooking*, even though, in China, many of these dishes are the staple fare of Szechwanese restaurants as well.

The selection of foods reflects everyday Szechwanese eating habits, and may seem slightly lopsided to an American. There are almost no desserts, because most Chinese meals end with fruit. Desserts are not the strong point of China's cuisine anyhow, and their near absence from Chinese menus in America is, for once, an accurate reflection of the art. Similarly, there are not many beef recipes. Beef was rarely eaten in the Szechwanese countryside where Mrs. Chiang grew up, and her repertoire reflects that fact. There are, on the other hand, a significant number of vegetable and bean curd dishes. Next to rice, the people of Szechwan ate more vegetables than anything else. They also ate a lot of bean curd; it was rich in protein, cheap, and delicious. We have included many noodle recipes; noodle dishes were extremely popular in Szechwan and deserve to be more so here.

A WORD ABOUT HOTNESS

Szechwanese food is often hot; approximately half the recipes in this book produce highly seasoned, peppery dishes. When you first taste an authentically prepared Szechwanese dish, the hotness may be overwhelming. But almost immediately you begin to taste the other flavors, made more delicious by the very pepperiness that at first seemed so formidable. The taste for hot food is acquired, but almost everyone who makes the effort quickly learns to love it. Friends of ours who initially balked at the spiciness of Mrs. Chiang's cooking now reach for the hot pepper oil in Chinese restaurants. Once you become accustomed to the cuisine of Szechwan, leaving out the hot peppers will be unthinkable.

On an absolute scale of hotness, Mrs. Chiang's dishes are not particularly fiery; they are actually rather moderately spiced. But they are hotter than most Americans, and most non-Szechwanese Chinese, are used to eating. This presents a real problem. It would be inconsiderate to ignore the fact that many people are not accustomed to hot food, but at the same time we do not want to alter Mrs. Chiang's recipes in any significant way. What we have done is what we did on the menu-planning lists—indicate which dishes are especially hot and put a fiery sign, ※, next to those ingredients which are the culprits. If you follow these recipes exactly, the end result will be completely authentic and fiery enough to delight any native or adopted son of Szechwan. If you are somewhat dubious about the ability of your family and friends to withstand the heat, you can reduce the amount of the hot ingredients. Try halving them initially and then slowly work your way up to the full degree of hotness. But don't leave them out. Omitting hot peppers can deform a Szechwanese dish, for in many cases it is the hotness that gives the food its distinction. All such dishes need some pepper, though they don't have to be very hot.

There are dozens of Szechwanese dishes that are not hot at all. At least half the recipes in this book produce mild and subtly seasoned food, from rich and flavorful meat stews to crispy fried breads and delicately steamed fish. Many of the most subtle and refined dishes in Mrs. Chiang's repertoire fall into this category, for the closer you get to Szechwanese *haute cuisine*, the less blatantly spiced the food becomes. Smoked Chicken, Fragrant, Crispy Duck, tiny Meat-Filled Omelets, Shrimps with Ginger and Wine: the list is long and delicious and includes many of our favorite dishes.

A WORD ABOUT MEASUREMENTS AND SERVINGS

We have tried to make the recipes as precise as possible, but nature is not precise. Vital Szechwanese seasonings like garlic, ginger, and scallions are not uniform in size and cannot be measured as accurately as things like soy sauce or salt. The measurements in our recipes are for average-sized vegetables and herbs. If your scallions are particularly fat or your garlic cloves particularly tiny, use your head and use less or more of them than the recipe stipulates. To make things easier, we have stated the measurements for ginger in terms of inches rather than teaspoons and tablespoons. Ginger doesn't come ready chopped, and it will save you a lot of work to measure it before you chop it rather than afterwards. Though ginger does vary in width, 1 inch of an average-sized piece should yield about 1 tablespoonful of finely chopped ginger. And, in any case, normal fluctuations in the amounts of chopped fresh ingredients do not make any difference in the final taste of a dish.

All our cooking times are expressed in what seem to be frighteningly precise figures—15 seconds here, 45 seconds there. We did this mainly to give you a concrete idea of how long, or usually how quickly, it takes something to cook. The times are short, but they are not sacred. You don't have to stand over your wok with a stopwatch in your hand, counting every second as you stir-fry a dish. It won't be ruined if you cook it an extra minute or two. Mrs. Chiang often does, for, like all natural cooks, she rarely prepares the same dish exactly the same way twice in a row, and her own cooking times deviate enormously. In addition, American stoves display extraordinary variations in the amount of heat they produce. Ingredients that cook in 3 minutes on one stove may need 4 or 5 on one with a less powerful flame. You may have to experiment with a few dishes in order to determine how closely your own stove conforms to the times in the recipes.

The number of servings is similarly flexible. The Chinese style of offering several different dishes at one meal makes it difficult to estimate the number of servings in each dish. So, rather than using an arbitrary or vague figure, we have decided not to specify any particular number of servings for each dish. The more people you plan to feed the more dishes you will have to prepare, for most Chinese recipes, especially those that require stir-frying, can't be doubled. Putting too much food into a wok invites disaster. The ingredients don't get hot enough; and meats in particular will simmer in their own juices, producing muddy sauces instead of the bright clear ones that characterize Szechwanese food.

PART III
THE RECIPES OF SZECHWAN

8 - MEAT

In Szechwan, meat meant pork. Everybody raised pigs. Mrs. Chiang's family had nine or ten, "big black ones that lived in three small huts in back of our house. They were raised for market; when they got to be three or four hundred pounds, my father would sell them. The buyers would come to our house and haggle for hours, and then they would all troop off to the nearest market to verify the price. But we always saved one pig for ourselves. My father would butcher it just before New Year's, and then my mother would have to rush to make a whole year's supply of sausages, hams, and salted meats before the holiday feasting began."

The meat from the family's pigs was incredibly fragrant and delicious, a far cry from the bland products of our chemically raised porkers. This was because the pigs ate almost as well as the family. Not only did they get table scraps, but they were also fed a special fodder plant called *saocai*, which was so fragrant and flavorful that the family used to eat it as well. Even better was the meat that came from pigs that died before they were fully grown. When the children saw sausages, ham, and salted meats suddenly sprout from the rafters of a neighboring house, they knew that a pig had just died. Such an event inspired nothing but envy at the thought of all the sweet and tender dishes that were being enjoyed next door.

Though pork predominated, it was not the family's only meat; they also ate beef, rabbit, and goat, but not very often:

"We kept two goats, and we children had the job of leading them to the cemetery and tying them up where they could eat grass. We also kept about fifteen rabbits. They were cuddly and white and we made pets of them. They were kept in a little mud house next to the pigsty, and we fed them bits of grass and vegetable. We used to get upset when one was killed, but when we smelled my mother's delicious rabbit dish we forgot how sad we were. Not everyone in Szechwan ate rabbit, but we loved it. There was a little shop in Chengtu that sold the most aromatic roast rabbit in the world. Whenever anyone went into the city they bought some; it was always rich and tender.

"We didn't have beef cattle; beef came from water buffalo, and they were raised as work animals. So we didn't eat much beef, although we kept a water buffalo. But my father loved beef; he believed it was good for you. It wasn't available very often, but whenever he heard of some for sale at a nearby market he would rush off and buy it. The meat was tough, since it came from a work animal, but it was also full of flavor. My mother cooked it a long time; it was too tough for stir-frying."

Lamb, which was really what we call mutton, was even less common than beef in Szechwan. It was hardly ever eaten by itself, but was made into a soup that was fed mainly to young children to help them develop bladder control. Veal was nonexistent.

In this cookbook, we have included recipes for only those kinds of meat that are easy to get in this country. I know of no butcher who carries goat, though one may exist.

Because the Chinese cook their meat differently than we do, they butcher it differently. A visit to a Chinese market will confront you with new cuts of meat—long slabs of lean pork as free from bones and fat as a filet mignon and big hunks of fresh bacon, two-thirds fat and one-third lean. Fortunately, you don't have to make a special pilgrimage to Chinatown to get most of the meat you need for the recipes in this book. The pork section of your neighborhood supermarket should suffice.

Most ordinary stir-fried dishes call for either shredded or sliced pork. For these we use pork chops. It is also possible to obtain the kind of completely lean meat needed for shreds and slices by cutting up a larger piece of pork, but pork chops are both easier to use and always available. There are a few famous Szechwanese dishes that require special cuts of meat, a fresh ham for a *tipan* or fresh bacon for Double-Cooked Pork, or *huiguo-rou*. These are always specified in the recipes. You may have to order them in advance or badger your butcher a bit to get them. Chinese grocers usually carry them. Ground pork is another type of meat commonly used in Szechwanese cooking. Mrs. Chiang's repertoire of ground pork dishes is so delicious and ground pork so easy to obtain that we have included a lot of recipes that call for it.

There are few beef dishes in this cookbook because we are presenting the real peasant food of Szechwan. To offer more beef recipes as a concession to American eating habits would be a misrepresentation, even though it is perfectly possible that if beef had been more available in Szechwan it would have been a more important part of the diet.

Since American beef can be stir-fried, it can be substituted for pork in most meat and vegetable dishes such as String Beans and Pork Shreds. It isn't as good though, for stir-fried beef doesn't taste quite as Chinese as pork. The most felicitous substitutions would be in long, slow-cooked dishes like Red-Cooked Meat, or *hongshao rou*, and in chopped meat dishes. Lean cuts of beef, top and bottom round, rump or sirloin, provide the best meat for most of Mrs. Chiang's recipes. Cheaper cuts of beef are usable, but tend to be either stringy or else taste too strongly of beef fat.

蹄膀

FRESH HAM (*tipan*)

Weddings were a time for feasting in Szechwan. No expense was spared, and the guests were offered the most elegant dishes the kitchen could prepare. In Mrs. Chiang's family it was traditional to serve three special banquet dishes, or *dacai*, at a wedding—a soup made out of a whole chicken, a whole duck, and a fresh ham, or *tipan*. Other delicacies could be added, but these three were crucial. All the guests could appreciate the extravagance of using a whole chicken just for a soup, and they knew how much effort went into preparing the duck, with its tender meat and crisp skin.

But it was the fresh ham that dominated the feast. It would appear majestically at the table, a mountainous hunk of meat bathed in a fragrant, mildly anise-flavored sauce and resting on a bed of bright green vegetables. Everybody would tear into the tender flesh with their ivory chopsticks, offering the choicest pieces to the most honored guests. The best part of the *tipan* was the fat that covered the meat in a thick, translucent layer, so soft and luscious that it literally melted in the mouth. Perhaps the reason why Western gourmets do not prize fat the way Chinese ones do is simply that Western cooking does not produce anything that is as pure, sweet, and fragrant as the succulent layer of fat on a *tipan*.

For such a spectacular dish, a *tipan* is sinfully easy to make. There is no chopping or stir-frying involved. All you do is simmer the fresh ham in a large pot for several hours with some ginger, scallions, soy sauce, wine, and spices. Though the actual cooking time is long, the amount of human effort required is not much more than that needed to scramble an egg. Yet you end up with a magnificent Chinese banquet dish, a real *dacai*. It is also a *dacai* that, like all long-simmered dishes, can be made way in advance and reheated just before serving. Only the spinach garniture must be freshly prepared. We usually use half of a fresh ham, weighing 6 or 7 pounds, for a *tipan*. It is a lot of meat, so plan your menu accordingly. We treat it as the equivalent of two or three smaller dishes.

When you serve a *tipan*, accompany it with a batch of steamed Flower Rolls, or *huajuan* (page 331). You need something starchy to mop up the sauce with, and *huajuan* are the traditional accessory.

Though the recipe calls for red peppers, this is not a hot dish. The peppers make the *tipan* lively, not hot.

PREPARATION

½ *fresh ham (about 6 or 7 pounds)*	Before cooking the ham, tie it in several places with a piece of string so it will not fall apart while it is cooking.
4 *scallions*	Clean the scallions, then cut them in half, using both green part and white.

5-inch piece fresh
  ginger
10 large or ½ cup
  smaller dried
  mushrooms

Smash the ginger with the side of a cleaver,
  but don't peel it.
Wash the dried mushrooms carefully. They
  do not have to be soaked.

COOKING

4 quarts water,
  approximately
(scallions, ginger, and
  mushrooms)
3 whole star anise or
  the equivalent in
  pieces
✿ 4 dried red peppers
1 tablespoon
  Szechwan pepper-
  corns

Put the ham in a very large pot and cover
  it with water.
Bring the water to a boil, then add the scallions, ginger, dried mushrooms, star
  anise, dried red peppers, and Szechwan
  peppercorns. Let the ham boil about 1
  minute, then remove as much as you can
  of the foam that has risen to the surface
  of the liquid. Cover the pot and let it boil
  fairly heavily for anywhere from 1 to
  1½ hours, until the liquid in the pot has
  been reduced to half its original amount.
  Turn the ham over once if you think it
  may not be cooking through evenly.

1 cup soy sauce
½ cup Chinese rice
  wine or cooking
  sherry
3 tablespoons
  granulated sugar

Add the soy sauce, wine, and sugar, then
  reduce the heat and let the ham simmer
  for 1 hour longer.

1 tablespoon sesame
  oil
2 teaspoons salt

Add the sesame oil and the salt and continue to cook the ham until the liquid has
  boiled down to about a quarter of its
  original amount.
(At this point, the ham is cooked. You can
  serve it right away or you can let it sit for
  several hours—or even days—in the
  refrigerator. Reheating will not hurt it.)
Just before you are ready to serve the ham,
  prepare its garnish of fresh spinach.

SPINACH GARNISH

1 *package (10 ounces) fresh spinach*

4 *cups water*

1 *teaspoon salt*

Wash the spinach carefully.

Bring the water to a full boil in a regular saucepan. Add the salt and then the spinach. Wait until the water boils again, then let the spinach cook for 2 or 3 minutes; don't overcook it. Drain the spinach, then arrange it decoratively on a large platter. Put the ham in the middle of the platter and remove the strings from it. Spoon the sauce over both the ham and the spinach and serve.

Note: It is a good idea to taste the mushrooms before you serve them with the *tipan*; they may have absorbed too much salt from the soy sauce during the cooking process. If so, discard them.

Be sure to try some of the layer of fat on the outside of the ham; it will literally melt in your mouth.

紅燒肉

RED-COOKED MEAT (*hongshao rou*)

"When my maternal grandmother visited us my mother would make a big pot of *hongshao rou*, red-cooked meat," recalls Mrs. Chiang. "My grandmother had lost her teeth, and her stomach couldn't tolerate peppers any more, but she loved to eat, especially rich meat dishes. A *hongshao rou* was the perfect way to honor her. When properly prepared, it is simmered for so long that the meat is almost disintegrating and is as soft as paste. Its rich, dark sauce is spicy and fragrant with star anise, but it is not hot.

"In a sense, this is a Shanghai-style dish because it contains no hot peppers or hot pepper paste, as do most Szechwanese *hongshao*. And it uses sugar, which is typical of the region around Shanghai."

Pork is so rarely stewed in America that you will probably have to get the meat for this dish specially cut. Fresh shoulder, ham, or butt are good. You can also substitute beef, though it doesn't have the rich flavor of pork. If you add the optional carrots and potatoes to the meat, you will end up with something that looks just like a regular stew. You could serve it that way, with rice of course. This is a useful dish for entertaining, especially if you don't have the time for a more elaborate Chinese meal. The recipe can be doubled and the whole dish can be prepared way in advance. It actually improves on standing.

PREPARATION

2 *pounds pork (the cut is unimportant)*	Chop the meat into 2-inch cubes. If the meat has bones, leave them in; they add richness to the dish.
2 *medium carrots (optional)*	Peel the carrots and slice them diagonally into chunks, roughly the same size as
2 *medium potatoes (optional)*	the pieces of meat. Peel the potatoes and cut them into chunks as well.
3 *scallions*	Clean the scallions and tie them together in a bunch.
2-*inch piece fresh ginger*	Smash the ginger with the flat side of the cleaver; you don't have to peel it. Do the
5 *cloves garlic*	same thing to the garlic cloves, but peel them after they have been smashed.

COOKING

3 *tablespoons peanut oil*	Heat your wok or pan over a moderate flame for 10 seconds, then add the oil. Let the oil get warm, but nowhere near as hot as it usually gets when you cook Chinese food.
1 *tablespoon granulated sugar*	Add the sugar and stir it very carefully for 20 seconds with your cooking shovel or spoon to make sure it doesn't burn. It will turn dark brown.
(ginger, pork cubes)	Turn up the flame and add the ginger and

the pork cubes. Stir-fry them for 1 minute, using your cooking shovel or spoon to scoop the pork cubes off the sides of the pan and then stir them around in the middle. Make sure they are all well coated with the caramelized sugar.

(garlic)

Add the garlic cloves and continue to stir-fry everything for another 1½ minutes.

(carrots and potatoes)

Now toss in the scallions, the optional carrots and potatoes and the star anise, wine, soy sauce, and salt.

4 whole star anise or the equivalent in pieces

2 tablespoons Chinese rice wine or cooking sherry

Bring the liquid to a boil and let it cook for 3 minutes, without stirring, then cover the pan and continue cooking the pork about 7 more minutes.

6 tablespoons soy sauce

½ teaspoon salt

¾ cup water

Add the water. Bring it to a boil over a high flame and let it boil vigorously for 5 minutes before covering the pan and lowering the heat.

Simmer the pork for 1 hour, or until it becomes very soft. Serve immediately, or reheat and serve later.

回 鍋 肉

DOUBLE-COOKED PORK (*huiguo rou*)

Mrs. Chiang remembers that "Chinese New Year was the biggest celebration of the year in the Szechwan countryside. We children got new clothes, shiny new coins, and special treats of candy, nuts, and oranges. My father would be very grave about weighing out each child's portion so none of us felt cheated.

"But the eating was even better than the gifts. Each branch of the family gave a banquet for everyone else; my uncle's was on the second day after the New Year, and my family's was on the fifth. The food was wonderful; my father slaughtered a pig just before the New Year so there was a lot of meat. We had several kinds of sausages and salted meats, fresh hams and rich meat stews. Best of all were the big platters of Double-Cooked Pork."

Double-Cooked Pork, or *huiguo rou*, is such a famous Szechwanese dish that many Chinese restaurants and cookbook authors in this country call it simply Szechwanese Pork. In a sense the name really isn't wrong, for the juxtaposition of clashing tastes and textures in authentic Double-Cooked Pork is quintessentially Szechwanese. It is hot, rich, fragrant, salty, and, because of the unusual presence of hoisin sauce, even a little bit sweet. Many Szechwanese dishes combine and contrast flavors, but what makes Double-Cooked Pork so special is its method of preparation and the particular cut of meat that is used in making it. It is a dish that plays upon the crispness and richness of pork fat, qualities that are highly prized by Chinese gourmets. An authentic *huiguo rou* must be made with fresh bacon, with its clear stripings of lean and fat. In Szechwan the meat Mrs. Chiang's mother used for Double-Cooked Pork came from such large pigs that, instead of containing several stripes of lean meat, each piece was half fat and half lean. When it was cooked, the meat would curl up into the shape of a tiny bowl, which was so similar to that of a Chinese oil lamp that the cooked pieces of *huiguo rou* were called "little oil lamps."

The meat in Double-Cooked Pork *is* cooked twice. First it is boiled, then fried, and it is the second cooking that is the crucial one. If it is done right, the slices of partially cooked fresh bacon will fry in their own fat. This requires a very hot flame, for otherwise the meat will simply stew in its own juice. This may seem to be an esoteric matter, but it is just the kind of thing that makes the difference between authentic Szechwanese food and a dismal approximation thereof. A real *huiguo rou* should have practically no sauce. Each piece of meat should be rather dry and coated with the savory remnants of the condiments rather than bathed in them.

All the other ingredients are secondary to the meat. Some cooks use green peppers, some don't. Leeks are generally *de rigueur*, but can be substituted for in an emergency by scallions and increased amounts of garlic. Though you can make a good Double-Cooked Pork using a different and leaner cut of meat, it won't be fully authentic. Fresh bacon is always available in Chinese markets, but it can be difficult to find elsewhere. Try pestering your butcher; it's worth it.

PREPARATION

1 *pound fresh bacon or similar* very fatty *cut of pork, in one piece*

4 *cups water, approximately*

Put the pork in a saucepan and cover it with water, first cutting the meat into several chunks, if necessary, to fit it into the pan. Bring the water to a boil and cook the meat for about 3 minutes, then remove the meat from the pan. Drain it and let cool. The pork will not be completely cooked; don't worry, it has a second chance. (You can, if you want, reserve the cooking liquid for making some other dish, like a vegetable or soup).

3 *leeks*

Slice the leeks in half lengthwise and wash them thoroughly, then cut them into pieces 2 inches long. Use both the white and the green part.

2 *green peppers*

Wash the green peppers, then cut them into pieces approximately 1 inch square.

4 *cloves garlic*

Smash the garlic cloves with the side of your cleaver, then peel. Chop the garlic into pieces the size of a match head.

(pork)

If you have used fresh bacon, slice the partly cooked meat across the grain as thinly as you can. Each slice should measure roughly 2 inches long and 1 inch wide. If you have a different cut of meat, try to cut it into pieces of this size.

COOKING

1 *tablespoon peanut oil*

Heat your wok or pan over a fairly high flame for about 20 seconds, then pour in the oil. It will be ready to cook with when the first tiny bubbles form and a few small wisps of smoke appear.

(green peppers)
½ *teaspoon salt*

When the oil is ready, add the green peppers and the salt. Lower the heat slightly and stir-fry the peppers, using your cooking shovel or spoon in a scooping motion to toss the pieces around in the pan so they all come into contact with the hot oil. (It doesn't make any difference if the peppers char slightly, so you don't have to be too conscientious about stir-frying them. Just make sure they all cook.) After 2 minutes, remove the peppers from the pan.

(leeks)

Put in the leeks without adding any more oil and stir-fry them over a medium flame for about 2 minutes, until they are limp. Then remove them from the pan.

2 *tablespoons peanut oil*
(6 *fatty slices pork*)

Reheat the pan over the same moderately high flame and add the oil. When it is ready for cooking, toss in about 6 of the fattiest slices of the meat. Stir-fry them, pressing them against the sides of the pan until most of their fat has been rendered.

(garlic)
✿ *1 tablespoon hot pepper paste*
1½ *tablespoons hoisin sauce*
(meat)

Now add the chopped garlic, hot pepper paste, hoisin sauce, and the rest of the partially cooked meat. Stir-fry these ingredients vigorously while you add them to the pan and continue to do so for about 2½ minutes. The mixture will be quite dry; it should be.

(green peppers and leeks)

Return the green peppers and the leeks to the pan and stir-fry them, together with the pork, for a final 2½ minutes, then serve immediately.

凉拌拼盤

MIXED COLD PLATE (*liangban pinpan*)

The traditional introduction to an elegant Chinese banquet is usually a Mixed Cold Plate. It consists of an elaborately arranged assortment of thinly sliced meats and other delicacies. Since a cold plate lies within the realm of *haute cuisine*, its appearance is very important. Its preparation presents an ambitious Chinese cook with an excellent opportunity to indulge himself artistically. We have encountered some extraordinary manifestations of this genre, including one plate of cold meats arranged in the form of a peacock. Although the creation of such esoteric masterpieces is normally the province of a professionally trained chef, any home cook can turn out an extremely decorative cold plate, consisting of tastefully arranged slices of meat, eggs, and other ingredients.

Mrs. Chiang says, "This was my father's favorite dish. It was prepared especially well at a local restaurant where he and his friends would gather to drink wine and play cards; I have always suspected that the wine and card playing were an excuse to eat there. My own cold plate is easier to make than most because everything is boiled together in the same rich, anise-flavored sauce. It uses red peppers to make the sauce bright but not hot."

Cooking the ingredients is the easiest step in constructing a mixed cold plate; slicing everything after it has been cooked is the most difficult. It is tedious and demanding work that is surprisingly time consuming. Arranging the sliced ingredients provides some compensation; it can be fun to express yourself artistically in the unusual medium of food. And while there are no set rules for laying out a cold plate, in this area of cuisine as in all others, Mrs. Chiang stresses unusual contrasts of textures and colors.

Be forewarned: if you follow this recipe exactly, you will produce an enormous amount of food, enough for several gigantic platters. This is because culinary tradition demands that a cold plate contain equal portions of each item. To avoid being overwhelmed by a mountain of anise-flavored cold cuts, simply reduce the number of ingredients you use. We have included a full panoply in the recipe in order to provide instructions for preparing each item. The overall combination is the essence of Chinese cuisine, with its emphasis on innards and on foods with unusual textures. But it is perfectly acceptable to prepare a cold plate containing only one or two items; and in fact, each major ingredient, like the duck or the pork loin, can easily be treated as a separate dish.

Note that you can boil all the ingredients of your cold plate a day in advance, leaving only the slicing and final arrangement of the dish for the day you plan to serve it. Even the final arrangement can be done hours in advance, as long as the platter is covered and doesn't dry out.

Note also that this dish is made by boiling a variety of meats and other things together in a large pot. Since different items are added at different points in the boiling, it is rather difficult to make the usual distinction between cooking and preparation in this recipe. Allow about 2 hours for cooking the cold plate and another 30 minutes for arranging it.

PREPARATION AND COOKING

8 *cups water* 1 *cup soy sauce* 2½ *tablespoons granulated sugar* 5 *whole star anise, or the equivalent in pieces* ❀ 6 *dried red peppers* 2 *tablespoons Szechwan peppercorns*	Put the water, soy sauce, and sugar in a large pot and bring them to a boil over a high flame. Then add the star anise, dried red peppers, and Szechwan peppercorns.
4 *scallions*	Clean the scallions, then fold them in half and tie them together in a bunch. Add them to the pot.
4-*inch piece fresh ginger*	Don't peel the ginger; just smash it with the side of your cleaver and put it in the pot.
1 *duck (4 to 5 pounds)*	Clean the duck carefully and remove the fatty sacs around the tail. Chop it in

half lengthwise down the breastbone (a cleaver or poultry shears will do the job). Put the halved duck in the pot. (You will use only one half of the duck in your cold plate. However, since the cooked duck will keep for several days, cook both halves. You can always serve the extra duck cold at another meal.)

3 *feet of dried kelp, approximately*

6 *cups warm water, approximately*

Put the dried kelp in a large bowl and cover it with the warm water. Let it soak for about 20 minutes.

2 *pork tongues*

4 *cups water*

Put the pork tongues in a medium saucepan and cover them with the water. Bring them to a boil and let them cook for about 2 minutes before removing them from the pan. Cool them off quickly by placing them in cold water. Then, using a small sharp knife and your fingers, peel the skin off the tongues. This is a tedious task; the skin doesn't come off easily, even though the parboiling should help somewhat. When the tongues are fairly well skinned, add them to the pot.

5 *large dried black mushrooms*

Rinse the mushrooms off under cold running water and add them to the pot.

¾ *pound fairly lean boneless pork, in one piece*

Put the pork in the pot.

4 *eggs*

4 *cups water, approximately*

Put the eggs in a medium saucepan, cover them with water, and bring them to a rolling boil. Reduce the heat and let the eggs boil for about 10 minutes, then remove them from the pan and run them under cold water. Set aside.

3 *squares bean curd (see note below)*

Put the bean curd in another saucepan, cover with water, and bring to a boil.

4 *cups water, approximately*

(kelp)

1 *tablespoon salt*

Simmer over a moderate flame for 15 minutes, then drain and set aside.

After the kelp has soaked for about 20 minutes and become soft and gelatinous, drain it. Then rinse it very carefully under cold running water. Use the salt, as you might use a kind of scouring powder, to rub into the kelp in order to scrub off all the impurities. When the kelp is clean, divide it in half and roll each half into a compact bundle. Tie each bundle together with string if the kelp itself won't hold together. Then add the kelp to the pot.

(eggs)

Peel the cooled hard-boiled eggs. Then, using a small knife or a taut piece of thread, make tiny parallel slashes about ¼ inch apart all over the surface of the eggs. (This will help the eggs absorb the flavor of the liquid in which they will be boiled.) Set the eggs aside.

1 *whole pork liver (about 1¼ pounds)*

Rinse the liver under cold running water and remove as much of the white membrane around it as you can. Set the liver aside.

1 *tablespoon salt*

½ *cup Chinese rice wine or cooking sherry*

(pork liver)

(eggs)

(bean curd)

2 *tablespoons sesame oil*

After all the ingredients in the large pot have boiled for at least 30 minutes, add the salt and the wine, then the pork liver. Cover the pot, but don't lower the flame.

Wait about 15 minutes, then add the hard-boiled eggs, bean curd, and sesame oil. Cover the pot again and let it boil over the same hot flame for about 5 more minutes.

Reduce the heat and let everything simmer, covered, for a final 15 to 20 minutes.

Turn off the flame, but don't begin to take the ingredients out of the pot. Let them cool in the pot for at least 30 minutes before you remove them and begin to prepare them for the cold plate. Reserve the cooking liquid and discard the mushrooms.

SERVING

The elegant nature of a Mixed Cold Plate requires that it be presented on a very large and attractive platter or tray. Every ingredient is sliced very thin and then arranged decoratively on the platter.

(lean pork)
(pork liver)
(pork tongue)
(bean curd)
Slice the lean pork, against the grain, as thinly as possible. Arrange the slices on the platter so they overlap slightly. Do the same with the liver, tongue, and bean curd.

(duck)
Use only one of the duck halves. Cut the drumstick off the duck and then chop the carcass crosswise, bones and all, into pieces about ½ inch thick. Chop the drumstick into ½ inch sections, too. Arrange them all on the platter.

(eggs)
Slice each egg lengthwise into sixths. Put the slices on the platter.

(kelp)
Cut the kelp bundles crosswise into pieces about ¼ inch thick. Arrange them on the platter.

1 tomato (optional)
After you have laid out all the meats, eggs, seaweed, and bean curd in some kind of design on the platter, you can, if you wish, garnish the center with a tomato rosette. Create it by making 8 lengthwise cuts two-thirds of the way down

from the top of the tomato and about ¼ inch deep, no deeper than the outside flesh of the tomato, and then bending each segment down like the petal of a flower.

4 to 6 tablespoons of the cooking liquid

Right before serving the cold plate, spoon the cooking liquid over it. Use enough liquid to moisten all the sliced ingredients, but not enough to drown them.

2 tablespoons sesame oil

Finally, sprinkle the sesame oil over the ingredients and serve.

Note: If you have laid out your cold plate ahead of time and refrigerated it, be sure to let it come back to room temperature before you serve it. There is nothing less attractive than the congealed fat of a chilled cold plate.

In this recipe, do not use the soft Japanese bean curd or the kind you make from a mix. Try to get slightly older and tougher bean curd. You can also use, if the Chinese stores have it, a form of slightly pressed bean curd with a brownish skin called *doufu gan*.

魚 香 肉 絲

PORK IN THE STYLE OF FISH (yuxiang rousi)

A malodorous quality clings to the literal English translation of the name of this celebrated Szechwanese specialty. But no fish are used in its preparation, and there is nothing fishy about the actual taste of the dish. The "fish" in its name refers to the fact that this particular method of cooking—and Mrs. Chiang makes many other things besides pork shreds in the style of fish—was originally similar to that used in preparing fish. By now it has evolved into a very specific recipe, which obtains its delicious result by using sugar and vinegar in addition to the more customary Szechwanese condiments. It is a highly complicated dish that tastes hot, sweet, and tart all at the same time.

Mrs. Chiang's version of this famous dish features an equally unusual interplay of textures. She gets it by adding fresh water chestnuts and tree ears to the pork shreds and chopped ginger and garlic. The combination lets you experience crunchy, gelatinous, fibrous, and soft textures all in one mouthful.

Do not use canned water chestnuts in this dish. If fresh ones are unavailable, leave them out. The texture may be less intriguing, but the taste will be authentic. It will also be hot. Some Szechwanese dishes are more fiery than others; this is one of them. It can be toned down somewhat by reducing the amount of hot pepper flakes in oil. Don't omit them though; *yuxiang rousi* should be hot.

PREPARATION

3 medium pork chops (for a yield of ¾ pound meat, approximately)

Remove all the fat and bone from the pork and slice it into very thin shreds, 2 inches long and ⅛ inch thick, or about the size and shape of a wooden matchstick. (It is always easier to cut meat into very fine slices if you first put it in the freezer for about 10 minutes, until it is slightly stiff, but not frozen.)

4 scallions

Clean the scallions; then cut them (both green part and white) into shreds about the same size as the pork.

(pork)
¼ teaspoon salt
1 teaspoon sesame oil
¼ teaspoon ground roasted Szechwan peppercorns
⅛ cup dried tree ears
1 cup boiling water

Take half of the scallion shreds and put them in a bowl with pork shreds. Add the salt, sesame oil, and ground roasted Szechwan peppercorns to the meat and scallions. Mix thoroughly and let stand for 30 minutes.

Put the tree ears in a small bowl, pour the boiling water over them, and let them soak for at least 10 minutes.

1½ inch piece of fresh ginger
4 cloves garlic

Peel the ginger and the garlic and mince them together very fine, until they almost reach the consistency of farina.

5 *water chestnuts* (*optional*) — Cut off the dark outside part of the water chestnuts and chop them into tiny pieces the size of a match head. (The water chestnuts should not be minced quite as fine as the ginger and garlic.)

(*tree ears*) — Before you drain the tree ears, make sure that they have become soft and slightly gelatinous. Then rinse them thoroughly and pick them over carefully to remove any impurities, such as little pieces of wood, that may still be embedded in them. Slice the tree ears into shreds approximately the same size as the pork and scallion shreds.

1 *teaspoon cornstarch*
1 *teaspoon water* — Combine the cornstarch and water, then add to the pork mixture and stir thoroughly.

COOKING

3 *tablespoons peanut oil* — Heat your wok or pan over a fairly high flame for 15 seconds, then pour in the oil. It will be hot enough to cook with when the first tiny bubbles form and a few small wisps of smoke appear.

(*garlic, ginger*)
❀ 1½ *teaspoons hot pepper paste*
❀ 1½ *teaspoons hot pepper flakes in oil*
(*tree ears, water chestnuts, and scallions*)
½ *teaspoon granulated sugar*
(*pork and marinade*)
1 *tablespoon water, approximately (optional)* — When the oil is ready, quickly add the ginger, garlic, hot pepper paste, hot pepper flakes in oil, tree ears, water chestnuts, scallions, sugar, and, finally, the meat mixture. As you throw in the various ingredients, agitate them around in the bottom of the pan with your cooking shovel or spoon so that the little pieces of ginger, garlic, and water chestnuts cook without burning. Then stir-fry everything together, using your shovel or spoon in a scooping motion to toss the ingredients around in the pan so all are

equally exposed to the hot oil. If the mixture seems too dry and is sticking to the pan, add a little water to it.

Continue to stir-fry the pork shreds until they are thoroughly cooked; they will have stiffened and turned pale. This whole process should take only about 3½ minutes.

¼ *teaspoon rice wine*
vinegar
Salt to taste

Add the vinegar and mix thoroughly; then taste for salt and serve immediately.

醬 爆 肉 絲

PORK SHREDS WITH HOISIN SAUCE (*jiangbao rousi*)

A *jiangbao* dish is one very quickly fried (the word *bao* literally means "explosively fried") in hoisin sauce, that thick, dark brown paste, made out of sweetened wheat flour, which in Mandarin is called *tianmian jiang.* According to Mrs. Chiang, *jiangbao* is a fairly common way to cook chicken and shrimps, as well as meat, in Szechwan. It is not a hot dish; it is rich and sweet. The barely cooked, slightly crunchy scallions provide a much-needed contrast both in taste and texture to the heavy sauce and chewy, fibrous pork shreds. In some ways, this combination of scallions and hoisin sauce is reminiscent of northern Chinese food. Scallions and hoisin sauce are, after all, the standard accompaniment to Peking Duck. This dish is as easy to make as it is delicious, and should not take more than 20 minutes to prepare. The cooking itself takes only 5.

PREPARATION

5 *medium pork chops*
(for a yield of 1¼
pounds meat, ap-
proximately)

Trim the fat and the bones off the pork chops, but reserve the fat from one of the chops. Slice the meat into slivers that are about the size and shape of wooden matchsticks, 2 inches long and ⅛ inch thick. (It is always easier to cut meat into fine slices if you first put it in the freezer for about 10 minutes, until it becomes slightly stiff, but not frozen.) Dice the reserved fat into pieces approximately the size of uncooked grains of rice. Keep the diced fat separate from the meat shreds.

10 medium scallions

Clean the scallions, then cut them, both green part and white, into 2-inch lengths. Slice these into shreds of about the same size as the meat slivers.

(pork)
1⅓ tablespoons soy sauce
1 teaspoon Chinese rice wine or cooking sherry
1 teaspoon sesame oil
1 egg white

Add half of the shredded scallions to the meat slivers, along with the soy sauce, wine, sesame oil, and egg white. Mix everything together thoroughly.

1-inch piece fresh ginger

Peel the ginger and cut it into shreds about ⅛ inch wide, the width of a matchstick. Set aside.

(meat mixture)
1 tablespoon water

Just before you are ready to begin cooking the meat, add the water and stir the mixture up.

COOKING

¼ cup peanut oil
(ginger)
(diced pork fat)

Heat your wok or pan over a high flame for 15 seconds, then add the oil. The oil will be hot enough to cook with when the first tiny bubbles form and a few small wisps of smoke appear. When the oil is ready, throw in the shredded ginger and the diced pork fat. Stir-fry them together over a high heat for about 30 seconds, using your cooking shovel or spoon to agitate them around in the bottom of the pan so they don't burn.

2 *tablespoons hoisin sauce*	Add the hoisin sauce and continue stir-frying the ingredients in the pan for another 15 seconds.
(pork and marinade) *(scallions)*	Now toss in the meat mixture and the rest of the shredded scallions. Stir-fry the meat for 3 more minutes. (You do not have to hover over the pan, stirring it continuously. Just scrape up the ingredients once in a while to make sure that all the pork is exposed to the hot oil and that nothing is sticking to the pan.) The meat will be completely cooked when it has stiffened slightly and turned a light grayish-brown color.
1 *tablespoon soy sauce*	Add the soy sauce, stir-fry for an additional 15 seconds, then remove from the heat.
Salt, if necessary	You will probably not need to add any salt, because there is plenty in the soy sauce. But you should taste the dish for salt just to make sure that the flavor is clear and bright.

黑豆豉青椒炒肉絲

BLACK BEANS, GREEN PEPPERS, AND PORK SHREDS
(*heidouchi qingjiao chao rousi*)

Dried, salted black beans entered Szechwan from the outside, probably either from Canton or Hunan. Because they were not indigenous, Mrs. Chiang's mother rarely cooked with them, though when she did the results were always delicious. She used them mainly in simple stir-fried dishes, for the black beans have such a strong and complicated flavor that they dominate any dish to which they are added. They also have an affinity for hot foods, a combination any good Szechwanese cook would be bound to exploit. Mrs. Chiang uses them to add an unusual new dimension to an otherwise ordinary dish of green peppers and pork shreds. The pleasantly salty-sour flavor of the beans sets off the fresh hotness of the long green peppers in a particularly delicious way. Though you can make this recipe using the regular green peppers, once you have tried it with the hot ones, any other way of making it will seem too bland. Because this dish is supposed to stimulate your visual and tactile senses as much as your taste buds, don't overcook the peppers; they should be crisp and bright green. If you can't find hot green peppers, use the regular peppers, but add ½ teaspoon of hot pepper flakes to the dish.

PREPARATION

¾ *cup dried salted black beans*	Rinse the black beans thoroughly under cold water for 1 minute. Put them in a small bowl and set them aside.
3 *medium pork chops (for a yield of ¾ pound meat, approximately)*	Cut the fat and the bone away from the pork chops, then slice the lean meat into shreds about 3 inches long and ⅛ inch wide, the width of a wooden matchstick. (It is easier to slice meat very fine if you first put it in the freezer for about 10 minutes, until it becomes slightly stiff, but not frozen.)
2 *scallions*	Clean the scallions, then cut them, both the green part and white, into 3-inch lengths. Slice these into shreds approximately the same size as the meat shreds.
(pork) 1 *teaspoon sesame oil* 2 *tablespoons soy sauce*	Put the shredded scallions on a plate with the sliced pork. Add the sesame oil and soy sauce and mix thoroughly. Set aside to marinate until you are ready to begin cooking.
❊ 4 *hot green peppers, each 3 inches long, or 2 green peppers*	Slice the peppers in half lengthwise and remove the seeds, then cut them into shreds approximately the same size as the pork.
4 *cloves garlic*	Smash the garlic cloves with the side of your cleaver, then peel. Chop the garlic rather coarsely, into pieces about the size of peppercorns.

COOKING

1 tablespoon peanut oil

Heat your wok or pan over a hot flame for 15 seconds, then add the oil. It will be ready to cook with when the first tiny bubbles form and a few small wisps of smoke appear.

(green peppers)

As soon as the oil is ready, throw in the green pepper slices. Stir-fry them vigorously for 30 seconds, using your cooking shovel or spoon in a scooping motion to toss the pepper shreds around in the pan so every piece is exposed to the hot oil.

½ teaspoon salt

Add the salt and continue to cook the pepper shreds for about 2 more minutes, stirring occasionally, until they have become slightly limp. Then remove the peppers from the pan.

3 tablespoons peanut oil
(garlic)
(black beans)
1 teaspoon granulated sugar
(meat mixture)
(peppers)

Reheat the wok or pan and pour in the fresh oil. When it seems hot enough to cook with, throw in the chopped garlic and stir-fry vigorously for 15 seconds. Quickly add the black beans and the sugar and stir-fry them for 1 minute.

Now add the meat mixture and the partially cooked peppers. Stir-fry for 3 more minutes, until the pork has lost all of its pinkish color and is thoroughly cooked.

Salt, if necessary
2 tablespoons water, approximately (optional)

Just before you are ready to serve the dish, taste it. You probably won't have to add any salt, because the black beans are extremely salty. In fact, the dish may be too salty for your taste. If that is the case, just add a few tablespoonfuls of water and stir thoroughly.

Then serve.

洋芋青椒炒肉絲

POTATOES, GREEN PEPPERS, AND PORK SHREDS
(yangyu qingjiao chao rousi)

Why is it so hard to think of the potato as a Chinese vegetable? Potatoes came to China, as they came to Europe, after the discovery of the New World. Even though they were not greatly liked, they spread quickly, and were soon cultivated all over China. Sinification did not change the spud; and, according to Mrs. Chiang, Szechwanese potatoes are exactly the same as the ones from Maine or Idaho. The difference lies in the way the potatoes are cooked. Mrs. Chiang treats them not as a starch, but as a vegetable. She uses them in stir-fried dishes the way she uses carrots or string beans or any nonleafy vegetable. Cooked in this manner, potatoes do seem less starchy and more vegetablelike.

This recipe accentuates the vegetable side of the potato, its crispness and fresh flavor. It is a simple combination of potatoes, green peppers, and pork shreds that plays upon the contrasting textures, tastes, and colors of the ingredients. Even though this is an authentic Szechwanese dish, you will be amazed at its mildness—unless, of course, you elect to use hot green peppers instead of ordinary green bell peppers.

PREPARATION

3 medium potatoes	Peel the potatoes, then slice them into shreds about 2 inches long and ⅛ inch wide, the size and shape of a wooden matchstick. Put the shreds in a bowl and cover them with cold water so they will remain crisp.
3 medium pork chops (for a yield of ¾ pound meat, approximately)	Cut all the fat and bone away from the pork chops, then cut the lean meat into shreds about the same size as the potatoes. (This is easier to do if you first put the pork into the freezer for about 10

minutes, until the meat becomes slightly stiff but not frozen.)

3 *scallions*

Clean the scallions, then cut them, both the white part and about one-third of the green, into 1-inch lengths.

3 *tablespoons soy sauce*
½ *teaspoon sesame oil*
2 *teaspoons corn-starch*
(pork)

Add the scallions, soy sauce, sesame oil, and cornstarch to the pork shreds. Mix thoroughly, until each shred is coated with the mixture, then set aside.

2 *green peppers or*
❋ 5 *small hot green peppers*

Slice the peppers into shreds the same size as the potato and pork shreds.

1 *leek (optional)*

Cut the leek in half lengthwise and wash thoroughly, then cut into slivers the same size as the other shredded ingredients.

(potatoes)

Just before you are ready to begin cooking, drain the potatoes thoroughly.

COOKING

3 *tablespoons peanut oil*

Heat your wok or pan over a high flame for about 15 seconds, then pour in the oil. It will be hot enough to cook with when the first tiny bubbles form and a few small wisps of smoke appear.

(potatoes)
½ *teaspoon salt*
1 *teaspoon rice wine vinegar*

When the oil is ready, add the shredded potatoes, salt and vinegar. Stir-fry vigorously for about 2 minutes, using your cooking shovel or spoon in a scooping motion to toss the potato shreds around in the pan so every piece is exposed to the hot oil. When the potatoes have become slightly limp but are still white, remove them from the pan.

3 tablespoons peanut oil

¼ teaspoon salt

(green peppers)

(leek)

(meat mixture)

(potatoes)

⅛ teaspoon ground roasted Szechwan peppercorns

Reheat the pan and pour in the fresh oil. When the oil is ready for cooking, add the green pepper and leek shreds and the salt. Stir-fry for about 30 seconds, then add the meat mixture and the partially cooked potato shreds. Continue to stir-fry all these ingredients fairly vigorously for about 2 more minutes.

Add the ground roasted Szechwan peppercorns and continue stir-frying until the pork is thoroughly cooked, which should take no more than 3 or 4 minutes. (It is important not to overcook this dish, because the potatoes should not lose their crisp texture.)

Salt, if necessary

Taste the dish just before you are ready to serve it. You may need to add more salt in order to bring out the bright taste of the green peppers and the slightly rich flavor of the pork.

白菜炒肉絲

CABBAGE AND PORK SHREDS (*baicai chao rousi*)

Regular round cabbage is a Chinese vegetable, too, and, as in Europe, it is associated with real peasant cooking. Probably for the same reason, too—it's cheap and easy to grow. According to Mrs. Chiang, it was by far the cheapest vegetable available in Szechwan. As far as growing it went, each head could grow very large without taking up much space or requiring very much effort on the part of the cultivator.

Because its robust flavor was considered unrefined, it was prepared in very simple ways, as in this lusty pork dish. Mrs. Chiang has dressed the recipe up a bit with tree ears and mushrooms, but its rural origins are still easy to discern in the simplicity of its seasonings and its ease of preparation. If you yearn for true peasant cooking, you can easily omit the extra ornamentation. Either way, it's delicious.

PREPARATION

½ cup tree ears
4 large dried black
mushrooms
2 cups boiling water,
approximately

Put the tree ears and mushrooms in a small bowl and cover them with boiling water. Set aside to soak for at least 20 minutes.

3 medium pork chops
(for a yield of ¾
pound meat,
approximately)

Cut the fat and bones away from the pork chops, then cut the lean meat into slivers about 2 inches long and ⅛ inch wide, the size and shape of a wooden matchstick. (It is always easier to slice meat very fine if you first put it in the freezer for about 10 minutes, until it becomes slightly stiff but not frozen.) Put the meat shreds in a bowl.

2 scallions
3 tablespoons soy
sauce
2 teaspoons sesame
oil
1½ teaspoons
cornstarch
½ small head
cabbage

Clean the scallions; then cut them, both green part and white, into slivers approximately the same size as the pork shreds. Add these to the meat, along with the soy sauce, sesame oil, and cornstarch. Mix well.

Peel off and discard the outer leaves of the cabbage, then slice the cabbage into shreds, just as if you were making cole slaw; you should get about 6 cups of loosely packed cabbage shreds.

(tree ears and
mushrooms)

Drain the tree ears and mushrooms. Rinse the tree ears very carefully under cold running water, picking them over in order to remove any impurities, like little bits of wood, that might still be sticking to them. Slice the tree ears into shreds, the same size as the other ingredients. Rinse the mushrooms, remove their tough stems, and then shred them, too. Keep them separate from the tree ears.

COOKING

2 *tablespoons peanut oil*	Heat your wok or pan over a high flame for 15 seconds, then add the oil. When the oil is just at the point of smoking, add the cabbage.
(cabbage) 1¼ *teaspoons salt*	Stir-fry the cabbage for 45 seconds, using your cooking shovel or spoon to scoop the cabbage shreds off the sides of the pan and then stir them around in the middle, then add the salt and continue to stir-fry the cabbage for 1 more minute. Remove it from the pan.
5 *tablespoons peanut oil* *(mushrooms)*	Wipe the pan out with a paper towel, then reheat it over a high flame for a few seconds. Pour in the fresh oil and wait until the first few bubbles form and a few tiny wisps of smoke appear. When the oil is ready, add the mushrooms. Stir-fry them for 30 seconds.
1 *tablespoon water* *(pork and its marinade)* *(tree ears)*	Combine the water with the meat mixture and mix thoroughly, then add the meat to the pan. Stir-fry it, together with the mushrooms, for about 10 seconds, then add the tree ears and stir-fry for another 1½ minutes.
(cabbage)	Finally, return the partially cooked cabbage shreds to the pan. Stir-fry everything together for about 3 minutes, or until the meat is thoroughly cooked (slightly grayish in color and stiff), and the cabbage, though no longer raw, is still green and not yet limp. Serve immediately.

四季豆炒肉絲

STRING BEANS AND PORK SHREDS (*sijidou chao rousi*)

This is the kind of plain meat and vegetable dish that Mrs. Chiang's mother served her family for dinner almost every day. The proportions of meat and vegetable would vary in accordance with the availability of meat at the time. Mrs. Chiang's version probably uses more meat than the original did, but it is still a simple and unpretentious dish. It calls for only the most minimal of seasonings—just a little soy sauce and sesame oil—and takes no more than 15 minutes to make.

PREPARATION

¾ pound string beans	Wash the string beans, break off the ends, and slice them into shreds.
4 medium pork chops (for a yield of 1 pound meat, approximately)	Cut the meat off the bone and remove the fat. Chop the pork fat into little pieces about the size of grains of uncooked rice and set them aside separately. Slice the lean meat into shreds 2 inches long and ⅛ inch wide, the size and shape of a wooden matchstick, and put them in a small bowl. (It is always easier to cut meat very fine if you first put it in the freezer for about 10 minutes, until it is stiff but not frozen.)
4 scallions	Clean the scallions, then cut them, all the white part and most of the green, into 2-inch lengths. Slice these into shreds and add them to the pork slivers.
1 teaspoon granulated sugar *1 tablespoon cornstarch* *1 teaspoon sesame oil* *3 tablespoons soy sauce*	Add the sugar, cornstarch, sesame oil, and soy sauce to the pork shreds and mix thoroughly.

COOKING

2 *tablespoons peanut oil*	Heat your wok or pan over a high flame for 15 seconds, then add the oil. The oil will be hot enough to cook with when the first tiny bubbles form and a few small wisps of smoke appear.
(string beans) 1½ *teaspoons salt*	When the oil is ready, add the string beans. Stir-fry them for 45 seconds, using your cooking shovel or spoon in a scooping motion to spread the beans around in the pan. Add the salt and continue to stir-fry the beans for 2½ to 3 minutes longer. Then remove them from the pan to a serving dish.
¼ *cup peanut oil* *(pork fat)*	Wipe out the pan with a paper towel and reheat it over a high flame for 15 seconds. Pour in the fresh oil, and, when it is ready for cooking, add the diced fat and fry it for about 1 minute, pressing it against the sides of the pan with your cooking shovel or spoon to make sure that most of the fat is rendered.
1 *tablespoon water* *(pork shreds)*	Combine the water and the meat mixture and mix thoroughly, then add to the pan and stir-fry vigorously for 30 seconds.
(string beans)	Return the partially cooked string beans to the pan and cook, stirring occasionally, for about 3 minutes, or until the pork is thoroughly cooked (slightly grayish in color and stiff). Don't cook the dish too long, or the beans will wilt and lose their fresh, green color.

涼拌三絲

PORK, CUCUMBER, AND CELLOPHANE
NOODLE SALAD (*liangban sansi*)

"The summers in Szechwan were murderous, hotter and stickier than anywhere else in China," recalls Mrs. Chiang. "It was often too hot to sleep, and we would all stay outside in the courtyard. The adults would sit talking and fanning themselves, and we children would be allowed to stay up and play until quite late. Any time we were hungry we would get ourselves a bowl of congee (rice gruel) or a piece of fruit. We ate all our meals outside, and my mother made mostly salads and cold dishes. One of the best is this unusual combination of shredded pork, cucumbers, and cellophane noodles in a spicy sauce. I particularly like the contrasting textures of crisp cucumbers, resilient noodles, and fibrous pork shreds."

In many ways this dish resembles the classic Szechwanese cold dish, Bon Bon Chicken. Both feature cucumbers and cellophane noodles, but the sauce for Bon Bon Chicken contains sesame paste, while the sauce for this pork salad does not. In addition, this dish doesn't have to be highly spiced. It is equally good with or without hot peppers.

Mrs. Chiang often serves this salad with some thin Pancakes, or *baobing* (page 329). You put a few tablespoonfuls of salad inside a pancake and then roll it up and eat it with your fingers. It's very much like Moo Shu Pork that way, though cold.

PREPARATION

4 *cups water*

4 *medium pork chops (for a yield of 1 pound of meat, approximately)*

Bring the water to a boil in a medium-sized saucepan. Add the pork chops, and when the water boils again reduce the flame and let the meat simmer for 10 to 15 minutes, depending on the thickness of the pork chops.

2 *packages (2 ounces each) cellophane noodles*

Put the cellophane noodles in a medium-sized bowl and pour the hot water over them. Let soak for 10 minutes.

2 *cups hot water*

2 *cucumbers*   Peel the cucumbers and cut them in half crosswise. Cut each half lengthwise down the center and scoop out all the seeds in the middle, then slice the firm meat of the cucumbers into shreds 2 inches long and ⅛ inch wide, about the size and shape of a wooden matchstick. Put the shreds in a bowl.

1 *teaspoon salt*   Sprinkle the salt over the shredded cucumbers, mix well, and set aside for 10 minutes.

(pork chops)   When the pork chops have boiled long enough for the meat to be cooked through, take them out of the pan and set them aside to cool for a few minutes. (Don't discard the water in which they were cooked; you'll need it for boiling the cellophane noodles.)

(cellophane noodles) Drain the cellophane noodles. Bring the pork chop water to a furious boil, then drop the noodles into it. Let them boil for all of 3 minutes, drain them and rinse them under cold water.

(pork chops)   When the pork is cool enough to handle, cut away the bones and the fat and slice the lean meat into shreds, roughly the same size as the cucumbers.

(cucumbers)   Squeeze all the excess liquid out of the cucumber shreds with your hands. Put them into an attractive serving bowl and add the pork shreds to them.

(cellophane noodles) Drain the cellophane noodles well and then chop them into segments about 3 inches long. Add them to the pork and cucumbers.

4 *scallions*   Clean the scallions, then cut them, both white part and green, into 2-inch

lengths. Slice these into very fine slivers. Add the scallion shreds to the salad.

THE SAUCE

6 *cloves garlic*

Smash the garlic cloves with the side of your cleaver, then peel. Put them in a small, steep-sided bowl or mortar.

½-*inch piece fresh ginger*

1 *teaspoon salt*

Peel the ginger, then chop it into tiny pieces, about the size of a match head. Put, along with the salt, into the same bowl as the garlic. Using the handle of your cleaver, a wooden spoon, or a pestle, mash these ingredients together into a thick paste.

5 *tablespoons soy sauce*

1 *teaspoon sesame oil*

3 *teaspoons rice wine vinegar*

✿ 1 *to 2 teaspoons hot pepper flakes in oil (optional)*

½ *teaspoon ground roasted Szechwan peppercorns (optional)*

Add the soy sauce, sesame oil, vinegar, optional hot pepper flakes in oil and optional ground roasted Szechwan peppercorns to the smashed garlic and ginger. Stir the sauce thoroughly before you pour it over the salad, then mix the salad well so all the ingredients are covered with the sauce.

Note: Because this dish is best served cold, you can prepare it in advance and chill it for a few hours before you eat it.

黄瓜炒肉絲

PORK SHREDS AND CUCUMBERS (*huanggua chao rousi*)

This is the kind of plain meat and vegetable dish that takes no more than 15 or 20 minutes to prepare. It is easy to make and mild enough for small children. Besides cucumbers, Mrs. Chiang's mother used to use many varieties of home-grown squashes and melons in this recipe. We have called for cucumbers here mainly because they are so easy to get in America, though they are larger and less tasty than the Chinese ones. All the other ingredients are equally easy to find, the most exotic things required being soy sauce and sesame oil. Instead of shredding the pork and cucumbers, you can cut them into slices about 3 inches long by 1 inch wide. If you do this, increase the final cooking time by 1 minute.

PREPARATION

3 medium cucumbers	Peel the cucumbers and cut them in half crosswise. Slice each half lengthwise down the middle and scoop out the seeds. Cut the outer shell of the cucumbers into thin shreds about 3 inches long and ⅛ inch wide, the width of a wooden matchstick.
½ teaspoon salt	Put the cucumber shreds in a bowl, and add the salt. Mix thoroughly and let stand for at least 15 minutes.
4 medium pork chops (for a yield of 1 pound of meat, approximately)	Cut the bones and fat away from the pork chops, then slice the lean meat into very fine shreds. (It is always easier to slice meat into thin slivers if you first put it into the freezer for about 10 minutes, until it becomes slightly stiff but not frozen.)
4 scallions	Clean the scallions, then cut them, both the white part and about two-thirds of the green, into 2-inch lengths. Slice these into shreds.
(pork) *3 tablespoons soy sauce* *1 teaspoon sesame oil* *1 egg white*	Add the scallion shreds to the meat, along with the soy sauce, sesame oil, egg white, and cornstarch. Mix everything together well and set aside.

1 tablespoon corn-
   starch
(cucumbers)   Just before you are ready to begin cooking,
                              drain the cucumbers very well, using
                              your hands to squeeze out all the excess
                              liquid.

                             COOKING

1 tablespoon peanut   Heat your wok or pan over a high flame,
   oil   then add the oil. It will be ready to cook
                              with when the first tiny bubbles form
                              and a few small wisps of smoke appear.
(cucumbers)   When the oil is ready, toss in the cucum-
                              bers and stir-fry for about 1 minute, us-
                              ing your cooking shovel or spoon to
                              scoop the cucumbers off the sides of the
                              pan and stir them around in the middle.
                              Remove the cucumbers from the pan
                              onto a serving platter.
¼ cup peanut oil   Wipe out the pan with paper towels, then
                              reheat over a high flame and pour in the
                              fresh oil.
1 tablespoon water   While you are waiting for it to get hot,
(meat)   combine the water and the meat mixture
                              and mix thoroughly.
                             When the oil is ready, toss the meat mix-
                              ture into the pan and stir-fry for 1 min-
                              ute. (The meat will bc only partially
                              cooked at this point.)
(cucumbers)   Return the cucumber shreds to the pan
1 tablespoon soy   and add the soy sauce. Stir-fry the meat
   sauce   and cucumbers together for about 1½
                              minutes, or until the meat is completely
                              cooked through (slightly grayish in color
                              and stiff).
Freshly ground black   Just before you serve this dish you can, if
   pepper (optional)   you want, sprinkle some regular black

pepper on the top of it. Black pepper is a rarely used spice in Chinese cooking, but it adds a pleasant touch of piquancy to a mild dish like this.

DEEP-FRIED PORK CHOPS (*zha paigu*)

When we lived on Taiwan, we used to eat these crisp-fried pork chops almost every other day. Here in America we enjoy serving them to our friends because they can't believe they are Chinese. They look just like the simple fried pork chops they are, plain pieces of meat coated with batter and fried in deep fat. No exotic sauce or garniture of sliced ginger betrays their Oriental origin. But underneath their crisp exterior these pork chops are very Chinese, indeed. They have been marinated in soy sauce, shredded ginger, scallions, and sesame oil, a process that gives them a rich, nutlike flavor no American pork chops have ever known. And because they are still just pork chops, they are equally at home in either an American or a Chinese setting. Sometimes Mrs. Chiang serves them with some rice and a plate of stir-fried vegetables; sometimes she serves them as the topping for a simple dish of boiled noodles (see Pork Chop Noodles, page 296). Either way, they are a crisp and subtle departure from more customary Chinese or American fare. We love them.

PREPARATION

4 *very thin pork chops (even with the bones, they shouldn't weigh more than a pound)*

Trim most of the fat from the pork chops, but do not remove the bones. Score the meat lightly on both sides in a tiny diamond pattern, with the cuts about ½ inch apart. Then use the back of your cleaver or some other heavy utensil to pound the meat as you would pound and flatten veal scallops. Do this on both sides so the meat becomes very thin, then put the pork chops on a large, flat plate.

4 *scallions*

Clean the scallions, then smash them with the flat side of your cleaver. Cut the smashed scallions into 2-inch lengths and sprinkle these over the meat.

1-inch piece fresh ginger

Peel the ginger, then cut it into thin slivers, about ⅛ inch wide, the width of a wooden matchstick. Add to the meat.

3 tablespoons soy sauce
1 teaspoon sesame oil
1 teaspoon granulated sugar

Sprinkle the soy sauce, sesame oil, and sugar over the pork chops. Turn the chops over and over until they are covered with the marinade. Set aside for 10 minutes.

COOKING

1 cup peanut or other cooking oil
½ cup cornstarch

Heat your wok or whatever pan you normally use for deep-fat frying over a high flame for 15 seconds, then pour in the oil. While you are waiting for the oil to heat up, a process that will take several minutes at least, pour the cornstarch onto a flat plate.

(pork chops)

Remove the pieces of scallion and ginger from the pork chops and dip each chop into the cornstarch. Make sure each piece of meat is thoroughly coated with cornstarch; press it in with your hands, if necessary.

When the oil in the pan is smoking lightly and seems hot enough for cooking, put in the pork chops; they are so thin they will cook very quickly. Turn them over after 30 seconds and fry them for about 1 minute on the second side, then turn them over again to fry for a final 15 to 30 seconds. They are done when both sides are a deep, golden brown.

Drain the fried pork chops on some paper towels for a few seconds and serve.

糖 醋 排 骨

SWEET AND SOUR SPARERIBS (*tangsu paigu*)

John and I share an embarrassing weakness for barbecued spareribs. Every once in a while, we venture out to a local chop suey palace to indulge ourselves. Although it would be difficult to vouch for their authenticity, the bright red, sweet, and sticky spareribs that most Chinese-American restaurants feature are, in their way, quite delightful, for pork and sugar have a delicious affinity for each other.

Mrs. Chiang's spareribs are equally marvelous. They are marinated in a simple mixture of soy sauce, sugar, and vinegar and then deep fried until they are crisp. The contrast between the spareribs' tangy sweet and sour flavor and their delightfully crunchy texture is quite extraordinary. Since they are easily prepared and can be eaten with the fingers, these unusual spareribs are an excellent party food. They can be fried in advance and then reheated in the oven just before serving.

PREPARATION

1½ pounds spareribs

Rinse off the spareribs and then cut them into individual ribs. Make tiny slashes along the sides of the meat every ¼ inch or so, and if the spareribs are particularly fatty cut off some of the excess fat. Put the ribs in a shallow bowl or plate.

1½ teaspoons salt
1½ teaspoons granulated sugar

Sprinkle the salt, sugar, soy sauce, and vinegar over the spareribs.

2 *tablespoons soy*
   sauce
1 *tablespoon rice wine*
   vinegar
1-*inch piece fresh*
   ginger

Peel the ginger and cut it into shreds about ⅛ inch wide, the width of a wooden matchstick. Sprinkle them over the spareribs.

2 *scallions*

Clean the scallions, then smash them with the side of your cleaver. Cut the smashed scallions, both white part and green, into 2-inch lengths. Add these to the spareribs.

Mix all the ingredients very thoroughly with the spareribs, then set aside to marinate at room temperature for at least 30 minutes.

COOKING

2½ *cups peanut or*
    other cooking oil,
    approximately

Heat your wok, or whatever pan you use for deep-fat frying, over a high flame for 15 seconds, then pour in the oil. It may take 5 or 10 minutes until the oil is hot enough for cooking; it should be practically smoking.

(*spareribs*)

When the oil is ready, put in the spareribs. (Depending on the amount of oil you use, you may want to cook the spareribs in several batches.) Fry the spareribs for 5 minutes, or until they have turned very dark brown and are quite dry and crisp, then remove them from the oil with chopsticks or a slotted spoon and let them drain for about 1 minute on some paper towels. Serve immediately.

獅 子 頭

LIONS' HEADS (*shiz tou*)

Lions' Heads came originally from Yangchow, near Shanghai, though the dish is now also a specialty of Peking. Lions' Heads are big, soft meatballs, simmered in a rich, dark sauce and served on a "mane" of barely cooked Chinese cabbage. By the time the recipe reached Szechwan, almost everything but the name was changed. True, Szechwanese Lions' Heads are meatballs, but they are smaller and firmer and come in a clearer and less elaborate stock, one that contains carrots and cellophane noodles as well as Chinese cabbage. The finished product is a savory meatball stew, at once lighter and yet more filling than the original.

Mrs. Chiang's recipe for Lions' Heads is representative of a style of cooking called *daguocai*, or "big pot food." Dishes prepared in this manner resemble American casseroles in that all the ingredients are cooked and served together in one large pot. Also like American casseroles, they are the easiest way to feed a lot of people, especially when cold weather demands hot and filling food. They are meals in themselves, and no other dishes are ever served with them. Mrs. Chiang's mother used to prepare these hearty peasant stews for the men when they were planting and harvesting rice. We serve them at informal family suppers, where the meatballs and cellophane noodles make a big hit with the kids.

PREPARATION

8 *large dried black mushrooms* 1 *cup boiling water*	Wash the mushrooms very carefully under cold running water. Then put them in a small bowl and pour the boiling water over them. Let soak for at least 20 minutes.
1 *package (2 ounces) dried cellophane noodles* 2 *cups boiling water*	Put the dried cellophane noodles into a bowl and cover them with boiling water. Set aside to soak.

4 *scallions*	Clean the scallions, then chop them, both the white part and most of the green, into tiny pieces, approximately the size of a match head.
2-*inch piece of fresh ginger*	Peel the ginger and chop it very fine, until it reaches the consistency of coarse cornmeal.
6 *fresh water chest-nuts (optional)*	Cut off the black outer part of the water chestnuts and chop the inner parts into tiny pieces, the size of a match head.
1 *pound ground pork* (*scallions*) (*ginger*) (*water chestnuts*) 2 *tablespoons soy sauce* 1 *tablespoon sesame oil* 2 *egg whites* 1 *teaspoon ground roasted Szechwan peppercorns* 1 *teaspoon salt* ¼ *cup cornstarch*	Put the pork in a bowl and add the chopped scallions, ginger, and water chestnuts to it, along with the soy sauce, sesame oil, egg whites, ground roasted Szechwan peppercorns, salt, and cornstarch. Mix well.
1 *medium head Chinese cabbage (see note below)*	Separate the leaves of the Chinese cabbage. Discard the tough outer ones and wash the rest carefully, then chop them into segments 2 inches wide.
2 *small carrots*	Peel the carrots and cut them into 3-inch lengths. Cut these pieces into very thin slices about ⅛ inch in width.
(*mushrooms*)	Drain the mushrooms, reserving the liquid they soaked in. Cut off the hard stem, and then, if any of the mushrooms are very large, cut them into quarters.

COOKING

¼ cup peanut oil	Heat your wok or pan over a high flame for about 10 seconds, then add the oil. It will be hot enough to cook with when the first tiny bubbles form and a few small wisps of smoke appear.
(carrots and mushrooms)	When the oil is ready, put the carrots and mushrooms into the pan and stir-fry them for 30 seconds, using your cooking shovel or spoon to scoop the ingredients from the sides of the pan and then stir them around in the middle.
(cabbage) (mushroom liquid) 3 cups water, approximately	Now add the cabbage shreds, stirring them very carefully in order to keep them from spilling over the sides of the pan. Cook the cabbage for about 3 minutes before adding the mushroom liquid and enough extra water to make 4 cups of liquid. Bring the liquid to a boil over a high flame.
(meat mixture)	While you are waiting for the liquid to boil, you can begin to form the meatballs.
	Use a wet spoon and your hands to shape the meat mixture into balls about the size of large plums. You should get about 9 or 10 of these balls.
	Place the meatballs on top of the cabbage and cover the pan. As soon as the liquid is boiling heavily, reduce the heat and let the meatballs simmer for 45 minutes. Then remove the meatballs from the pan.
(cellophane noodles)	Drain the cellophane noodles and rinse them thoroughly under cold water. Add them to the simmering liquid.

1 tablespoon salt,
    approximately
    (meatballs)

Taste the soup and, if it needs it, add some salt.

Return the meatballs to the soup and let them simmer for 2 minutes before serving.

SERVING

This is a real one-dish meal. The best way to serve it is to give each person a soup bowl and then ladle out his portion of meatballs, vegetables, cellophane noodles, and soup into it. You won't need rice.

Note: In a pinch, you can use regular round cabbage in this dish, but it has a much stronger taste when cooked.

蛋 夾

MEAT-FILLED OMELETS (danjiao)

This is Mrs. Chiang's most elegant dish, the one she makes when she wants to impress a special guest. It consists of tiny omelets, each one filled with a delicately flavored meat mixture, covered with a subtle, clear sauce, and accompanied by such exotic vegetables as tree ears and lily buds. The contrasting colors and textures of its ingredients, the care required in its preparation, and its mild, yet luscious, taste elevate it into the realm of Szechwanese *haute cuisine*. Although making the omelets and stuffing them adds a few extra steps to the preparation of the dish, there is nothing difficult about the procedure. The cries of pleasure that invariably greet a large platter of *danjiao* will more than reward your exertions.

PREPARATION

¼ cup dried tree ears
¼ cup dried lily buds
2 cups boiling water

Put the dried tree ears and lily buds in a small bowl and pour the boiling water over them. Let soak for 20 minutes.

4 scallions

Clean the scallions, then chop them, both white part and green, into tiny pieces about the size of a match head.

1-inch piece fresh
  ginger

Peel the ginger, then chop it very fine until it reaches the consistency of coarse bread crumbs.

½ pound ground pork
(ginger)
(scallions)
2 tablespoons soy
  sauce
1 teaspoon sesame oil
1 egg white
¼ teaspoon salt
1 tablespoon corn-
  starch

Put the ground pork in a bowl and add the ginger, three-fourths of the scallions, the soy sauce, sesame oil, egg white, salt, and cornstarch. Mix thoroughly until all the ingredients are well blended.

1 small or ½ large
  cucumber
½ teaspoon salt

Peel the cucumber, then slice it in half lengthwise. Scrape out all the seedy pulp in the middle. Cut the firm outer part of the cucumber into the thinnest possible slices. Put these slices in a bowl and sprinkle the salt over them. Mix thoroughly and let stand.

3 eggs
3 tablespoons all-
  purpose flour
⅛ teaspoon peanut
  oil, approximately

Beat the eggs and flour together in a small bowl until you have a smooth batter.

The next step is to make tiny omelets out of this batter. Heat a small, flat frying pan over a high flame. Add a tiny bit of oil and swirl it around until the bottom of the frying pan is covered with it.

(egg batter)

Pour a very scant tablespoonful of the egg batter into the frying pan, tilting the pan so that the batter covers a circle roughly 3 inches in diameter. Cook the egg until it has barely set and is still soft, but not runny, in the middle. Using a metal spatula, quickly remove it from the pan to a warm plate.

Cook the rest of the egg batter in the same way. You should end up with about 2 dozen little omelets.

Now you are ready to begin filling these omelets with the meat mixture.

1 egg
(meat mixture)
(omelets)

Beat the egg.

Take about 1 teaspoonful of the meat mixture and place it in the middle of one of the little omelets. Moisten the edges of the omelet with the beaten egg, then fold the omelet over the filling and press the edges together. Don't worry if the edges aren't completely sealed; this isn't the kind of filling that will ooze out of any little gaps.

(tree ears and lily buds)

Drain and rinse the tree ears and lily buds. While you are rinsing the tree ears, pick them over carefully to remove any impurities, like little pieces of wood, that might still be embedded in them.

Tear each lily bud lengthwise with your fingers into 3 or 4 shreds.

(cucumbers)
1½ tablespoons cornstarch
3 tablespoons water

Drain the cucumber slices.

Mix the cornstarch and water together in a small bowl and set aside.

COOKING

1 tablespoon peanut oil

Heat your wok or pan over a high flame for about 15 seconds, then add the oil. It will be ready to cook with when the first tiny bubbles form and a few small wisps of smoke appear.

(cucumbers)

When the oil is ready, add the cucumber slices and stir-fry them, using your cooking shovel or spoon to scoop the cucumbers off the sides of the pan and then

2½ tablespoons pea-
nut oil
(scallions)
(tree ears and lily
buds)
½ teaspoon salt

1 cup water
(filled omelets)

(cucumbers)
⅛ teaspoon ground
roasted Szechwan
peppercorns
(cornstarch and water)

stir them around in the middle. After you have cooked the cucumbers for 1 minute, remove them from the pan.

Clean out the pan with a paper towel, then reheat it over a high flame. Pour the fresh oil in and wait until it is hot enough to cook with, then toss in the rest of the chopped scallions, the tree ears, lily buds, and salt. Stir-fry for about 30 seconds.

Add the water and then, gently, put the filled omelets in the pan. Wait until the liquid is boiling, then cover the pan and let it cook over a moderate flame for 5 minutes.

Return the partially cooked cucumbers to the pan, along with the ground roasted Szechwan peppercorns.

Stir the cornstarch and water to make sure it is well combined, then pour the mixture into the pan, stirring gently all the while. When the sauce has thickened slightly and turned clear again, the dish will be ready to eat; this should take only 15 or 20 seconds.

黃瓜釀肉

STUFFED CUCUMBERS (*huanggua niangrou*)

"Szechwan winters could get very cold," recalls Mrs. Chiang. "On the coldest days I would stay in bed, dozing under thick quilts. The only heat we had came from earthenware braziers, and when I had to get up I would warm my clothes on one before I dressed. There was a big one under the dinner table, and each of us had a little one to warm our feet while we ate. Even the hot food helped warm the room. In cold weather my mother made a lot of steamed dishes, and the steam helped heat the kitchen. Her steamed dishes were delicious, and these delicate stuffed cucumbers would lure even the coldest child out of bed."

For such an attractive dish, stuffed cucumbers are surprisingly easy to prepare. All you do is hollow out raw cucumbers, fill them with a rich mixture of ground pork and spices, and steam them. Somehow the savory stuffing and slightly bitter cucumber complement each other perfectly. Since you can interrupt the cooking process at any one of a number of points, this is a useful dish for dinner parties. It looks as if it must have been hard to make, and everybody loves it.

PREPARATION

4 *cucumbers* 1 *teaspoon salt*	Peel the cucumbers, then cut each one in half crosswise and scoop out all the seeds from the inside of each piece, leaving a hollow shell made of the firm outer meat of the cucumber. Put the cucumbers in a dish and sprinkle the salt over them. Make sure that the salt is thoroughly distributed over the cucumbers, then set them aside for 15 minutes.
½-inch piece fresh ginger	Peel the ginger, then mince it until it reaches the consistency of farina.
3 *scallions*	Clean the scallions, then chop them, both the white part and the green, into tiny pieces, about the size of a match head.
½ pound ground pork *(ginger)* *(scallions)* 4 *teaspoons soy sauce* 1 *teaspoon sesame oil* *¼ teaspoon ground roasted Szechwan peppercorns* 1 *egg* *½ teaspoon salt* 1 *tablespoon cornstarch*	Put the ground pork in a bowl. Add the chopped ginger and the scallions to the pork, along with the soy sauce, sesame oil, ground roasted Szechwan peppercorns, egg, salt, and cornstarch. Mix well. Drain the cucumbers, then stuff them with the pork mixture and put them on a plate. You are now ready to steam them.

COOKING

(stuffed cucumbers)

As soon as you have assembled your steamer (see page 54), bring the water inside it to a boil. Put the plate of stuffed cucumbers on the rack, cover it, and let the cucumbers steam over a high flame for 20 minutes. Reduce the heat. First check the water level inside the steamer, adding some more water if it is needed, then let the cucumbers steam for another 10 minutes. Remove them from the steamer.

Cut each cucumber half into about 5 slices and arrange them decoratively on a serving dish.

½ teaspoon sesame oil

Save the juice that exuded from the cucumbers while they steamed. Add the sesame oil, stir it up, then pour it over the cucumber slices just before serving them.

Note: This dish can be made in advance and reheated in a steamer for a few minutes just before you are ready to eat it.

珍 珠 圓 子

PEARL BALLS (*zhenzhu rouyuan*)

Mrs. Chiang considers this a dish for company. It contains no exotic ingredients and is not hard to make, but some of the steps in its preparation take a long time. They do not, however, require much effort, and most of the work can be done in advance. What you end up with is a dish of delicately flavored steamed meatballs, each one covered with a pearly coating of glutinous rice.

PREPARATION

The first step, soaking the glutinous rice, takes at least 3 to 4 hours. Be fore-warned and allocate your time accordingly.

¾ cup glutinous rice
2 cups water,
    approximately

Put the glutinous rice in a bowl and cover it with the water. Set it aside to soak for at least 3 or 4 hours. (It won't hurt if the rice soaks even longer, so you can start your evening meal at breakfast time if you aren't going to be in the kitchen during the day.)

After the glutinous rice has soaked for its allotted time, drain it and set it aside.

1 pound ground pork
½-inch piece fresh
    ginger

Put the ground pork in a bowl.

Peel the ginger and then chop it as fine as you can, until it reaches the consistency of farina. Add it to the pork.

4 scallions

Clean the scallions, then chop them, both green part and white, into tiny pieces, about the size of coarse bread crumbs. Add the chopped scallions to the ground pork.

1 tablespoon soy
    sauce
1 tablespoon sesame
    oil
1 teaspoon salt
½ teaspoon ground
    roasted Szechwan
    peppercorns
1 egg white
1 heaping tablespoon
    cornstarch

Now add the soy sauce, sesame oil, salt, ground roasted Szechwan peppercorns, egg white, and cornstarch to the pork and mix everything together thoroughly.

Using a tablespoon and your hands, shape the pork mixture into small balls, about the size of a walnut; you should get about 18 meatballs.

(glutinous rice)

Roll each ball in the glutinous rice until the outside of the ball is completely covered. Press the rice into the balls with your hands, then put the meatballs in a shallow bowl or plate for steaming.

COOKING

If you have a Chinese steamer, set it up; if you don't, you can devise one from a large covered pot or a wok and its cover (see page 54).

(meatballs)

When the water in the bottom of the steamer is boiling, put the plate of sticky rice-covered balls on the rack over the water and cover the steamer. Steam the balls for 1 hour. Keep the flame fairly high and check the steamer occasionally to make sure that the water in the bottom has not all boiled away.

After the hour is up, the meatballs will be ready to serve. (You may want to transfer them to a cooler plate for serving.)

Note: The meatballs can be prepared ahead of time and kept in the refrigerator for several hours until you are ready to steam them.

藕　圓

LOTUS ROOT BALLS (*ouyuan*)

The lotus is a versatile as well as beautiful plant. The Chinese eat its seeds and its roots, wrap seasonal pastries in its leaves, and celebrate its flowers as the Buddhist symbol of beauty and purity because they bloom so gloriously in the most uninviting environments. Fresh lotus root, which is sold by the pound in most Chinese markets, looks like a potato. It is approximately the size and shape of a potato and even has a light brown, potatolike skin. Inside, however, the crisp white meat is laced with air holes, which provide the bouyancy needed to keep the plant afloat and produce a lovely starlike pattern when the lotus root is sliced crosswise.

Mrs. Chiang utilizes the crispness of a fresh lotus root to produce these fragrant and delicate little meatballs. Deep-fat frying makes them as crunchy on the outside as the lotus root makes them on the inside. They are not difficult to prepare, and can be served as a regular course in a Chinese meal or as an hors d'oeuvre. They would be completely at home on the end of a toothpick.

PREPARATION

¾ pound ground pork (this meat should be quite fatty, if possible)

1 tablespoon soy sauce

1 tablespoon sesame oil

2 egg whites

Put the ground pork in a bowl and add the soy sauce, sesame oil, and egg whites to it. Mix well.

1-inch piece fresh ginger

Peel the ginger, then mince it very fine, until it reaches the consistency of coarse cornmeal. Add to the pork.

3 scallions

Clean the scallions, then chop, both the white part and one-third of the green, into tiny pieces, about the size of a match head. Add the chopped scallions to the pork.

piece of lotus root about 4 inches long and 3 inches wide

Cut the outer skin off the lotus root, then chop it into little pieces, about the size of grains of uncooked rice. You should get approximately 1 cup of chopped lotus root. Add it to the pork.

¼ cup cornstarch

1 teaspoon salt

2 teaspoons ground roasted Szechwan peppercorns

Now add the cornstarch, salt, ground roasted Szechwan peppercorns, and water to the pork mixture. Use a wooden spoon to mix the pork and other ingredients very thoroughly, giving it about

1 *tablespoon water*	50 strokes to get a smooth, well-blended mixture.

COOKING

2 *cups peanut or other cooking oil, approximately*	Fill your wok or whatever pan you normally use for deep-fat frying with about 2 inches of oil. Heat the oil over a moderate flame until it is hot enough for frying. This may take 5 or 10 minutes; the oil should be practically smoking.
(meat mixture)	Using a wet teaspoon, form the meat mixture into little balls about the size of a walnut. (Keep a dish of water handy, so your teaspoon stays wet.)
(meatballs)	When the oil is ready, drop the little meatballs into it and let them cook, turning them gently, until they are a deep golden brown all over. This should not take more than 2 or 3 minutes.
	Remove the meatballs from the hot oil to a paper towel to drain before serving.

乾燒牛肉絲

DRY-FRIED BEEF (*ganshao niurousi*)

This is one of the most famous Szechwanese dishes of all, and one of the few that actually require beef. We were first introduced to it by an ancient Chinese bookseller in Hong Kong who took us out to lunch at a marvelously old-fashioned Szechwanese restaurant that looked as shabby and worn as some of the secondhand books he was selling. Yellowing calligraphy covered the walls, and the waiters, genuine antiques themselves, treated the patrons with stylized irreverence and called out the dishes in the traditional manner reminiscent of Chinese opera. The whole meal, with its strong overtones of another era, remains unforgettable to this day. Somehow it seemed especially appropriate to receive our introduction to Dry-Fried Beef in such a place, for it is a dish totally unlike any other in flavor and texture.

All too often, American Chinese restaurants produce what they call a Szechwanese Dry-Fried Beef covered with vegetables and swimming in gravy. Nothing could be farther from the genuine article, for this is a dish where dry really means dry. In a properly prepared Dry-Fried Beef, like Mrs. Chiang's, everything has been cooked for so long that the meat has literally dried out and has become hard and crunchy. The shredded carrots and celery that cooked with the meat have all but melted away, leaving behind a few soft threads and a deep, savory flavor. The entire dish is transcendently perfumed with *huajiao*, or Szechwan pepper.

According to Mrs. Chiang, the beef should cook, or rather dry out, over the tiniest possible flame for several hours. The procedure can be somewhat abbreviated by using a higher flame, but that requires more attention to keep the meat from burning. Although time consuming, this is a good dish for a dinner party; it can be made in advance and reheated quickly just before serving. As you plan your menu, take into account the fact that as the beef cooks it shrinks; you will end up with about half the volume of food you had in the beginning.

PREPARATION

1 *pound beef, preferably a very lean cut like top or bottom round*	Slice the beef into very thin slivers, about 3 inches long and ¼ inch wide. (It is easier to cut meat into little shreds if you first put it into the freezer for about 10 minutes, until it has stiffened slightly but is not yet frozen.)
2 *scallions*	Clean the scallions, then chop one of them, both green part and white, into 1-inch lengths. Cut the other scallion into very fine slivers, about 2 inches long.
½-*inch piece fresh ginger*	Peel the ginger and slice it into shreds, the size of a wooden matchstick.
(beef)	Put the beef shreds on a plate with the
(ginger)	ginger and the scallion that has been

(scallion lengths)

½ *teaspoon granu-
lated sugar*

3 *tablespoons soy
sauce*

1 *tablespoon Chinese
rice wine or cooking
sherry*

1 *teaspoon sesame oil*

½ *teaspoon ground
roasted Szechwan
peppercorns*

3 *carrots*

1 *teaspoon salt*

4 *stalks celery*

½ *teaspoon salt*

❀ 5 *dried red peppers*

cut into 1-inch lengths. Then add the sugar, soy sauce, wine, sesame oil, and ground roasted Szechwan peppercorns. Combine very thoroughly, so every piece of the meat is coated with the marinade. Set the beef mixture aside and let it stand for about 30 minutes.

Peel the carrots and slice them into shreds about the same size as the meat. Put them in a bowl, add the salt, and mix thoroughly. Let the carrot shreds stand in the salt for about 15 minutes, then pour the brine off.

Slice the celery into slivers the same size as the carrots. Put the celery shreds into yet another bowl; add the salt, mix, and let stand for about 5 minutes. Pour the brine off.

Slice each dried red pepper lengthwise into 3 or 4 strips. (Removing the seeds from the inside of the peppers will make the dish somewhat less hot.)

COOKING

1½ *tablespoons
peanut oil*

(carrots)

Heat your wok or pan over a fairly high flame for about 15 seconds, then pour in the oil. It will be hot enough to cook with when the first tiny bubbles form and a few small wisps of smoke appear.

When the oil is ready, lower the heat slightly and add the carrot shreds. Stir-fry the carrots over a medium flame for about 1 minute, using your cooking shovel or spoon in a continuous scooping motion to toss the carrot shreds around in the pan so every bit is exposed to the hot oil.

(celery) Now add the shredded celery. Continue to cook the carrots and celery, stirring frequently, for about 6 minutes. When the carrot and celery shreds are slightly cooked but still crunchy, remove them from the pan and set them aside.

Clean out the pan by wiping it out with a paper towel.

(beef mixture) When you are ready to cook, carefully remove all the scallions from the beef mixture.

1½ tablespoons peanut oil
(red peppers)
(beef mixture) Reheat the pan and pour in the fresh peanut oil. When the oil is hot, add the sliced dried red peppers and the beef mixture. Stir-fry everything together over very high heat, using your cooking shovel or spoon to scoop the ingredients from the sides of the pan and then stir them around in the middle. Continue cooking the beef shreds in this way until all the liquid in which they were marinated has completely evaporated; this may take up to 10 minutes.

Lower the heat and continue to cook the meat shreds for about 30 seconds more, until they become rather dry.

(carrots and celery) Now add the partially cooked carrots and celery and stir-fry them, together with the beef, for another 30 seconds.

(scallion slivers) Reduce the heat until the flame is barely flickering (or in the case of an electric stove, adjust the burner to the lowest setting or transfer to another burner set

to low). Add the scallion slivers, mix them thoroughly, and continue cooking the meat and vegetable shreds together, stirring occasionally, for at least 20 minutes, until the mixture has become quite dry and the beef has shrunk and turned dark brown. (Twenty minutes is the bare minimum for this dish; if you have the time and the patience, you can let it cook for up to 1 hour. The longer the meat cooks, the darker, drier, and crisper it becomes.)

At this point, you can set the whole pan of meat shreds aside for several hours. The beef should be so thoroughly desiccated that a few hours' rest will not affect it. (The only problem is that it tastes so good it will be hard to refrain from nibbling at it!)

1 teaspoon sesame oil   Just before you are ready to serve the dish, turn up the heat again and add the sesame oil. Stir-fry everything together for about 30 seconds, to allow the sesame oil to penetrate all the little pieces of beef, then serve.

青椒炒牛肉絲

PEPPER STEAK (*qingjiao chao niurousi*)

Pepper Steak, that old warhorse of the chow mein palace, occupies an honorable place in the cuisine of Szechwan as well. If Mrs. Chiang's version seems more Spartan than Szechwanese in its simplicity, this is as it should be. An authentic Pepper Steak is a very plain, down-to-earth dish that relies on only the most minimal seasonings to bring out the natural flavors of the beef and green peppers. It is not hot.

This is *the* perfect recipe for a novice. A friend who had never cooked Chinese food before claimed that it took her all of 20 minutes to prepare. The ingredients are uncomplicated and readily available. And once you have mastered the basic recipe, any number of variations come to mind. Try pork and broccoli.

PREPARATION

1 *pound round steak or any similarly lean cut of beef*	Cut away all the fat from the steak and slice the lean meat into slivers about 2 inches long and ⅛ inch wide, the size and shape of a wooden matchstick. (It is always easier to cut meat into fine shreds if you first put it in the freezer for about 10 minutes, until it becomes slightly stiff but not frozen.)
1½-inch *piece fresh ginger*	Peel the ginger, then cut it into very thin slivers, about 1 inch long.
4 *scallions*	Clean the scallions, then cut them, both the white part and most of the green, into 1½-inch lengths. Slice these into slivers as well.
(beef) 2 *tablespoons soy sauce* 1 *tablespoon sesame oil* 1 *tablespoon cornstarch*	Add the shredded ginger and scallions to the beef, along with the soy sauce, sesame oil, and ˙cornstarch. Mix well and set aside to marinate.
3 *medium green peppers*	Wash the green peppers, then cut them in half and remove the seeds. Cut the peppers into shreds about ⅛ inch wide.

COOKING

1 *tablespoon peanut oil*	Heat the pan over a high flame for 10 seconds, then add the oil. It will be hot enough to cook with when the first tiny bubbles form and a few small wisps of smoke appear.

(green peppers)	When the oil is ready, toss in the green pepper shreds. Stir-fry them vigorously for about 2 minutes, using your cooking shovel or spoon to scoop the peppers off the sides of the pan and then stir them around in the middle. Remove them from the pan.
¼ cup peanut oil	Rinse the pan well and dry it out with paper towels. Reheat the pan over a high flame and pour in the fresh oil; it should be hot enough for cooking after about 2 minutes.
1 tablespoon water *(meat mixture)*	Combine the water and the meat mixture and mix thoroughly. When the oil is ready, put the meat mixture in the pan and stir-fry for 45 seconds.
(green peppers)	Return the peppers to the pan and continue to stir-fry for another 30 seconds.
1 to 2 tablespoons soy sauce	Add soy sauce to taste. Stir-fry the meat and peppers for 1 more minute, then serve.

9 - INNARDS

Innards were the filet mignon of the Szechwanese countryside—expensive delicacies to be cooked with reverence and served only on special occasions.

Mrs. Chiang says, "My father loved pork liver, kidneys, brains, and stomach. There was a tiny restaurant attached to the local general store, and he and his cronies used to meet there to drink wine and play cards and nibble on a plate of cold liver. But women and children didn't go to restaurants, and innards were too expensive for family dinners, so the rest of us hardly ever ate them.

"Innards were prized partly because they were considered beneficial to human internal organs. Heart was good for the heart, liver for the liver, and so on."

Western science may dispute these specific benefits, but it accepts the general nutritional value of innards, which are full of protein, iron, and vitamins.

Because Americans have traditionally had such a barbaric attitude toward innards, they have been among the cheapest of all meats. Mrs. Chiang was delighted to discover how inexpensive innards are here, and as she began to make them into one exquisite dish after another, we quickly came to share her pleasure. Prepared in the Szechwanese manner, variety meats are far more succulent and interesting than when made in ordinary Western ways. Chinese cooking methods, especially stir-frying, work particularly well with innards. Overcooking can ruin such things as liver and kidneys, but stir-frying cooks them so quickly that they don't become tough. Red-cooked innards are also delicious. Mrs. Chiang simmers them for hours in a rich, dark, mildly anise-flavored sauce. Unlike other meats, they don't fall apart after such long cooking, and can be sliced and served cold as an elegant introduction to a special meal.

凉拌芝蔴腰子

COLD KIDNEYS IN SESAME SAUCE (*liangban zhima yaoz*)

Mrs. Chiang's combination of cold, cooked kidneys with a rich and spicy sesame paste–based sauce is as delicious as it is unusual. Because she barely cooks the kidneys, they have a delightful, crunchy texture. The sauce is one that goes with many cold dishes. Although few Chinese restaurants in this country use sesame sauce, it is a basic Szechwanese condiment. This dish uses its opulent, almost meaty, flavor to tone down the raw and powerful ones of the garlic, ginger, and hot peppers in a rich and subtle way.

Preparing kidneys takes more time than preparing other cuts of meat, for they must be soaked and rinsed to get rid of the unpleasant trace of ammonia that otherwise detracts from the flavor of cooked kidneys. They also have to be carefully sliced and then scored on the outside of each slice. The scoring makes the kidneys look nice and, more important, helps them cook quickly. The worst catastrophe that can befall a kidney is to be overcooked. Tough kidneys are even more unappealing than uncleaned ones.

Because this is a cold dish and must be made in advance, it is a useful one for entertaining.

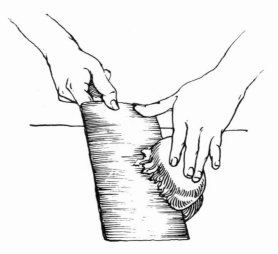

Slicing a kidney

PREPARATION

6 *pork kidneys*

Slice each kidney in half lengthwise. Remove the core from each piece and discard, leaving only the brownish outside part of each kidney. (This is a time-consuming chore but a necessary one.) Score the smooth outside of each piece lightly with two sets of parallel lines about ⅛ inch apart, so that you get an allover pattern of tiny diamonds. Then cut the kidneys into slices about the width of a pencil.

Put the sliced kidneys in a bowl, cover with cold water, and let soak for 15 minutes.

2 *tablespoons Chinese rice wine or cooking sherry*

Drain the kidneys, then put them back in the bowl. Add the wine, toss, and let soak for another 10 minutes. (The extended soaking helps the kidneys lose the peculiarly strong taste and odor that many people find offensive about kidneys.)

While the kidneys are soaking, you can begin to prepare the sauce.

8 *cloves garlic*

Smash the garlic cloves with the flat side of your cleaver, then peel. Chop the garlic very coarsely.

2-*inch piece fresh ginger*

Peel, then chop the ginger coarsely as well.

½ *teaspoon salt*

Take the coarsely chopped ginger and garlic and put them in a small steep-sided bowl or mortar. Mash them, together with the salt, until they turn into a thick paste, using either the handle of your cleaver, a wooden spoon, or a pestle. (The salt not only heightens the flavors of the garlic and the ginger, but its action in drawing out their juices also aids in the process of pulverization.) This procedure may take you several minutes, but the longer you pound it, the more pungent and delicious the finished product will be.

3 *scallions*

Clean the scallions, then chop them, both the white part and about one-third of the green, into pieces the size of a match head.

COOKING

2 *cups water*
(*kidneys*)

Bring the water to a boil in a saucepan and add the kidney slices. Let them boil over a moderate flame until they are thoroughly cooked, but for no more than 3 minutes. *Don't cook them too long or they will become tough.*

Drain the kidneys and rinse them thoroughly under cold water to remove all

(garlic and ginger
   paste)
(chopped scallions)
½ teaspoon granu-
   lated sugar
❋ 2 teaspoons hot
   pepper flakes in oil
½ teaspoon rice wine
   vinegar
1½ tablespoons soy
   sauce
1 teaspoon sesame
   paste
1 teaspoon sesame oil
½ teaspoon ground
   roasted Szechwan
   peppercorns

the scum that exuded from them while they were cooking.

Put the kidneys in a bowl. Add the garlic and ginger paste, the chopped scallions, sugar, hot pepper flakes in oil, vinegar, soy sauce, sesame paste, sesame oil, and the ground roasted Szechwan peppercorns.

Mix very thoroughly to make sure that all the kidney slices are coated with the sauce, then put on a serving dish and serve.

Note: Since this dish can be eaten cold, it can be made far in advance and kept in the refrigerator until just before serving. Remember to stir it up well right before you serve it.

腰 花 炒 雪 豆

KIDNEYS AND SNOW PEAS (*yaoz chao xuedou*)

This simple stir-fried dish of kidneys makes it easy to understand why Chinese gourmets treasure innards so highly. According to Mrs. Chiang, the only trick involved in preparing kidneys is to clean and rinse them very, very thoroughly; this will eliminate the unpleasant taste and odor that otherwise accompanies these delicious organs. This recipe combines them with crisp snow peas in a straightforward, relatively mild dish.

PREPARATION

¼ cup dried tree ears
1 cup hot water,
   approximately
4 pork kidneys

Put the tree ears in a small bowl and cover them with the hot water. Set aside to soak for at least 20 minutes.

Rinse off the kidneys, then cut each one horizontally into 3 or 4 slices. Cut out and discard the core in the middle of each piece of kidney, putting the usable brown outer parts of the kidney in a bowl of cold water as you finish each piece. Score one side of each piece of kidney in a diamond pattern by making incisions about ¼ inch deep and ¼ inch apart. Then cut each piece crosswise into slivers about ½ inch wide. Rinse the kidneys again very thoroughly under cold running water. Squeeze out as much excess moisture as you can with your hands and then put the slivered kidneys in a bowl.

2 scallions

Clean the scallions, then cut them, both the white part and most of the green, into 3-inch lengths; cut each piece into very fine shreds. Add the shredded scallions to the kidneys.

½-inch piece fresh ginger

Peel the ginger, then cut it into very fine shreds. Add these to the kidneys.

½ teaspoon granulated sugar
½ teaspoon salt
1 tablespoon cornstarch
1 teaspoon sesame oil
3 tablespoons soy sauce
1 tablespoon Chinese rice wine or cooking sherry

Add the sugar, salt, cornstarch, sesame oil, soy sauce, and wine to the kidneys and mix thoroughly.

6 ounces fresh snow peas

Wash the snow peas carefully and break off the tough tips at each end.

(tree ears)

Drain the tree ears, then rinse them thoroughly and pick over them carefully to remove any impurities, such as little pieces of wood, that may still be embedded in them.

COOKING

2 *tablespoons peanut oil*	Heat your wok or pan over a very hot flame for about 15 seconds, then pour in the oil. It will be hot enough for cooking when the first tiny bubbles form and a few small wisps of smoke appear.
(snow peas)	Quickly toss in the snow peas and stir-fry them for 30 seconds, using your cooking shovel or spoon to scoop the snow peas off the sides of the pan and spread them around in the middle.
½ *teaspoon salt* 1 *tablespoon water*	Add the salt and continue to stir-fry the snow peas for 45 seconds, then add the water and stir-fry the snow peas for about 30 more seconds before removing them from the pan to a serving dish.
¼ *cup peanut oil* *(tree ears)* ¼ *teaspoon salt*	Return the pan to the same high flame and pour in fresh oil. When the oil is ready for cooking, add the tree ears and the salt and stir-fry them for 15 seconds.
(kidneys and their marinade)	Now add the kidneys and their marinade. Stir-fry them for 30 seconds.
(snow peas)	Return the partially cooked snow peas to the pan and stir-fry them, together with the kidneys, for about 2 minutes. As soon as the kidneys are cooked all the way through, serve them; overcooking will make the kidneys too tough and the snow peas too limp.

紅燒腦花

RED-COOKED BRAINS *(hongshao naohua)*

Brains seldom appear on Chinese menus or in Chinese cookbooks in America; they have been sacrificed to American eating habits. This is a loss, because Szechwanese-style brains are delicious. They were a favorite of Mrs. Chiang's family, although they were such a luxury they were reserved for special occasions. On Taiwan, where brains were easily available, she often made them for us. Like bean curd, their soft, custardlike texture and mild flavor make a splendid foil for the complex and powerful seasonings of Szechwan.

Mrs. Chiang's recipe contains ginger, scallions, hot pepper paste, Szechwan pepper, and garlic, but it is easy to make and cooks in a flash. Depending on how much time you may have to spend cleaning the brains, the whole procedure, including 20 minutes' worth of marinating, shouldn't take more than half an hour from start to finish.

Pork brains are traditionally used, but, since they are almost impossible to find, even in Chinatown, we use calves' brains.

PREPARATION

2 *whole calves' brains (about 1½ pounds)*	Clean the brains very carefully, using a toothpick or similar pointed implement to remove the membrane surrounding the brains and to pull out any blood vessels that are still attached to them. Rinse the brains thoroughly under cold running water, then cut them into pieces roughly 1 inch in diameter. Put the pieces into a large bowl.
4 *scallions*	Clean the scallions, then chop them, both white part and green, into tiny pieces, about the size of a match head. Add the scallions to the brains.
1½ *-inch piece fresh ginger*	Peel the ginger, then chop it as fine as you can, until it reaches the consistency of farina. Add the chopped ginger to the brains.
1 *teaspoon salt* 1¼ *teaspoons granulated sugar* 2 *teaspoons sesame oil* 3 *tablespoons soy sauce*	Add the salt, sugar, sesame oil, soy sauce, ground roasted Szechwan peppercorns, wine, and cornstarch to the brains. Mix well, then set aside to marinate for at least 20 minutes.

2 *teaspoons ground roasted Szechwan peppercorns*

2 *tablespoons Chinese rice wine or cooking sherry*

1½ *tablespoons corn-starch*

8 *cloves garlic*

While the brains are marinating, peel the garlic and chop it into tiny pieces, about the size of a match head. Set aside.

COOKING

5 *tablespoons peanut oil*

Heat your wok or pan over a fairly high flame for 15 seconds, then pour in the oil. The oil will be hot enough to cook with when the first tiny bubbles form and a few small wisps of smoke appear.

(garlic)

When the oil is ready, add the chopped garlic. Stir-fry it for 30 seconds, using your cooking shovel or spoon to stir it around in the hot oil and make sure it doesn't burn.

❖ 2 *tablespoons hot pepper paste*

(brains and their marinade)

Quickly add the hot pepper paste and stir-fry it, along with the garlic, for another 30 seconds. Then add the brains and their marinade and continue to stir-fry, over the same high flame, for 1 minute, using your cooking shovel or spoon to scoop the contents of the pan off the sides and then stir them around in the middle.

Cover the pan, but don't reduce the heat. Cook the brains, stirring occasionally, for 4 or 5 minutes. Then, when the brains are thoroughly cooked, serve immediately.

豬肝炒雪豆

LIVER AND SNOW PEAS (*zhugan chao xuedou*)

This is a simple stir-fried dish whose clear, bright sauce contains the standard array of Szechwanese spices. But liver is a special food in Szechwan as in the rest of China; no Chinese gourmet would consider this dish an ordinary one.

Mrs. Chiang's combination of textures and colors is very special. The bright green snow peas, orange carrots, crisp white water chestnuts, and gelatinous black tree ears provide the kinds of visual and textural contrasts that an expensive delicacy like liver deserves. In America the situation is reversed; liver is not exotic but the vegetables are. Because frozen snow peas are not crisp enough and canned water chestnuts taste wrong, these vegetables must be fresh; they will probably require a trip to Chinatown.

PREPARATION

¼ *cup dried tree ears* 2 *cups boiling water, approximately*	Put the tree ears in a small bowl and pour the boiling water over them. Set them aside to soak.
1 *pound pork or beef liver*	Pull off the whitish membranes around the liver, then cut it crosswise into very thin slices, about 2 inches long and ⅛ inch thick. (It is easier to slice meat very thin if you have first put it in the freezer for about 10 minutes, until it becomes slightly stiff but not frozen.) Put the sliced liver in a bowl.
1-*inch piece fresh ginger*	Peel the ginger, then cut it into slivers about ⅛ inch thick, the width of a wooden matchstick. Add half the ginger shreds to the liver and reserve the rest.
1 *scallion*	Clean the scallion, then cut it, both white part and green, into 2-inch lengths and then into slivers. Add the scallion to the liver.

3 tablespoons soy sauce

1½ teaspoons sesame oil

1 tablespoon Chinese rice wine or cooking sherry

½ teaspoon granulated sugar

1 tablespoon cornstarch

Now add the soy sauce, sesame oil, wine, sugar, and cornstarch to the liver. Mix well, so all the liver slices are covered with the marinade, and let stand.

3 fresh water chestnuts (optional)

Cut off the dark outer skin of the water chestnuts, then slice the meat as fine as you can.

1 small or ½ large carrot

Peel the carrot and cut it crosswise into similarly thin slices. (Mrs. Chiang adds a decorative touch by first incising 5 small, wedge-shaped channels lengthwise around the outside of the carrot, so each slice comes out shaped like a flower.)

1 cup snow peas (about 4 ounces)

(tree ears)

Wash the snow peas. Break off the tough tips at both ends.

Drain the tree ears, then rinse them and pick over them carefully to remove any impurities, such as little pieces of wood, that may be embedded in them.

COOKING

1 tablespoon peanut oil

Heat your wok or pan over a high flame for 15 seconds, then add the oil. It will be hot enough to cook with when the first tiny bubbles form and a few small wisps of smoke appear.

(snow peas)

When the oil is ready, put the snow peas in and stir-fry them, using your cooking shovel or spoon in a scooping motion to spread them around in the pan and

	make sure they are all exposed to the hot oil.
(carrots and water chestnuts)	After about 45 seconds, add the carrots and water chestnuts and stir-fry them, together with the snow peas, for about 30 seconds.
1 *teaspoon salt* *(tree ears)*	Add the salt and the tree ears to the vegetables and continue to stir-fry them over a high flame for another 30 seconds.
¼ *cup water*	Pour in the water and cook the vegetables for about 20 more seconds, stirring occasionally. Then remove them from the pan.
5 *tablespoons peanut oil*	Clean out the pan by wiping it with some paper towels. Reheat it over a high flame for 15 seconds, then pour in the fresh oil.
2 *tablespoons water* *(liver)*	While you are waiting for the oil to heat up, add the water to the liver slices and mix thoroughly.
✿ 1 *tablespoon hot pepper paste* *(ginger)*	When the oil is hot enough for cooking, add the hot pepper paste and the reserved ginger shreds. Stir-fry vigorously for 10 seconds, making sure that the ginger doesn't burn.
(liver)	Add the liver slices and stir-fry them for about 1 minute over the same high flame.
	Return the vegetables to the pan and stir-fry them, together with the liver, for a final 1½ minutes. Serve immediately.

凉拌肝舌

ANISE LIVER AND ANISE TONGUE (*liangban ganshe*)

Anise Liver and Anise Tongue are both constituents of the Mixed Cold Plate on page 98, but there is no reason why either of them cannot be cooked and served separately. A dish of cold, sliced anise-flavored tongue or liver would make a pleasant introduction to a larger meal, as well as an unusual entree in itself. Since they are cold foods they must be made in advance—an added advantage. If you are only going to cook one innard, halve the amounts of seasonings (from the soy sauce through the ginger) as given on page 99, and use water to cover. The tongue should simmer for about 1 hour and 10 minutes, the liver no more than 30 minutes.

10 - POULTRY

"Chicken was something of a luxury in the Szechwan countryside, but we raised our own and ate it every week. We ate eggs several times a week," recalls Mrs. Chiang. "We kept about a hundred chickens, feisty, independent birds that roosted in a rough shed behind the house and ran free in the yard, scratching up insects and little bits of grain left over from the harvest. They were all raised for our dinner table, although my father sometimes sold eggs fertilized by his best rooster to the neighbors, who would add the chicks to their own flocks.

"We raised all the birds we ate. Fifteen or twenty ducks lived on the bank of the canal, and wandered around the rice paddies. It was the children's job to herd them back to the canal at night; if a duck got lost we had to scour the neighborhood for it. There were only a few geese, because they are bad-tempered and nobody liked to clean up the mess they made. A colony of pigeons flew around quite free but nested on our land.

"Ducks and geese and their eggs were usually cheaper than chickens because they were bigger, but we ate more chicken because we raised so many. We saved our ducks and geese for special occasions, like New Year's or visits from relatives. My mother would make rich, golden soups from whole fat chickens, and stew a whole goose in an aromatic, anise-flavored sauce. Ducks would be steamed or fried or, at New Year's, salted. My mother soaked the duck in salt for ten days and hung it up outside to dry. By the time it reached the table its meat was bright red."

Chickens and ducks can be used interchangeably in many of Mrs. Chiang's recipes featuring whole fowls, although ducks need to be cooked longer. Chickens are better for stir-frying. Most of our stir-fry recipes call for chicken breasts because they are the only part of the bird that yields pieces uniform enough in size and texture.

燻 鷄

SMOKED CHICKEN (*xunji*)

Szechwan is famous for its camphor-smoked ducks. Most Szechwanese dishes are too highly spiced for formal occasions, but camphor-smoked ducks—whose flesh is dark red and tastes like ham—have become part of the national *haute cuisine*. Like most banquet dishes, they are not made at home; camphor chips aren't available in America anyhow. Mrs. Chiang's mother smoked duck and chicken in other ways; her favorite recipe uses an aromatic mixture of Szechwan peppercorns, tea leaves, cinnamon, and other spices. The result doesn't taste like ham, but it has such a rich, smoky flavor that it is hard to believe it is only chicken or duck.

Both chicken and duck can be smoked the same way. It is a major production because it takes a lot of time and some ingenuity, but it doesn't require any special equipment, and the result is worth every minute. The bird is first marinated for 3 days, then steamed, dried, and finally smoked. Ducks are harder to deal with because they are fatter. They also have to be steamed longer, about 1½ hours as opposed to 1 hour.

A smoked chicken is a useful thing to build a banquet around, since it can be prepared and stored in the refrigerator for several days. This is hazardous, for few mortals can resist smoked chicken, and you risk finding your majestic bird reduced to a few bones and shreds of skin. The vandals will have made a mistake; magnificent as a cold smoked chicken is, it is even better when eaten at room temperature.

PREPARATION

1 *whole chicken (3½ to 4 pounds)*	Clean the chicken thoroughly inside and out. Remove the fat sacs near the tail and the tail as well. Cut off the wings. Put the chicken in a large shallow bowl.
2-*inch piece fresh ginger*	Don't peel the ginger, but cut it into tiny slivers about 2 inches long and ⅛ inch wide, the size and shape of a wooden matchstick.
5 *scallions*	Clean the scallions; give each one a few whacks with the side of your cleaver, then cut into 2-inch lengths.
(ginger) ¼ *cup salt* 2 *tablespoons Szechwan peppercorns* 1 *tablespoon granulated sugar* 1 *tablespoon Chinese rice wine or cooking sherry*	Put the scallions in a bowl, along with the ginger, salt, Szechwan peppercorns, sugar, and wine. Stir to combine, then rub the mixture thoroughly into the chicken, inside the cavity as well as all over the skin.
	Put the marinade-covered chicken in a bowl, cover, and let sit for 3 days at room temperature. Turn the chicken over at least once a day.

COOKING

After the marinating period is up, the chicken is ready to be steamed.

If you don't own a special Chinese steamer, you can make one using either a wok or a large pot with a rack and cover (see page 54).

Fill the bottom of the steamer with water, then place the bowl containing the

(chicken)
⅓ *cup Chinese rice
wine or sherry*

chicken and its marinade on a rack over the water. Pour the additional wine over the chicken, then bring the water to a boil over a high flame. Cover the steamer and let the chicken steam for 30 minutes.

After that time, check to make sure there is enough water in the bottom of the steamer. Add more, if necessary, then lower the heat and steam the chicken for an additional 30 minutes.

Remove the chicken from the steamer, let it cool off slightly, then hang it up to dry. (Yes, hang it up to dry! Since this is not a very commonly employed cooking technique, I know of no special equipment designed for hanging chicken. You will have to exercise your ingenuity on the problem. Mrs. Chiang ties the chicken's legs together with some string, which she then hangs from a conveniently placed hook over the kitchen sink. Any device will do that suspends the chicken in such a way that it is exposed to the air on all sides. If you don't hang it over the sink, be sure to put something under it to catch the liquid that drips out of it.)

The longer the chicken hangs, the better. At least 2½ or 3 hours is required; you could hang it overnight.

After the chicken has hung sufficiently, it is ready for smoking. For this you will need a large pot with a cover and an open rack inside it on which to place the chicken. (Mrs. Chiang uses a regular wok and its top, and makes a serviceable rack by placing about ten chopsticks crisscross in the middle of the wok.)

4 *sticks cinnamon*

¼ *cup Szechwan pep-*
percorns

⅓ *cup raw rice*

¼ *cup dried tea leaves*

5 *whole star anise or*
the equivalent in
pieces

¼ *cup granulated*
sugar

1 *tablespoon salt*

2 *tablespoons sesame*
oil, approximately

Break the cinnamon sticks into several pieces and put them in the bottom of the pot, along with the Szechwan peppercorns, raw rice, tea leaves, star anise, sugar, and salt. Mix these ingredients thoroughly, then place the chicken directly on the open rack over them.

Put the pot over a medium flame, then, when the ingredients in the bottom really begin to smoke, cover the pot and smoke the chicken for 10 minutes. (Don't worry about smoking up your kitchen; the spices give this smoke an incredible fragrance.)

After 10 minutes, the smoke should have turned the chicken a lovely light golden color. Remove it from the rack and brush the sesame oil all over it.

Remove the chicken meat from the bones and cut into small strips. Arrange the strips decoratively on a flat plate and serve.

Note: Smoked chicken keeps for quite a long time in the refrigerator, so you can prepare it several days before you want to eat it. Just remember to take it out of the refrigerator several hours before serving, as it is best at room temperature.

棒棒鷄

BON BON CHICKEN (COLD CHICKEN, CUCUMBERS, AND CELLOPHANE NOODLES IN SESAME SAUCE) *(bangbangji)*

This is the ultimate chicken salad—a beautiful arrangement of cold steamed chicken, shredded cucumbers, and cellophane noodles covered with a hot and garlicky sesame paste-based sauce. Mrs. Chiang claims that the dish got its unusual name from its appearance. The shredded chicken was supposed to look like sticks of kindling, or *bangbang*.

Really too large and elaborate for a family meal, Bon Bon Chicken is a good dish for a dinner party. Though it takes more time to prepare than a regular stir-fried dish, it's prettier, and can be made ahead of time. The various components of the dish—chicken, cellophane noodles, cucumbers, and sesame sauce—are all prepared separately, and are only combined at the final moment, right before serving. The chicken is the only ingredient that requires any significant amount of preparation and you can, if you want, marinate and steam it several hours before you fix the rest of the dish. Then, when the dish is complete, store it, covered with plastic wrap or aluminum foil, in the refrigerator for 3 or 4 hours. Pour the sauce over it only at the last minute.

PREPARATION

2 *whole chicken breasts (about 1½ to 2 pounds)*	Split each breast in half, but leave the skin and bones intact. Put the chicken in a shallow bowl while you prepare a marinade for it.
1-*inch piece fresh ginger*	Peel the ginger, then cut it into slivers about ⅛ inch wide, the width of a wooden matchstick.
6 *scallions*	Clean the scallions, then smash 3 of them, both white part and green, with the side of your cleaver; cut each of them into 2-inch lengths. Slice the remaining scallions crosswise into the thinnest possible pieces; set these aside.
1 *teaspoon salt* 1 *tablespoon Chinese rice wine or cooking sherry* 1 *tablespoon Szechwan peppercorns*	Combine the slivered ginger and the scallion lengths with the salt, wine, and Szechwan peppercorns. Rub this mixture all over the chicken breasts, then set the chicken aside, in a shallow bowl, to marinate at room temperature for at least 1 hour, turning it over several times while

(chicken breasts)

*1 package (2 ounces)
cellophane noodles*

*4 cups boiling water,
approximately*

2 cucumbers

½ teaspoon salt

it is marinating.

Put the cellophane noodles in a medium-sized bowl and pour the boiling water over them. Let soak for 20 minutes.

Peel the cucumbers, then cut them lengthwise down the middle and scoop out all the seedy pulp in the center. Cut each cucumber half into 3 sections, each about 2 inches long, and slice each section lengthwise as thin as you can.

Put the cucumber slices in a bowl and sprinkle the salt over them. Mix well and set aside.

COOKING

After the chicken has marinated for at least 1 hour, you are ready to steam it. If you don't have a special Chinese steamer, you can devise a perfectly serviceable one out of your wok or a large pot (see page 54).

(chicken)

Once the steamer has been constructed and filled with several inches of water, put the bowl of chicken, in its marinade, on the rack over the water. Bring the water to a boil over a moderately high flame, cover the steamer, and let the chicken steam for 30 minutes, checking occasionally to make sure that the steamer doesn't run out of water.

Remove the chicken from the steamer and let it cool.

*4 cups water,
approximately*

(cellophane noodles)

Bring the water to a boil in a medium-sized saucepan. Drain the softened cellophane noodles and add them to the boiling water. After the water boils again, cook the noodles for all of 2 or 3 minutes. Drain them and rinse them under cold water, then drain them again, thoroughly, and set them aside.

The last step before assembling the various components of the dish is to make the sauce:

8 *cloves garlic*

Smash the garlic cloves with the side of your cleaver, then peel. Put them in a small, steep-sided bowl or mortar.

1-*inch piece fresh ginger*

Peel the ginger, then chop it until it reaches the consistency of coarse bread crumbs. Put the ginger in the small bowl with the garlic.

½ *teaspoon salt*

Add the salt to the garlic and ginger, then, using the wooden handle of your cleaver, a wooden spoon, or pestle, mash them all together until they turn into a coarse paste. (The salt not only heightens the flavors of the garlic and ginger, but its action in drawing out their juices also aids in the process of pulverization.)

2 *teaspoons granulated sugar*
2 *teaspoons ground roasted Szechwan peppercorns*
❀ 1 *tablespoon hot pepper flakes in oil*
3½ *teaspoons rice wine vinegar*
3 *tablespoons sesame paste*
1 *tablespoon sesame oil*
5 *tablespoons soy sauce*
1½ *tablespoons water*

After the contents of the bowl are pulverized, add the sugar, Szechwan peppercorns, hot pepper flakes in oil, vinegar, sesame paste (first stirred thoroughly), sesame oil, soy sauce, and water.

(chopped scallions)	Add the chopped scallions to the other ingredients and stir them all together until the sauce is thoroughly blended.
(cucumbers)	Drain the cucumbers, using your hands to squeeze out as much excess water from them as you can. Select a large flat platter and cover it evenly with the cucumber slices.
(cellophane noodles)	Put the cooked and drained cellophane noodles on the chopping block and cut across them several times to make the individual noodles a more manageable size. Then spread the noodles in a layer over the cucumbers.
(chicken)	Bone the cooked chicken meat and pick off any little pieces of ginger, scallion, or brown peppercorns that are still sticking to it from the marinade. Then, leaving on the skin, chop the chicken into slices about the width of a lead pencil.
	Arrange the sliced chicken in an attractive way on top of the cellophane noodles.
(sauce)	Spoon the sauce over the chicken and serve.
	Note: This dish can be served either cold or at room temperature. If you plan to make it in advance and chill it for a while, remember not to add the sauce until just before you serve it.

紅燒八角鷄

ANISE CHICKEN (*hongshao bajiao ji*)

"When I was young our house was always full of people," remembers Mrs. Chiang. "Our friends would come to play and stay for supper, and all the cousins who lived in my father's parents' big house across the fields treated our house as their second home. When older relatives showed up for dinner, it would be a formal occasion. We kept the family scrolls and our wooden tablets inscribed with the names of ancestors in a room next to the kitchen, and my mother would set up a table there for dinner. Children and young women weren't allowed to eat there; only the men and older women did. Everyone sat according to rank; the most honored guest faced the door, with his back to the ancestral tablets. The food was always special, meaning as many meat dishes as possible—fresh pork or fish when we had it, sausages or salted meats any time. And there was always a freshly killed chicken, usually this rich, dark anise-flavored stew. My mother's Anise Chicken was magnificent; I always thought my uncles invented reasons to visit at dinner time just to eat it."

Anise Chicken improves with age. It should be made far enough in advance so it can be served lukewarm. Room temperature brings out the luscious flavor of the dish in a much more interesting way than either chilling or heating does. We serve Anise Chicken at most of our dinner parties, too. It is delicious, it can be made a day or more ahead of time, and it is one of the few recipes of Mrs. Chiang's that can be doubled. Increasing the amount of ingredients in most stir-fried dishes means that there will be too much liquid in the pan for proper cooking, but no reasonable amount of additional liquid can spoil a slow-simmered dish like this.

Mrs. Chiang likes to use chicken breasts for this dish, as they can be cut into nice, meaty pieces of a uniform size.

PREPARATION

10 *dried black mushrooms* 2 *cups boiling water*	Rinse the mushrooms off thoroughly, then put them in a bowl and pour the boiling water over them. Soak the mushrooms for about 20 minutes, or until they are soft, then cut off the hard stems and cut the larger mushrooms in half. Do *not* discard the water in which they soaked; you will use it later for cooking.
¼ *cup dried tree ears* 1 *cup boiling water*	Put the tree ears in a small bowl. Pour the boiling water over them and let soak for at least 10 minutes.

4 scallions	Cut 2 of the scallions, both green part and white, into 2-inch lengths. Tie the remaining scallions, whole, into a bunch.
1½ pounds chicken pieces, preferably breasts	Pull the skin off the chicken, but leave the bones in. Chop the chicken, bones and all, into 2-inch cubes, roughly the size of a walnut. (Mrs. Chiang is always careful to make sure that all the pieces are about the same size.) Put the chicken in a shallow dish and add the cut-up scallions and the wine. Set aside to marinate for 15 minutes.
(cut-up scallions)	
1 tablespoon Chinese rice wine or cooking sherry	
2-inch piece fresh ginger	Peel the ginger and cut it into 4 slices.
(tree ears)	When the tree ears are soft and slightly gelatinous, rinse them thoroughly and pick them over carefully to remove any impurities, such as tiny pieces of wood, that may still be embedded in them.

COOKING

¼ cup peanut oil	Heat your wok or pan for about 15 seconds over a moderate flame, then pour in the oil. The oil will be hot enough to cook with when the first tiny bubbles form and a few small wisps of smoke appear.
(ginger)	When the oil is ready, quickly throw in the ginger, red peppers, sugar, whole scallions, and chicken mixture, making sure you stir the ingredients well while you add them. Continue to stir-fry for about 30 seconds, using your cooking shovel or spoon to scoop the ingredients from the sides of the pan and then stir them around in the middle, so every piece of chicken is exposed to the hot oil.
❉ *5 dried red peppers*	
1 tablespoon granulated sugar	
(whole, tied scallions)	
(chicken mixture)	
4 whole star anise, or	Add the star anise, then reduce the heat

*the equivalent in
pieces*

2 *tablespoons Chinese
rice wine or cooking
sherry*
6 *tablespoons soy
sauce*
*(mushrooms and their
soaking water)*
1 *cup water,
approximately*

(tree ears)

1 *tablespoon sesame
oil*
1 *teaspoon salt, or to
taste, if necessary*

slightly, and continue to cook, stirring occasionally, for about 5 more minutes, until the chicken stiffens and turns white.

Add the wine and the soy sauce, bring to a boil, and continue to cook, over a moderate flame, for 3 minutes more.

Now add the mushrooms and the water in which they were soaked, and pour in enough additional water to barely cover the chicken; you will probably need about a cupful. Wait until the liquid boils, then lower the heat, cover the pan, and let the chicken simmer slowly for 1 hour.

After this period, the chicken should be very soft and the sauce should be reduced to almost half its original amount. At this point add the soaked tree ears and let them cook with the chicken for about 5 minutes more.

Finally, add the sesame oil and stir thoroughly.

Because the soy sauce has become so concentrated during the cooking process, the chicken may not require any additional salt. Make sure that you taste the sauce *before* you add any.

Note: This dish can be prepared way ahead of time and then brought to room temperature, when it is actually at its best, just before serving. It can also be kept for several days in the refrigerator without harm.

官保鷄丁

GRAND DUKE'S CHICKEN WITH PEANUTS (*gongbao jiding*)

There is some debate as to just which grand duke gave his title to this celebrated chicken dish, usually called simply Grand Duke's Chicken on Chinese-American menus. As in Europe, it was not uncommon for a celebrated Chinese gourmet to allow his name to be used for a classic dish, one his sensitive criticism may have helped perfect. Whoever he was, our anonymous grand duke must have been a gentleman of impeccable taste, for his chicken with peanuts is one of the great dishes of Szechwan. Many gourmets feel it epitomizes the true taste of the province.

Debate also surrounds the composition of the dish; some cooks use only dried red peppers, while others, including Mrs. Chiang, add green peppers. But everybody uses peanuts.

When she can get them, Mrs. Chiang likes to use hot green peppers instead of the regular round variety. Together with the dried red ones, they produce a very hot chicken dish. Her *gongbao jiding* is light and aromatic, as brilliantly flavored as it is lovely to look at.

The peanuts for this dish must be fresh; neither roasted nor salted ones will do. You can get fresh peanuts at health food stores as well as at Chinese markets.

Perfectly prepared, a *gongbao jiding* will have very little sauce, although it may be covered with a thin film of oil. Szechwanese food occasionally seems oily; this is not a flaw but a sign that the cook respected his ingredients enough not to adulterate them with any prepared sauce.

PREPARATION

½ cup fresh *peanuts*
1 cup boiling water
(*optional*)

If the peanuts still have their dark red skins on, put them in a small bowl and pour boiling water over them. Let the peanuts soak for about 3 minutes, then drain them; the skins will practically pop off. (If the peanuts have already been skinned, omit this step.)

1 *large whole chicken breast (about 1 pound)*

Remove all the skin and bones from the chicken breast and cut the meat into cubes roughly 1 inch in diameter.

1⅓ *tablespoons soy sauce*

½ *teaspoon granulated sugar*

1 *teaspoon sesame oil*

1 *teaspoon Chinese rice wine or cooking sherry*

1 *egg white*

1 *scant tablespoon cornstarch*

Put the chicken pieces in a bowl and add the soy sauce, sugar, sesame oil, wine, egg white, and cornstarch. Mix thoroughly and set it aside to marinate while you prepare the other ingredients.

2 *green peppers or* ✿ *3 large hot green peppers*

Wash the peppers and cut them into squares that are approximately the same size as the chicken pieces.

10 *cloves garlic*

Smash the garlic cloves with the flat of your cleaver, then peel. Chop the garlic into little pieces, about the size of a match head.

½-*inch piece fresh ginger*

Peel the ginger and mince it into slightly smaller pieces than the garlic.

✿ 5 *dried red peppers*

Cut each of the red peppers into about 4 pieces.

2 *scallions (chicken)*

Clean the scallions, then chop them, both green part and the white, crosswise into ¼-inch pieces. Add the scallions to the chicken.

COOKING

3 *tablespoons peanut oil*

Heat your wok or pan for 15 seconds over a medium flame before you pour in the oil. The oil should be hot enough to cook with when the first tiny bubbles form and a few small wisps of smoke appear.

(peanuts)

When the oil is ready, add the peanuts. Stir-fry them for 2 or 3 minutes, using your cooking shovel or spoon in a scooping motion to agitate them around in the pan so all are exposed to the hot oil. (They can burn easily, so watch them carefully.) As soon as the peanuts have turned a golden brown, remove them from the pan.

(green peppers)
½ teaspoon salt

Add the green peppers to the oil in the bottom of the pan. Stir-fry them for 30 seconds over a fairly high flame, then add the salt and continue to stir-fry for another 45 seconds before taking the peppers out of the pan.

¼ cup peanut oil

Remove the pan from the heat and wipe it out carefully with paper towels. Return it to the stove and reheat over a fairly high flame for 15 seconds before pouring in the fresh oil.

(garlic, ginger, and dried red peppers)

As soon as the oil is ready for cooking, add the garlic, ginger, and red peppers. (Mrs. Chiang tests the oil by floating a tiny piece of ginger in it. If the ginger sinks to the bottom the oil is too cold; if it turns brown immediately, it is too hot. The ginger should float on the surface, sputtering and hissing.) Cook the ginger, garlic and red peppers for 20 seconds, stirring constantly.

(chicken and its marinade)

Then add the chicken and its marinade and stir-fry for 1 minute.

(partially cooked green peppers)

Now return the green peppers to the pan and stir-fry them together with the chicken for another minute.

1 tablespoon soy sauce

Add the soy sauce to the chicken and stir-fry for about 15 seconds, or until the chicken is cooked through. The chicken

<table>
<tr><td></td><td>is ready when it has stiffened and turned white.</td></tr>
<tr><td>(peanuts)</td><td>Finally, return the peanuts to the pan. Stir-fry everything together for 30 seconds longer, then serve.</td></tr>
</table>

醬 爆 鷄 丁

CHICKEN WITH HOISIN SAUCE (jiangbao jiding)

This simple and delicious chicken dish belongs to an important Szechwanese family of dishes called *jiangbao*—literally, "explosively fried with sauce"—all of whose members contain hoisin sauce as their main seasoning. Though definitely of Szechwanese origin, *jiangbao* dishes are not hot; they have a surprisingly rich, sweet taste. *Jiangbao* is a particularly felicitous way to cook chicken; the rich, dark sauce goes beautifully with the mild chicken, and the color contrast is attractive as well.

You may notice that in the finished dish some of the oil separates and floats on top of the sauce. This happens in many authentic Szechwanese dishes. Though the free oil may seem unappetizing by Western standards, it is an authentic Szechwanese characteristic—and, in any case, is infinitely preferable to a thick and muddy sauce.

PREPARATION

2 *whole chicken breasts (about 1½ to 2 pounds)*	Bone the chicken and pull off all the skin. Chop the meat into 1-inch cubes and put them in a bowl.
6 *scallions*	Clean the scallions, then cut them, the white part and most of the green, into ½-inch lengths.
3 *tablespoons soy sauce*	Add the scallions to the chicken, along with the soy sauce, sesame oil, wine, and salt.
1 *teaspoon sesame oil*	Mix well and set aside to marinate for
1 *tablespoon Chinese rice wine or cooking sherry*	at least 15 minutes.

1 teaspoon salt
1-inch piece fresh
   ginger
5 to 6 cloves garlic

Peel the ginger, then chop it into tiny pieces, about the size of a match head. Smash the garlic cloves with the side of your cleaver, then peel. Chop the garlic as fine as the ginger.

COOKING

5 tablespoons peanut
   oil

Heat your wok or pan over a high flame for 15 seconds, then add the oil. It will be hot enough to cook with when the first tiny bubbles form and a few small wisps of smoke appear.

(garlic and ginger)

When the oil is ready, toss in the chopped ginger and garlic and stir it around in the hot oil for 10 seconds.

2 tablespoons hoisin
   sauce

Add the hoisin sauce and stir-fry for 30 seconds, using your cooking shovel or spoon to keep the ingredients moving so they don't burn or stick.

1 tablespoon water
(chicken mixture)

Combine the water and the chicken mixture and stir well, then add the chicken mixture to the pan. Cook, stirring occasionally, for about 5 minutes, or until the chicken is stiff and is completely cooked. Serve immediately.

成 都 鷄

CHENGTU CHICKEN (*chengdu ji*)

I have long considered celery, along with monosodium glutamate, one of the great banes of bad Chinese restaurants. Cooked celery has such a strong taste that it almost invariably overpowers every other ingredient in the dish. Yet, treated with moderation, celery is a wonderful vegetable, crisp and slightly bitter. Mrs. Chiang uses it in this otherwise simple chicken dish to provide an unexpected combination of textures and flavors. Because the celery is added just before serving, it is barely cooked. It remains crunchy, and its flavor, though pronounced, doesn't dominate the dish.

Like so much of the food of Chengtu, the culinary heart of Szechwan, this recipe calls for a liberal dosage of dried red peppers. If you are unaccustomed to such fiery fare, omit some of the peppers. Not all, though, for it is the peppers that keep the celery under control.

PREPARATION

2 *whole chicken breasts (about 1½ to 2 pounds)*	Chop the chicken into cubes, roughly the size of walnuts. Leave the bones in, though the skin is optional.
4 *ribs celery*	Rinse off the celery and trim it, then chop it into little pieces, about ¼ inch in diameter.
2 *scallions*	Clean the scallions, then chop them, both white part and green, into small pieces, roughly the same size as the celery.
1½-inch *piece fresh ginger*	Peel the ginger and chop it until the pieces are the size of match heads.
6 *cloves garlic*	Smash the garlic cloves with the side of your cleaver, then peel. Chop the garlic into the same size pieces as the ginger.
❀ 7 *whole dried red peppers* or ❀ 1 *teaspoon dried red pepper flakes*	If you are using the dried red peppers, cut them into little pieces, about the same size as the celery and scallion pieces.
2 *tablespoons cornstarch* 2 *tablespoons water*	Combine the cornstarch and water in a small bowl; mix well and set aside.

COOKING

6 *tablespoons peanut oil*	Heat your wok or pan over a high flame for 15 seconds, then add the oil. The oil will be hot enough to cook with when the first

tiny bubbles form and a few small wisps of smoke appear.

(garlic)
(ginger)

When the oil is ready, toss in the chopped garlic and ginger and stir-fry for about 30 seconds, using your cooking shovel or spoon to stir them around in the bottom of the pan and keep them from burning. Don't be alarmed if they turn brown right away.

(dried red peppers or
pepper flakes)

Now add the dried red peppers or pepper flakes to the pan and continue to stir-fry for another 25 seconds or so.

(chicken)
1¾ teaspoons salt

Add the chicken and the salt to the pan. Stir-fry them for about 1 minute 15 seconds, scooping the chicken pieces off the sides of the pan and spreading them around in the middle, so all are exposed to the hot oil.

2 tablespoons rice
wine or cooking
sherry

Add the wine and stir-fry for another 30 seconds.

(scallions)
¼ cup water

Add the scallions and the water. Cook the chicken, stirring occasionally, for about 2½ minutes, or until it is almost cooked through, then cover the pan and let the chicken cook over the same high heat for 3 minutes more.

1 teaspoon
granulated sugar

Uncover the pan, add the sugar, and stir-fry for another 45 seconds.

(cornstarch and water)
(celery)

Stir the cornstarch and water to make sure they are thoroughly combined, then add the mixture to the pan, along with the chopped celery. Stir-fry everything for 1 final minute, then serve. The sauce should have thickened and become clear, and the celery should be just barely cooked and still quite crunchy.

鶏 炒 黄 瓜 丁

CHICKEN AND CUCUMBERS (*ji chao huangguading*)

Szechwanese cucumbers are longer, thinner, and tastier than the American variety. Mrs. Chiang's family grew several kinds of cucumbers and cucumberlike squashes, which her mother cooked, pickled, and served raw in salads as well:

"We ate cooked cucumber often; we children loved its softness and its mild, faintly bitter flavor."

In this spicy chicken dish the cucumbers provide a nice contrast to the slightly fibrous texture of the chicken pieces and the overall pepperiness of the sauce.

One enormous advantage of this recipe is that it requires no exotic ingredients. Outside of the most basic Oriental staples, you can find everything you need at the corner grocery store or supermarket. It is also very easy to prepare, and, though the raw chicken should marinate for 30 minutes, the entire dish takes only about 5 minutes to cook.

PREPARATION

2 *whole chicken breasts (about 1½ to 2 pounds)*

Remove the skin from the chicken breasts and bone them, then chop the meat into small cubes, about ½ inch on each side. Put the chicken into a bowl.

2 *scallions*

Clean the scallions, then cut them, both white part and green, crosswise into pieces about ¼ inch long. Add these to the chicken.

½ *teaspoon granulated sugar*
½ *teaspoon salt*
1 *teaspoon sesame oil*
2 *tablespoons soy sauce*

Add the sugar, salt, sesame oil, soy sauce, wine, egg white, and cornstarch to the chicken. Using chopsticks or a wooden spoon, mix everything together well, so the egg white is thoroughly blended in with the other ingredients. Set the

1 tablespoon Chinese rice wine or cooking sherry	chicken aside to marinate at room temperature for at least 30 minutes.
1 egg white	
1 tablespoon corn-starch	
2 small cucumbers	Peel the cucumbers, then cut them in half lengthwise and scoop out all the seedy pulp in the middle. Chop the cucumber flesh into ½-inch cubes, roughly the same size as the chicken pieces. Put the cucumbers in a bowl. (You should get about 2 cups of chopped cucumber. If your cucumbers seem large, use only half of the second one.)
½ teaspoon salt	Sprinkle the salt over the cucumbers, stir, and set aside for 20 to 30 minutes.
❀ 4 dried hot red peppers	Cut the peppers into 3 or 4 pieces, each about ½ inch long.
10 cloves garlic	Smash the garlic cloves with the flat side of your cleaver, then peel. Chop the garlic coarsely, into pieces roughly the size of grains of uncooked rice.
(cucumbers)	Just before you are ready to begin cooking, drain the cucumbers, using your hands to squeeze out as much of their excess moisture as you can.

COOKING

1 tablespoon peanut oil	Heat your wok or pan over a high flame for 15 seconds, then pour in the oil. It will be ready to cook with when the first tiny bubbles form and a few wisps of smoke appear.
(cucumbers)	When the oil is ready, toss in the cucumbers, and stir-fry them fairly vigorously,

using your cooking shovel or spoon to scoop them off the sides of the pan and then stir them around in the middle, so all the cucumbers are exposed to the hot oil. Remove them from the pan after 1½ minutes and set aside.

1 *tablespoon water*
(chicken mixture)

Combine the water and the chicken mixture and stir well, so the cornstarch is thoroughly blended in.

¼ *cup peanut oil*
(garlic)

Wipe the pan out with paper towels, then reheat over the same high flame. Pour in the fresh oil, and, when it is hot enough, add the garlic, stirring it around in the pan for 15 seconds. Be careful to see that it doesn't burn.

(dried red peppers)

Add the dried red peppers and stir-fry them together with the garlic, for another 15 seconds.

(chicken mixture)

Give the chicken mixture one last stir and add it to the pan. Stir-fry for 1 minute.

❀ 2 *teaspoons hot*
pepper flakes in
oil
2 *tablespoons soy*
sauce
(cucumbers)

Add the hot pepper flakes in oil and stir-fry the chicken for another 15 seconds, then, finally, add the soy sauce and stir-fry the chicken for 15 seconds more.

Return the partly cooked cucumbers to the pan. Cook them, together with the chicken, over the same high heat for another 1 or 2 minutes, stirring occasionally to make sure that all the ingredients are equally exposed to the hot oil. The chicken will be fully cooked when it has stiffened and turned white. Test a piece for doneness, and when the chicken is ready, remove it quickly from the heat and serve. (Do not overcook this dish or the chicken will be tough and the cucumbers mushy.)

鶏肝炒青椒丁

CHICKEN LIVERS AND GREEN PEPPERS
(jigan chao qingjiaoding)

The Chinese consider the liver the most precious part of the bird; chicken livers were such a delicacy in Szechwan that Mrs. Chiang's mother cooked them only for important guests, such as her parents-in-law. Even on Taiwan chicken livers were expensive. The traditional Szechwanese way of preparing chicken livers is delicious, and, since chicken livers are inexpensive here, Americans can enjoy it often.

This dish can be made either with or without hot peppers. Although it is easy to prepare, you must take care not to overcook the chicken livers. Tender they are a delight; tough, a disaster.

PREPARATION

1 pound chicken livers

Rinse off the livers. Separate each pair and cut off all the white membranes and segments of fat, then cut each piece of liver in half and put them all in a bowl.

½-inch piece fresh ginger

Peel the ginger, then cut it into shreds ⅛ inch wide, about the width of a wooden matchstick. Add the ginger to the chicken livers.

1 scallion
½ teaspoon salt
½ teaspoon granulated sugar
1 tablespoon cornstarch
3 tablespoons soy sauce
1 teaspoon sesame oil

Clean the scallion then cut it, both white part and green, into 1-inch lengths. Add to the livers, along with the salt, sugar, cornstarch, soy sauce, sesame oil, and wine. Mix thoroughly and set aside to marinate.

1 tablespoon Chinese
  rice wine or cooking
  sherry

❀ 4 long hot green   Wash off the peppers and remove the
  peppers or 2   seeds. Cut the peppers into 1-inch
  green peppers   squares, roughly the same size as the
                               chicken livers.

6 cloves garlic   Smash the garlic cloves with the flat side of
                               your cleaver, then peel. Chop the garlic
                               coarsely, into pieces about the size of
                               grains of uncooked rice.

                            COOKING

2 tablespoons peanut   Heat your wok or pan over a high flame
  oil   for 15 seconds, then add the oil. The
                               oil will be hot enough for cooking when
                               the first tiny bubbles form and a few
                               small wisps of smoke appear.

(green peppers)   When the oil is ready, add the peppers.
                               Stir-fry for 30 seconds, using your cook-
                               ing shovel or spoon in a scooping motion
                               to spread them around in the hot oil.

½ teaspoon salt   Add the salt and continue to stir-fry the
                               peppers for 2 more minutes. Then re-
                               move them from the pan.

6 tablespoons peanut   Reheat the pan and pour in the fresh oil.
  oil   When the oil is hot enough for cooking,
(garlic)   add the garlic and the optional red pep-
❀ 3 dried red peppers   pers or hot pepper paste. Stir-fry care-
  or 1 tablespoon   fully for 40 seconds, then add the
  hot pepper   chicken liver mixture and stir-fry for
  paste (optional)   about 45 seconds longer.
(chicken livers)
(green peppers)   Return the partially cooked green peppers
                               to the pan and stir-fry everything to-
                               gether for 3 minutes.

½ *teaspoon granula-*
ted sugar

Add the sugar. Stir-fry the livers for a final 15 seconds, then, after testing them to make sure they are thoroughly cooked, serve.

香 酥 鴨

FRAGRANT, CRISPY DUCK *(xiangsu ya)*

Peking Duck is a much overrated bird. Its preparation and consumption are attended by so much ceremony that it is easy to forget that it is, after all, only a plain roast duck. And, propaganda aside, ducks are capable of greater things gastronomically.

In Szechwan, they achieve them. The two best Chinese ducks come from there, Camphor Smoked Duck and *xiangsu ya*, or Fragrant, Crispy Duck, often called Szechwan Duck. The former is indescribable, while the latter is merely the crispest and most fragrant bird I have ever eaten. Its rich flesh is soft and aromatic and its skin is dry and crunchy. Even its bones are delicious, as crisp and brittle as potato chips, but with a deep, perfumy flavor. Fragrant, Crispy Duck reaches this state of perfection by being first marinated, then steamed, then dried, and then, finally, fried.

Fragrant, Crispy Duck, like Peking Duck, cannot really be made at home. The dish needs the expertise and, above all, the special equipment that only a restaurant kitchen and a trained chef can provide. The kind of deep-fat frying required to produce the duck's transcendent crispness has to be a professional operation. A good home cook can, however, approximate the fragrance, if not the crispness, of a *xiangsu* duck. This is what Mrs. Chiang has been able to do. Her recipe for this Szechwanese classic is an excellent one; it produces a tender, aromatic bird with a crisp and flaky skin, the whole permeated with the special fragrance of Szechwan peppercorns. It takes hours of marinating for the aromatic spices of Szechwan to penetrate the flesh and bones of the duck, so give yourself at least an entire day to prepare it. The longer you dry and fry it, the crisper it gets. This recipe can also be used for making an equally fragrant, crispy chicken. In that case, reduce the steaming time from 2 hours to 1 hour 20 minutes.

Tradition demands that a *xiangsu ya* be served with a dish of seasoned salt (see below) and steamed Flower Rolls, or *huajuan* (page 331). You dip a crisp, fragrant piece of duck into the salt and then eat it encased in the soft, sweet bread. It is, I think, the greatest eating pleasure in the world.

PREPARATION

1 duck (about 4½ pounds)

Wash the duck well, especially on the inside. Pat it dry with paper towels. Then, to make sure that it is thoroughly dry, hang it up for about 30 minutes. (Since you will have to drain the duck this way later, it is a good idea to devise a convenient way to hang it up. Mrs. Chiang simply ties the duck's legs together with string, which she then hangs from a conveniently placed hook over the kitchen sink. It's not elegant, but it allows the air to circulate freely around the drying bird, which is the only thing that matters.)

3 whole star anise or the equivalent in pieces
⅓ cup salt
¼ cup Szechwan peppercorns

Break up the star anise into little pieces and put them in a pan with the salt and Szechwan peppercorns. Place the pan over a medium flame and stir-fry the spices for 4 or 5 minutes, using your cooking shovel or spoon in a continuous motion to spread them around in the bottom of the pan. Remove the spice mixture from the pan when it has become very fragrant and the salt has turned a pale tan in color.

(duck)

Rub 2 or 3 tablespoonfuls of the hot salt and spice mixture into the cavity of the duck; rub the rest into the skin. Put the duck in a shallow bowl and set it aside to marinate for at least 6 hours or overnight. Turn it over at least once while it is marinating; you don't have to refrigerate it.

3 *scallions*

Clean the scallions, then cut them, both white part and green, into 2-inch lengths.

3-inch piece of fresh ginger

Peel the ginger and cut it into slivers about ⅛ inch wide, the width of a wooden matchstick.

(*duck*)
1 *tablespoon soy sauce*

Don't scrape the salt marinade off the duck. Stuff a few tablespoonfuls of the ginger and scallions into the duck's cavity and cover the duck with the rest. Sprinkle the soy sauce over the duck and put it aside to marinate again, this time for about 4 hours, turning it over a few times during the marinating period.

COOKING

(*duck*)

Place the shallow bowl containing the duck and its marinade on the rack of a steamer partly full of boiling water. (If you do not own a steamer, see page 54 for instructions on how to improvise one.)

½ *cup rice wine or dry sherry*

Pour the wine over the duck. Adjust the flame under the steamer so that the water inside is boiling steadily. Cover the steamer and cook the duck for 2 hours, checking the water level inside the steamer occasionally and adding more water, if necessary. The duck will render a lot of fat while it steams.

Remove the duck from the steamer, let it cool off for a few minutes, and then hang it up to dry for at least 1½ hours. Make sure there is something underneath the duck to catch the juices that will drip from it.

Untie the duck. Use poultry shears or a cleaver to cut the duck in half down the backbone and along the breastbone. Scrape off all the spices and little bits of scallion and ginger that may still be sticking to the duck.

2 tablespoons soy sauce

½ cup all-purpose flour, approximately

3 or more cups peanut or other cooking oil

Sprinkle the soy sauce all over the duck, then coat the duck with the flour, patting it in carefully.

Heat a large wok or pan over a high flame for 15 seconds, then pour in the oil. It will take several minutes for the oil to get hot enough for cooking; wait until it just barely begins to smoke.

(duck)

When the oil is ready, put in one of the duck halves. Fry it for 2½ or 3 minutes, turning it several times to make sure every side is exposed to the hot oil. (Chopsticks are good for handling food in hot oil.) When the duck has turned golden brown on all sides and is very crispy, remove it from the hot oil and drain it on some paper towels. Fry the other half of the duck in the same way.

SERVING

Let the duck cool for a few minutes before you cut it into serving pieces.

First, cut off the drumsticks. Then use your cleaver or poultry shears to cut the rest of the carcass, bones and all, into slices about ¾ inch wide.

Arrange the duck decoratively on a serving platter. (Mrs. Chiang usually tries to re-form a cut-up fowl into its original shape.) It is best eaten slightly warm.

Traditionally, Fragrant, Crispy Duck is always accompanied by some kind of delicately steamed or fried bread. Flower Rolls, or *huajuan* (page 331), are what Mrs. Chiang always serves. She also serves a dish of seasoned salt for dipping the individual pieces of crunchy duck into.

1½ teaspoons salt
1 tablespoon freshly ground black pepper

Prepare the seasoned salt by combining the salt and pepper and then setting it out in small dishes for each diner to dip his piece of duck in.

凉拌八角鴨

ANISE DUCK (*liangban bajiao yaz*)

A rich, anise-flavored duck is invariably the focal point of the decorative Mixed Cold Plate, or *liangban pinpan* (page 98). But there's no reason not to cook and serve it separately. It's easy to prepare, since all you have to do is boil it, and that can be done far in advance. The directions for cooking the duck can be found on pages 99–100. This recipe is better for ducks than the one for Anise Chicken on page 167. Ducks do not take well to stir-frying and are better cooked whole, as they are for a *liangban pinpan*.

11 - FISH AND SEAFOOD

Fish cookery is one of the great glories of China's cuisine, and a whole fish is traditionally the penultimate course in a formal banquet. Nothing can perk up the flagging palate of an overfed gourmet as well as the sight of a beautiful fish in a fragrant sauce. Chinese cooks understand fish; they know that above all it must be fresh, and you can still find tubs of live carp in some of the more traditional markets of Chinatown. Many fish recipes, like the one for the famous Shanghai delicacy, West Lake Sour Fish, specify that the main ingredient remain alive until the final moment. There are even some dishes that feature the living animals. "Jumping" shrimp, as a matter of fact, were a specialty of several of our favorite Shanghai restaurants in Taipei. Though we had no qualms about eating raw fish in Japan, neither John nor I ever developed the courage to eat live, wriggling shrimps.

Salt-water fish and shellfish cannot be transported very far inland and stay fresh, so most traditional Chinese fish dishes use fresh-water fish or crustaceans. Szechwanese recipes, of course, use nothing else, and Mrs. Chiang's family ate fish fairly often:

"For a banquet my father would buy a large fish at the market, but more often he and my older brother would catch their own in a pond or irrigation canal. There were carp and many other kinds. During the rice-growing season, the rice paddies were flooded and thousands of tiny silver fingerlings swam in them. I used to love splashing around with my older brother, trying to scoop them up in a homemade net. If we only caught a few we fed them to the cats, but when we had a good catch my mother cooked them. They were very sweet, and she simply fried them in deep fat until they were crisp and golden. We also caught light green crayfish and fresh-water crabs, which hid under the bridges over the irrigation canals. They were delicious steamed with wine, or fried with ginger and eggs."

When Mrs. Chiang left Szechwan she encountered new and different types of fish and shellfish, but she had no trouble adapting them to her mother's recipes. She uses shrimp instead of crayfish, and sea bass instead of fresh-water fish. The cooking methods are the same and the results are just as delicious.

A NOTE ON FISH

Most of Mrs. Chiang's recipes use whole fish, with their heads on and the tails and bones still intact. Supermarkets specialize in filets and rarely carry fresh whole fish. Fish markets are better and Chinese fish markets are the best of all, for of course they sell exactly the right kinds of fish for cooking in the Chinese manner. The most important thing to look for in buying a fish is freshness. The best way to tell if a fish is fresh is to look it straight in the eye. The brighter and clearer its gaze, the fresher it is; dull red eyes belong to long-dead fish. The gills, however, should be red. Once you have chosen your fish, have it scaled and gutted, but make sure that the head is left on. Behead a fish and it loses some of its tastiest parts, as well as its regal appearance.

Some types of fish are better than others for cooking in the style of Szechwan. Fresh-water fish are best; but except for carp, which is a seasonal rarity, they are hard to find outside of Chinatown. Fortunate are those who catch their own. The rest of us must depend on the salt-water variety, of which the best, at least on the East Coast, is sea bass. Any mild-tasting, firm, white-fleshed fish will do. Red snapper and scup are fine, flounder is good for steaming. A 1½- to 2-pound fish is perfect. Smaller fish are acceptable, and, in fact, we have often cooked two trout instead of one larger fish. They are delicious, and easier to manage inside a wok.

A whole fish is a majestic creature, but even Mrs. Chiang finds cooking one a challenge, for it doesn't always fit snugly inside a wok. Usually either the head or tail or both will stick out of the oil and you will have to tilt the pan from side to side as you cook in order to get them fried. It is also hard to keep the skin from sticking to the wok. One trick is to tilt the wok and, holding the fish by the tail, ease it slowly into the pan head first. Slide the fish in and out of the hot oil a few times before you finally let it go. Even if the skin still sticks, it's no tragedy; taste is more important than appearance. That is why Chinese gourmets insist on a whole fish; they know that the head contains some excellent eating. The cheeks are firm and delicate, and the tongue has an interesting texture.

紅 燒 魚

RED-COOKED FISH (*hongshao yu*)

Whenever we want to test out an unfamiliar Szechwanese restaurant, we always order Red-Cooked Fish or *hongshao yu*. The only thing all red-cooked dishes have in common is soy sauce; what else goes into the wok depends on regional style and the ingenuity of the chef. Red-Cooked Fish is a good test of the talents of a chef and, more important, of the sensitivity with which he treats his ingredients. Even the most bravura performance should respect the fresh, pure flavor of the fish.

Mrs. Chiang's Red-Cooked Fish succeeds brilliantly by any standard. An epicurean Frenchwoman for whom Mrs. Chiang once made the dish went into Gallic superlatives about it, and declared that *carpe à la mode de Szechwan* surpassed anything her own cuisine could produce. The sauce, which is enlivened by minced garlic and ginger, is fresh and spicy, but not overwhelmingly so. Its bright, clear flavor complements the more delicate one of the fish.

The key ingredient in this dish is hot pepper paste, or *lajiao jiang*. If you are cooking a carp or other fresh-water fish, you can substitute hot bean paste or *ladouban jiang*. This will transform a red-cooked fish into an equally famous Szechwanese classic, Hot Bean Paste Fish, or *douban yu*. The change produces a richer and more pungent sauce.

PREPARATION

1½-inch piece fresh ginger	Peel the ginger. Slice it into slivers about ⅛ inch thick, the size of a wooden matchstick. Set aside a third of the ginger slivers and mince the remainder until it reaches the consistency of coarse cornmeal.
4 cloves garlic	Smash the garlic cloves with the flat side of your cleaver, then peel. Chop the garlic coarsely, into pieces the size of a match head. Add to the minced ginger.
4 scallions	Clean the scallions, then cut them, both white part and green, into pieces 1 inch long.
1 whole fish (about 1½ pounds), preferably sea bass or carp, or 2 small trout	Have the fish cleaned and scaled, but leave the head on. Cut about 8 shallow gashes on each side of the fish. (This will enable the flavors of the marinade and the cooking sauce to penetrate the fish more easily.)
¼ cup soy sauce (scallions) (ginger slivers)	Put the fish on a large plate and sprinkle the scallions, ginger slivers, and soy sauce over it. Let it marinate in this mixture for 20 minutes, turning it over once during that time. Then remove the fish from the marinade, but don't throw the marinade away.
1 tablespoon cornstarch *¼ cup cold water*	Mix the cornstarch and water together in a small bowl and set aside.

COOKING

5 tablespoons peanut oil	Heat your wok or pan over a moderately high flame for 15 seconds, then add the oil. The oil will be hot enough to cook with when the first tiny bubbles form and a few small wisps of smoke appear.

*(half the shredded
ginger and scallions
from the marinade)*

When the oil is ready, throw in about half of the shredded ginger and scallions from the marinade. Stir-fry for about 1 minute, using your cooking shovel or spoon in a scooping motion to agitate the ginger and scallions around in the hot oil so they won't burn and will fry equally. (Mrs. Chiang says that the fish has such a delicate flavor that it is necessary to fry the ginger and scallions first in order to alter the raw taste of the peanut oil.)

(fish)

After the scallions and ginger have cooked for about 1 minute, put the fish in the pan. Let the fish cook for 4 minutes on each side. Since it is impossible to stir-fry a whole fish, you should tip the pan occasionally from side to side to make sure that every part of the fish is exposed to the hot oil. If the scallions and ginger begin to turn brown, just remove them. After the fish has cooked on each side, take it out of the pan. Some of the skin of the fish may have stuck to the side of the pan; don't worry about it.

*(chopped garlic and
ginger)*
❀ *3 teaspoons hot
pepper paste*
*1½ teaspoons
granulated sugar*
*2 tablespoons soy
sauce*
¾ cup water
*1½ teaspoons rice
wine vinegar*
*(remaining fish
marinade)*

Now add the chopped garlic and ginger to the pan and stir-fry for 30 seconds. Continue to stir-fry the contents of the pan vigorously, at the same time adding the hot pepper paste, sugar, soy sauce, water, vinegar, and the remaining fish marinade.

(fish)

As soon as the contents of the pan have come to a boil, return the fish to the pan and let it cook in the boiling sauce for 1 minute.

1 tablespoon Chinese
rice wine or cooking
sherry

Add the wine and cover the pan. Let the fish continue to cook over a fairly high flame for about 5 minutes, then take off the cover, turn the fish over, and let it cook on the second side for 4 minutes longer. Remove the fish to a serving platter.

(cornstarch and water)

Stir the cornstarch and water to make sure they are thoroughly combined, then pour the mixture into the pan. Bring the sauce (which should be rather concentrated by this time, since it has already boiled over high heat for a while) to a boil, stir it occasionally until it thickens and turns clear, then pour it over the fish and serve.

紹 子 魚

FISH WITH MEAT SAUCE *(shaoz yu)*

This is one of Mrs. Chiang's most spectacular dishes—a whole fish cooked in a rich and spicy meat sauce. The combination, strange as it sounds, works. It exemplifies the Szechwanese taste for unusual juxtapositions of ingredients. Cooking in meat sauce, *shaoz*, is a favorite Szechwanese method. Mrs. Chiang makes noodles, bean curd, and eggplant that way. Like the fish, they are all marvelously spicy dishes, redolent with garlic and hot pepper paste, and are absolutely delicious.

PREPARATION

1 whole fish (1½ to 2
pounds), preferably

Have the fish cleaned and scaled, but leave the head on; make sure that the fish's

*sea bass, carp, or 2
small trout*

insides have been thoroughly gutted. Put the fish on a platter and cut shallow gashes about 1 inch apart on both sides of the fish. (These slashes will permit the flavor of the sauce to penetrate the entire fish.)

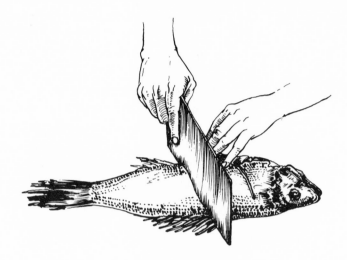

Scoring a fish

1 teaspoon salt

Sprinkle the salt over both the inside and the outside of the fish and rub it in fairly thoroughly. Set the fish aside for 30 minutes.

7 scallions

Clean the scallions, then chop them, both white part and the green, into tiny pieces, about the size of a match head.

½ pound ground pork
*2 tablespoons soy
sauce*
1 teaspoon sesame oil
*1-inch piece fresh
ginger*

Add 1 scallion's worth of the chopped scallions to the pork, along with the soy sauce and the sesame oil; mix it all together thoroughly.

Peel the ginger, then slice it into shreds about ⅛ inch wide, the width of a matchstick. Put half of the ginger shreds aside and chop the rest very fine, until they reach the consistency of coarse bread crumbs.

8 to 10 cloves garlic

Smash the garlic cloves with the side of your cleaver, then peel. Chop the garlic into tiny pieces, the size of a matchhead.

1 tablespoon corn-starch
3 tablespoons water

Combine the cornstarch and water in a small bowl and set aside.

COOKING

½ cup peanut oil

Heat your wok or pan (a large one) over a high flame for 15 seconds. (Before you add the oil, you can rub the inside of the heated pan with the cut end of a piece of ginger. Mrs. Chiang says this will help keep the fish from sticking to the pan.) Pour in the peanut oil. It will be ready to cook with when the first tiny bubbles form and a few small wisps of smoke appear.

(ginger shreds)

When the oil is ready, toss in the ginger shreds. Let the ginger cook by itself for 1 or 2 seconds.

(fish)

Now add the fish. (A good trick here is to hold the fish by the tail and slide it gently into the oil, head first, all the way up to your fingertips. Then pull it out and slide it into the oil on the other side. This also keeps the fish from sticking to the pan.)

Fry the fish over a high flame for 4 minutes, tipping the pan occasionally from side to side to make sure the hot oil reaches both ends of the fish. Then turn the fish over gently and let it cook for 4 more minutes on the other side. (It is quite possible that most of the ginger shreds have turned black by now; if so, try to remove them from the pan.)

After the fish has cooked on each side, remove it gently from the pan and deposit it on a large serving platter.

(chopped garlic and ginger)

Pour out about half the oil in the pan; you should have 4 or 5 tablespoons left. Reheat the oil over the same high flame, and, when it is hot enough for cooking, toss in the chopped garlic and ginger.

Stir-fry the garlic and ginger over a high flame for 1 minute, using your cooking shovel or spoon to stir the ingredients around in the bottom of the pan and keep them from burning.

❋ *2 tablespoons hot pepper paste*

1¼ teaspoons granulated sugar

(meat mixture)

Add the hot pepper paste and continue to stir-fry for 15 seconds.

Add the sugar and the meat mixture and stir-fry fairly vigorously for 45 seconds, taking particular care to break up any large hunks of meat that are sticking together.

5 tablespoons soy sauce

¾ cup water

Add the soy sauce and the water. Wait until the liquid comes to a boil, then let cook over a high flame for about 1 minute.

(fish)

(remaining scallions)

Now return the fish to the pan, along with the remaining chopped scallions. Let the fish cook in the boiling sauce for 2 minutes.

2 tablespoons Chinese rice wine or cooking sherry (optional)

Add the optional wine, then cover the pan, without reducing the heat, and let the fish cook for 5 minutes. Turn the fish over and cook it, covered, for 5 more minutes on the second side. Then remove it gently to the serving dish.

(cornstarch and water)

Stir the cornstarch and water to make sure they are thoroughly combined, then pour the mixture into the boiling sauce. Stir

the sauce until it turns clear and becomes slightly thick; this will probably
take about 15 seconds. Ladle the sauce
over the fish and serve.

清蒸魚

STEAMED FISH (*qingzhen yu*)

In Szechwan, fish were steamed as a special treat for the very young
and the very old, those pampered children and honored elders whose
palates occasionally needed a respite from the fiery everyday fare. Only
the freshest of fish got such a treatment. Mrs. Chiang's mother knew
how to use spices to disguise the flavor of a fish that had passed its
prime, but she used very little seasoning when she wanted to let a
really fresh fish speak for itself. Steaming is the best way to accentuate
the sweet flavor of a fish.

When Mrs. Chiang steams a fish, she follows her mother's recipe
and adds nothing but a few scallions, some ginger, wine, and a sprinkling of soy sauce and sesame oil. It is a simple recipe, one that
couldn't be easier to prepare. All you do is place the fish with its seasonings on a plate inside a steamer and let it steam; the recipe is fool-
proof. And if your fish is fresh, you will produce a subtle and elegant
dish.

PREPARATION

1 *whole,* fresh *fish* (*1½ pounds*), *preferably sea bass, carp, or flounder*	Have the store scale and clean the fish, but leave the head on. Before you cook it, rinse it under running water and make sure it is completely scaled and all the guts have been removed.
1½ *teaspoons salt*	Cut deep gashes into the side of the fish, about ¾ inch apart; it does not matter if the gashes hit the bone. Rub the salt all over the fish, inside the cavity as well as on the skin outside, then put the fish on a plate or in a shallow bowl.

2-inch piece of fresh ginger

Peel the ginger, then cut it into slivers about ⅛ inch wide, the width of a wooden matchstick.

4 scallions

Clean the scallions, then smash each one, both green part and white, with the side of your cleaver and cut into 1-inch lengths. Put about half the scallions, along with half the ginger, into the cavity of the fish.

1 tablespoon soy sauce
1 teaspoon sesame oil

Carefully sprinkle the soy sauce and sesame oil over the fish. Then spread the rest of the ginger and scallions on top.

Set the fish aside to marinate at room temperature for 15 to 20 minutes. After it has been marinating for a while, the fish's fragrance will be quite amazing.

COOKING

(fish and its marinade)
3 tablespoons Chinese rice wine or cooking sherry

If you don't have a Chinese-style steamer, you can improvise one out of a wok and its cover or a large pot (page 54). After you have set it up, fill the bottom of it with water and put the plate or shallow bowl containing the fish on the rack over the water. Sprinkle the wine over the fish.

Bring the water to a boil over a high flame, then cover the steamer and steam the fish for 20 minutes. Remove the plate from the steamer carefully and serve the fish immediately.

乾 炸 小 魚

DEEP-FRIED SMELTS (*ganzha xiaoyu*)

One of the more memorable seasonal treats of my own childhood was the large platters of fried smelts my family used to devour when those succulent little fish were in season. Modern freezing techniques have stretched the smelt season considerably. They are now available for much of the year and are refreshingly inexpensive.

As prepared by Mrs. Chiang, these tiny fish surpass my fondest memories. She marinates them in a mild sauce that seems to bring out all of their natural sweetness, then she fries them in deep fat until they become as crisp and crunchy as potato chips.

PREPARATION

1 pound smelts (about 40 fish roughly 4 inches long)	If the fish still have heads, chop them off. Then pull out the backbone with your fingers. (This is easier to do than it sounds. Simply grab the top of the backbone and pull it out and down; most of the larger bones attached to the backbone will come out, too.) Rinse off the fish.
1 teaspoon salt *1 tablespoon soy sauce*	Put the cleaned and partially filleted fish in a shallow bowl or plate and sprinkle the salt and soy sauce over them.
1-inch piece fresh ginger	Peel the ginger and chop it into tiny pieces, about the size of a match head. Sprinkle them over the fish.
4 cloves garlic	Smash the garlic cloves with the side of your cleaver, then peel. Chop the garlic into the same size pieces as the ginger. Add them to the fish.
	Stir well to make sure that all the ingredients are evenly distributed over the fish, then set the fish aside to marinate at room temperature for 30 minutes.
6 heaping tablespoons all-purpose flour	Just before you are ready to begin frying the fish, add the flour. Stir thoroughly to make sure that the flour is blended with the marinade, and that all the fish are coated with the thin batter that is produced.

COOKING

2½ *cups peanut or*
other cooking oil,
approximately

Heat a regular flat frying pan over a high flame for 15 seconds, then fill it with about an inch of oil. The oil should be ready for cooking when a slight haze has formed over it.

(smelts)

Gently drop the smelts into the hot oil (you may have to cook the fish in several batches depending on the size of your pan and the amount of oil you use) and fry the fish until they are quite hard and have turned a dark, golden brown; this may take up to 10 minutes.

Remove the cooked fish from the pan with chopsticks or a slotted spoon and drain them on paper towels.

Note: These fish can be eaten as soon as they are cooked or you can fry them in advance and serve them at room temperature. The only problem is that they are so crunchy and good you won't be able to *keep* from eating them.

紅燒魚片

RED-COOKED FISH SLICES (OR CHEEKS AND TONGUES)
(*hongshao yupian*)

The Chinese prize the cheeks and tongues of fish. The cheeks are firm and fleshy and the tongue has an unusual texture, both crunchy and gelatinous. They are difficult to obtain separately in America except in Boston, where codfish cheeks and tongues are an inexpensive regional specialty. In the hands of a talented cook like Mrs. Chiang, these unusual pieces of fish turn into a genuine delicacy. She cooks them in a rich and spicy sauce, Szechwanese in the complexity of its flavors and fragrant with a profusion of chopped garlic. Since fish cheeks and tongues are not always available, even in Boston, Mrs.

Chiang has discovered that she can use the same recipe for plain fillets of fish. It is particularly good with coarser, white-fleshed varieties like cod, whose resilient flesh is similar to that of a cheek or a tongue. Fillets of more finely textured fishes tend to disintegrate during stir-frying.

PREPARATION

1 *pound fish fillets, such as cod or sea bass, or cod cheeks and tongues*	Cut the fish into slices about ½ inch thick, about 3 inches long, and 1 inch wide. Put the fish slices in a bowl.
4 *scallions*	Clean the scallions, then cut them, both white part and green, into ½-inch lengths. Add the scallions to the fish.
½ *inch piece of fresh ginger*	Peel the ginger, then slice it into shreds, about ⅛ inch wide, the width of a wooden matchstick. Add them to the fish.
1 *teaspoon granulated sugar*	Add the sugar, salt, cornstarch, soy sauce, wine, and sesame oil to the fish and mix well.
½ *teaspoon salt*	
1½ *tablespoons corn-starch*	
3 *tablespoons soy sauce*	
1 *tablespoon Chinese rice wine or cooking sherry*	
1 *teaspoon sesame oil*	
6 *to 8 cloves garlic*	Smash the garlic cloves with the flat side of your cleaver, then peel. Chop the garlic into small pieces, the size of a match head.

COOKING

6 *tablespoons peanut oil*	Heat your wok or pan over a high flame for 15 seconds, then add the oil. The oil will

	be hot enough to cook with when the first tiny bubbles form and a few small wisps of smoke appear.
(garlic)	When the oil is ready, toss in the chopped garlic and stir it around in the hot oil with your cooking shovel or spoon for about 30 seconds. Don't worry if the garlic turns brown right away; just make sure it doesn't turn black.
✤ *1 tablespoon hot pepper paste*	Quickly add the hot pepper paste and stir-fry it, together with the garlic, for another 30 seconds.
(fish slices and their marinade)	Add the fish slices and their marinade and cook for 2 minutes, stirring the fish slices occasionally to make sure that all are exposed to the hot oil.
1 tablespoon rice wine vinegar	After the fish has cooked for 2 minutes, add the vinegar and stir-fry for another 30 seconds.
3 tablespoons water	Add the water, stir-fry everything for 30 more seconds, then cover the pan and let the fish cook, covered, over the same high flame for a final 2 minutes; serve immediately.

A NOTE ON SHRIMP

Any recipe that calls for the use of large shrimps introduces the vexatious problem of their shells. Mrs. Chiang and other Chinese cooks remove the shells from shrimps when they combine them with other main ingredients like vegetables or noodles. But when the shrimps are themselves the entire dish, the shells stay on, both for cooking and serving. This is not a form of sadism directed against the diner, but a way of making sure that the shrimps absorb the flavors of the sauce and do not dry out while cooking. Also, many Chinese and my husband as well like the crunchy texture of the shells. (I find that they always get caught between my teeth.)

Eating unshelled shrimps is bound to be messy, no matter what approach you adopt. I favor removing the shells with my fingers and then dipping the shrimps back into the sauce before I eat them. The authentic Chinese way is to chew on the whole thing and spit the shells out later. Whatever method you choose, you will have to overcome your inhibitions and use your fingers freely. Just be sure to provide a receptacle for the shells.

The size of the shrimps introduces another problem. The Chinese language contains several words for shrimps, each one denoting a different size. Mrs. Chiang provided a pragmatic solution to the question of what size to buy by explaining that in a dish where shrimps are the main ingredient, they should not be too big to absorb the flavor of the sauce, but should be large enough to be impressive. Shrimps that average about 20 to the pound are perfect, but smaller ones are also fine. In other recipes, smaller—and cheaper—shrimps can certainly be used.

乾 燒 明 蝦

SHRIMP IN RED SAUCE (*ganshao mingxia*)

While we were on Taiwan, we used to encounter this easily prepared dish of whole shrimps in a sweet red sauce at nearly every Szechwanese banquet we attended. Its ubiquity was probably due to its unusual taste, beautiful rosy color, and use of large shrimps, which, Mrs. Chiang explained, were an exotic luxury in Szechwan. When Mrs. Chiang cooked it for us, we were amazed to discover that one of the key ingredients in the recipe was ordinary tomato ketchup, a fascinating example of how Chinese cooks have skillfully assimilated a new ingredient into the traditional cuisine. The ketchup is used in much the same way as bean pastes are in other recipes. It adds to the final intriguing flavor of the sauce and to its color, but leaves no "ketchupy" taste. There is, of course, the tantalizing possibility that ketchup was not imported from the West at all, but was invented in China. When John became curious about its origin and looked it up in a few dictionaries, he found that the word "ketchup" originally came into English from a Chinese word in the Fukienese dialect, *ke-tsiap*, which could well mean "tomato paste." It is hard to guess what this primeval ketchup tasted like, and the product Mrs. Chiang uses today is the same stuff we pour on hamburgers. Still, it is intriguing to speculate that ketchup, like spaghetti, came from China.

PREPARATION

1 pound large raw shrimps (for a yield of 20 shrimps, approximately)

Rinse the shrimps well under running water. Pull off their legs, but leave the shells on. Using a scissors, cut a small slit about one-third of the way up the back of the shell. (This will allow the marinade and cooking sauce to penetrate the shrimps more easily. You can, if you want, also remove the dark intestine on the back of the shrimp. Mrs. Chiang does this by lifting up the intestine with a toothpick where it is exposed in the slit up the back and then slowly drawing the black vein out from under the shell.)

1 teaspoon salt
1 tablespoon Chinese rice wine or cooking sherry

Put the shrimps in a bowl and add the salt and wine.

2-inch piece fresh ginger

Peel the ginger and chop it into small pieces, about the size of a match head. Add 1 teaspoonful of the chopped ginger to the shrimps in the bowl and set the rest aside.

Stir the shrimps well, then let stand for at least 30 minutes.

3 scallions

Clean the scallions, then chop the white parts into the same size pieces as the ginger.

1 tablespoon cornstarch
¼ cup water

Mix the cornstarch and the water together in a small bowl.

COOKING

Pour off the excess liquid from the shrimps, but don't rinse them off. (It is all right for the little bits of ginger to remain on the shrimps.)

1 tablespoon peanut oil

Heat the pan over a fairly high flame for about 15 seconds, then add the oil. The oil will be hot enough to cook with when the first tiny bubbles form and a few small wisps of smoke appear.

(shrimps)
1 to 2 tablespoons water (optional)

Throw in the shrimps and stir-fry them over high heat for 1 or 2 minutes, until they are nearly cooked, using your cooking shovel or spoon in a scooping motion to toss the shrimps around in the pan so they are all exposed to the hot oil. When the shrimps are almost done, they will begin to turn pink and become slightly stiff. (If they seem too dry, you can add a little water during the stir-frying process.)

Lower the heat, cover the pan, and let the shrimps cook for 5 minutes more. Then remove them from the pan and set them aside.

3 tablespoons peanut oil
(remaining ginger and the scallions)
3 tablespoons ketchup

Clean out the pan by wiping it with a paper towel, then reheat it over a fairly high flame. Pour in the fresh oil. When it is hot enough, quickly add the rest of the chopped ginger, scallions, and ketchup and stir-fry vigorously for no more than 10 seconds.

5 tablespoons water
½ teaspoon sugar
¼ teaspoon salt
(shrimps)

Immediately add the water, sugar, and salt and let the mixture come to a boil. Let it cook for about 1 minute, then return the shrimps to the pan.

(cornstarch and water)	Stir the cornstarch and water thoroughly to make sure they are well combined, then pour the mixture into the pan. Stir-fry the shrimps and the sauce until the sauce has become clear and thick; this should not take more than about 30 seconds.
salt (optional)	Taste the sauce for salt before you serve it, and stir it up a little on the serving platter just before you bring it to the table. (This is to make sure that no film has formed on the sauce that would spoil its bright, fresh appearance.) *Note*: Make sure that each person gets some of the sauce along with his shrimps.

紅 燒 蝦

RED-COOKED SHRIMP (*hongshao xia*)

The only thing you can be sure of in a red-cooked, or *hongshao*, dish is that it contains soy sauce. Each regional cuisine has its own way of making red-cooked dishes. In Shanghai they contain sugar, in Peking they are plain and taste of soy sauce, and in Szechwan they are hot. Of course, an authentically prepared Szechwanese home-cooked *hongshao* dish is more than just hot; Mrs. Chiang's rich and spicy Red-Cooked Shrimp has a thick, dark sauce full of garlic, ginger, and chopped scallions whose bright, sharp tastes complement the sweet, fresh flavor of the shrimp. This is a very easy recipe; the actual cooking takes about 5 minutes.

PREPARATION

1 pound medium raw shrimps (for a yield of about 25	Rinse the shrimps well under running water. Pull off their legs, but leave the shells on. Using a scissors, cut a slit half-

shrimps)

way up the back of each shell. (This will allow the marinade and cooking sauce to penetrate the shrimp more easily.) Put the shrimps on a plate.

1 inch-piece fresh ginger
1 teaspoon salt

Peel the ginger, then chop it into tiny pieces, about the size of a match head, then sprinkle 1 teaspoonful of the chopped ginger and the salt over the shrimp. Make sure that the salt and the ginger are evenly distributed over the shrimp, then set aside to marinate for at least 15 minutes.

9 cloves garlic

Peel the garlic, then chop it coarsely, into pieces about the size of grains of un-cooked rice.

4 scallions

Clean the scallions, then slice them, both the white part and half of the green, crosswise into small pieces about ⅛ inch long.

1 tablespoon corn-starch
2 tablespoons water

Combine the cornstarch and the water in a small bowl and set aside.

COOKING

2 tablespoons peanut oil

Heat your wok or pan over a moderately high flame for 15 seconds, then add the oil. It should be hot enough to cook with when the first tiny bubbles form and a few small wisps of smoke appear.

(shrimps)

When the oil is ready, add the shrimps and stir-fry for 45 seconds, using your cooking shovel or spoon in a scooping motion to toss the shrimps around in the pan so they are all exposed to the hot oil.

1 tablespoon Chinese rice wine or cooking sherry

Pour in the wine, cover the pan, and let the shrimps continue to cook over a fairly high flame for another 45 seconds;

by that time they should have stiffened and turned slightly pink. Take them out of the pan and set them aside.

3 tablespoons peanut oil

(garlic and remaining ginger)

Wipe out the pan with paper towels, then reheat it over a moderate flame. Pour in the fresh oil. When it is hot enough to cook with, toss in the chopped garlic and the rest of the chopped ginger.

❀ 2 teaspoons hot pepper paste

2 tablespoons soy sauce

½ cup water

1¼ teaspoons granulated sugar

1¼ teaspoons rice wine vinegar

Stir-fry the garlic and ginger vigorously for 30 seconds, then reduce the heat slightly and stir in the hot pepper paste, soy sauce, water, sugar, and vinegar.

(shrimps)

(scallions)

Return the shrimps to the pan, along with the chopped scallions. Cover the pan and let cook over a moderately high flame for about 2 minutes.

(cornstarch and water)

Stir the cornstarch and water to make sure it is well combined, then pour the mixture into the pan. Continue to stir-fry until the sauce has become thick and clear; this should only take about 15 seconds. Serve immediately.

酒 燜 蝦

SHRIMP WITH GINGER AND WINE (jiumen xia)

It's a shame that we can't catch crayfish in New England, where we now live, for Mrs. Chiang insists that this delicate shrimp dish tastes even better made with crayfish. Szechwan was so far from the sea that salt-water shrimps were unknown there, and the recipes Mrs. Chiang uses for shrimp were originally created by her mother for the crayfish that lived underneath a bridge near the family's home. However, shrimps are so delectable prepared in this manner that it would be difficult to imagine anything better. Like many subtly flavored dishes, this one calls for only a few condiments. Wine and ginger are the main ones used, and, as they cook together with the shrimps, they combine to produce a delicate, almost buttery-tasting sauce. The essential simplicity of this dish means that it is as easy to prepare as it is delicious.

PREPARATION

1 pound medium-size raw shrimps (for a yield of 25 shrimps, approximately)	Rinse the shrimps well under running water. Pull off their legs, but leave the shells on. Using a scissors, cut a small slit halfway up the back of the shrimp. (This will allow the marinade and cooking sauce to penetrate the shrimps more easily.)
1½-inch piece fresh ginger	Peel the ginger, then chop it very fine, until it reaches the consistency of farina; you should get about 1½ tablespoons of chopped ginger.
2 scallions	Clean the scallions, then chop them, both the white part and most of the green, into tiny pieces, about the size of a match head.
(shrimps) *1¼ teaspoons salt* *(scallions)* *(1 tablespoon of the ginger)* *¼ teaspoon granulated sugar*	Put the shrimps in a dish. Add the salt and mix thoroughly, then add the chopped scallions, 1 tablespoonful of the chopped ginger, and the sugar. Make sure that everything is well combined, then let stand for at least 30 minutes.

COOKING

2½ tablespoons peanut oil	Heat your wok or pan over a moderately high flame for 15 seconds, then add the oil. It will be hot enough to cook with

(the remaining ginger)
(shrimps and their
    marinade)

when the first tiny bubbles form and a few small wisps of smoke appear.

When the oil is ready, throw in the rest of the chopped ginger and the shrimps and their marinade. Stir-fry over a moderately high flame for 2 minutes, using your cooking shovel or spoon in a scooping motion to toss the shrimps around in the pan so they are all exposed to the hot oil.

3 tablespoons Chinese
    rice wine or cooking
    sherry

Add the wine, then cover the pan, lower heat slightly, and let the shrimps cook for about 2 minutes longer.

As soon as the shrimps are cooked through, remove them from the pan and serve.

蝦圓

SHRIMP BALLS (xiayuan)

Despite its regional differences, China has essentially been, throughout most of its long history, one country with a unified culture. The written language bears this out, and so, too, does the food. Provincial cuisines are quite distinctive, but cooking methods like chao, or stir-frying, are much the same all over China. You can find chaomian, or fried noodles, everywhere. Shrimp balls are equally ubiquitous. We have no idea where these deep-fried chopped pork and shrimp balls originated. The lightest and most delicate ones in Taipei were served at a restaurant specializing in the food of Shensi, a province in northwestern China. The Szechwanese shrimp ball, as prepared by Mrs. Chiang, is somewhat more substantial, and extraordinarily fragrant due to the liberal use of ground Szechwan peppercorns.

Shrimp balls are not difficult to make. Since the batter can be prepared several hours in advance, they are convenient for dinner or cocktail parties. Cooked ones get soggy, however, if not eaten fairly soon after they are fried. Mrs. Chiang points out that the consistency of the balls depends on the fattiness of the pork you use—the fatter the pork, the lighter the Shrimp Balls. Water chestnuts are used to make each shrimp ball as crunchy inside as it is outside. Since fresh ones are often hard to find and canned ones no substitute, you may have to omit them. The texture of the shrimp balls will be less interesting, but the taste will be the same.

Fried foods are rarely eaten plain in China, but are usually accompanied by a dip sauce or a dish of seasoned salt. The best dip for these shrimp balls is a simple mixture of regular black pepper and salt.

PREPARATION

¾ *pound ground pork, preferably fatty*	Put the pork in a large mixing bowl and add the soy sauce and sesame oil to it.
3 *tablespoons soy sauce*	
2 *tablespoons sesame oil*	
4 *scallions*	Clean the scallions, then chop the white part into tiny pieces, about the size of a match head; add to the pork.
1½-*inch piece of fresh ginger*	Peel the ginger, then chop it very fine, until it reaches the consistency of coarse bread crumbs; add to the pork.
1 *pound medium shrimps*	Shell the shrimps and, if desired, devein them as well. Then chop—or rather pulverize—them. (The way Mrs. Chiang does this is by giving each shrimp a good solid whack with the flat side of the cleaver. Then, after all are mashed, she finishes the job by giving them about 100 strokes with the cleaver.) All the chopping should transform the shrimp into a sticky gray mass that resembles library paste far more than it does seafood. Add it to the pork.
7 *fresh water chestnuts (optional)*	Cut off the dark outer skin, then chop the water chestnuts into tiny pieces the same size as the chopped scallions; add them to the pork mixture.
2 *teaspoons salt*	Finally add the salt, egg whites, wine,

2 *egg whites*
1 *tablespoon Chinese rice wine or cooking sherry*
1¼ *teaspoons ground, roasted Szechwan peppercorns*
1 *cup cornstarch*

Szechwan peppercorns, and cornstarch to the meat. Mix well with a wooden spoon, giving the mixture at least 40 vigorous strokes to make sure it is thoroughly blended.

COOKING

3½ *cups peanut or other cooking oil, approximately*

Fill your wok or whatever pan you normally use for deep frying with about 4 inches of oil. Put it over a high flame and let the oil get really hot.

While you are waiting for the oil to get hot, you can start forming the shrimp balls. Use your hands and a large wet spoon to mold the meat and shrimp mixture into balls about the size of a large plum. (It helps to have a small bowl of water nearby to keep the spoon and your hands moist.) This recipe should yield about 15 or 16 balls, but, since a normal wok will only hold about 8 balls, you will have to cook them in several batches.

Drop the balls carefully into the hot oil, separating them so they don't stick together while cooking, then lower the flame slightly and let the shrimp balls cook for about 8 minutes, turning them gently, until they become a deep golden brown all over.

1½ *teaspoons salt*
1 *tablespoon freshly ground* black *pepper*

Remove them from the oil and let them drain on paper towels for 30 seconds before you serve them, accompanied by a dip made by mixing the salt and black pepper thoroughly together; put the mixture into individual small dishes and set them out on the dinner table.

蛋 炒 螃 蟹

CRAB AND EGG (*dan chao pangxie*)

The changing seasons determined the menu in the Szechwanese countryside. Spring was the time for delicate green vegetables; the tender young bamboo shoots that sprouted in the small grove next to the family's kitchen were spring foods, just as fresh fruits and melons were summer ones. Winter was the time for steamed dishes and big bowls of soup noodles, over which the children warmed their hands.

Crabs were also a seasonal delicacy. The food literature of China is full of mouth-watering descriptions of the crab-eating orgies that took place during September and October in the Yangtze delta. Though less renowned, the fresh-water crabs of Szechwan were just as delicious. Mrs. Chiang's mother would steam them or fry them with wine and ginger, and sometimes she would cook them with scrambled eggs. This was the children's favorite. The combination of the rich flavor of the eggs with the sweet crabmeat is delightful. It produces a subtle, delicate dish that is also very easy to prepare. You can make it with fresh or frozen crabmeat, shelled or unshelled. But you can't use canned crabmeat; both its taste and texture are wrong.

PREPARATION

2 *scallions*	Clean the scallions, then chop them, both the white part and about one-third of the green, into tiny pieces, about the size of a match head.
1-inch piece fresh ginger	Peel the ginger, then chop it quite fine, until it reaches the consistency of coarse cornmeal; you should have about 1 tablespoon of chopped ginger.
½ pound fresh or frozen crabmeat or	If the crabs are whole, chop them into 2-inch pieces. Put the crabmeat on a plate

crabs in their shells
(scallions)
½ tablespoon
  Chinese rice wine
  or cooking sherry
½ teaspoon salt
(2 teaspoons chopped
  ginger)

and add the scallions, wine, salt, and 2 teaspoons of the ginger. Mix thoroughly and let stand for 15 minutes.

2 eggs

Beat the eggs and set them aside.

COOKING

3 tablespoons peanut
  oil

Heat the pan over a moderately high flame for 15 seconds, then add the oil. It will be hot enough to cook with when the first tiny bubbles form and a few small wisps of smoke appear.

(crabmeat and
  marinade)
(remaining ginger)
¼ teaspoon granu-
  lated sugar

When the oil is ready, quickly add the crabmeat and its marinade, the rest of the chopped ginger, and the sugar. Stir-fry all these ingredients together very vigorously for about 1 minute, using your cooking shovel or spoon to scoop the ingredients from the sides of the pan and then stir them around in the middle, so everything is exposed to the hot oil.

1 teaspoon Chinese
  rice wine or cooking
  sherry
¼ teaspoon salt, or
  to taste

Continuing to stir-fry, pour in the wine. Taste the crabmeat for salt before you add it. (Since this is a slightly bland dish, it will probably need plenty of salt to bring out the subtle flavors of the ginger and crabmeat.)

(eggs)

After you have added the wine and salt, stir-fry the crabmeat for about 45 seconds more, then pour in the beaten eggs. Keep on stirring up the crab and eggs until the eggs are thoroughly cooked;

this should not take more than 1 minute.
As soon as the eggs are cooked, remove the
pan from the fire and serve.

螺 絲

SNAILS (*luosi*)

The French are not the only people who have discovered the glorious affinity between the lowly snail and the mighty garlic. In the heart of downtown Taipei, there were a few narrow streets full of tiny restaurants that featured the Chinese equivalent of short-order cooking. Foods already prepared were temptingly displayed in large containers in the front windows. Snails were always among the most attractive items, and for a few cents you could get a bowl of them covered with a lovely, garlicky sauce. We rarely resisted them, when we had time. The snails were tiny and not very filling, and it was a frustrating business trying to pull them out of their shells with toothpicks. But those that we succeeded in spearing were as delicious as the sauce that we invariably spattered all over our hands, arms, and shirtfronts during the removal process. When prepared in the Szechwanese way with garlic, ginger, and a chivelike vegetable called *jiucai*, a Chinese snail rivals anything that Burgundy can produce.

Chinese snails are smaller than French ones. In this country, Mrs. Chiang uses periwinkles. They are difficult to find; even in Chinatown they are only sporadically available. Once you buy them, you must soak them in water with a little bit of oil for several days to get the sand out of them. But after that they are not hard to cook. Mrs. Chiang's recipe for snails is so delicious that it would be criminal not to sample it merely because of the unavailability of the main ingredient. You might experiment with mussels if you can't get periwinkles. *Jiucai* is another problem; it is seasonal and often unavailable in those Chinese markets that do sell it. Fortunately, scallions are an acceptable substitute.

Eating snails (or periwinkles) is as great a challenge as finding them in the first place. Provide a good supply of toothpicks for snaring them and put out an empty plate for the empty shells. The process is bound to be messy, for it can't be done without using your fingers.

PREPARATION

1 *quart periwinkles*
or mussels

Allow 3 days between the time you purchase the periwinkles and the time you
are going to cook them. It takes that
long to get rid of all the sand inside the
shells.

4 *cups cold water,*
approximately
A *few drops peanut oil*

Put the periwinkles in a large bowl, cover
them with cold water, and add a few
drops of oil. Let them sit at room temperature for 3 days. Change the water
every day, each time rinsing the periwinkles well under running water and
adding new oil. (For some reason, the
oil forces the periwinkles to regurgitate
the sand they have swallowed.) By the
third day, they will be completely free
of sand and ready to be cooked.

Rinse the periwinkles thoroughly and pick
them over to get rid of any small stones
masquerading as periwinkles. Drain the
periwinkles and set them aside.

3 *bunches* jiucai *or*
scallions

If using the *jiucai*, pick it over and pull off
both ends of each stalk. Wash the *jiucai*
carefully, then cut it into ½-inch
lengths. If using scallions, clean them,
then cut them, both white part and
green, into ½-inch lengths.

1 *whole head of garlic*
(about 10 to 12
cloves)

Smash the garlic cloves with the flat side
of your cleaver, then peel. Chop the garlic into pieces about the size of grains of
uncooked rice.

3-inch piece fresh
ginger

Peel the ginger, then chop it into the same
size pieces as the garlic; you should get
about 3 tablespoons of each.

COOKING

6 *tablespoons peanut oil*	Heat your wok or pan over a high flame for 20 seconds, then pour in the oil. It will be ready to cook with when the first tiny bubbles form and a few small wisps of smoke appear.
(garlic and ginger)	When the oil is ready, toss in the garlic and ginger and stir-fry vigorously for 45 seconds, using your cooking shovel or spoon to agitate the garlic and ginger around in the bottom of the pan so they don't burn.
(periwinkles) *1½ tablespoons salt*	Then add the periwinkles and the salt. Stir-fry for about 1 minute, scooping the periwinkles off the sides of the pan and making sure every one is exposed to the hot oil.
1 tablespoon granulated sugar (jiucai) *3 tablespoons soy sauce*	Add the sugar and stir-fry all the ingredients for about 1½ minutes, then add the *jiucai* and the soy sauce and continue to stir-fry for another 1½ minutes.
¼ cup water *½ cup Chinese rice wine or cooking sherry*	Pour in the water and the wine and wait until the liquid boils, then cover the pan and let the periwinkles cook over the same high heat for 7 minutes. Serve immediately, making sure you provide plenty of napkins and a container for the empty shells.

12 - BEAN CURD

Every culture has its children's food—things that everybody eats but children dote on. In this country it might be hot dogs or pizza; in Szechwan it was bean curd. Older people loved rich meat dishes, but children had less developed palates and adored the clear, fresh taste and soft texture of bean curd. Mrs. Chiang's own favorite food when she was a child, the bean curd she ate was particularly delicious because it was homemade. The process was similar to that used in making cheese:

"My mother would grind fresh soybeans very fine, then combine them with water to make a kind of soybean "milk." When she added a certain chemical [probably gypsum] to this, it coagulated instantly. Then she hung the mixture to drain in a cloth bag for several days; at the end there was a mild, creamy bean curd with a texture as smooth as silk. We ate it several times a week. For breakfast we might have pickled bean curd, pungent and highly spiced, with plain boiled rice. When there were no guests for dinner, we would just have vegetables and a stir-fried bean curd dish. For formal dinners bean curd would be part of a cold plate or in a soup. Along with eggs it was our main source of protein."

Nutrition wasn't the main reason for the popularity of bean curd, however. Its texture and flavor adapted it perfectly to the vibrant seasonings and emphatic sauces that were essential to the family's favorite dishes.

Because bean curd played such a large role in Szechwan home cooking, we have given more recipes for it than most cookbooks do. We could have included twice as many, and only the fact that bean curd is not yet available in American supermarkets restrained us. Perhaps the soaring prices of meat and the vegetarian proclivities of the younger generation will someday bring bean curd into the American diet. If nothing else, it would give vegetarianism a much-needed gastronomic boost. In China, where religious Buddhists cannot kill animals for food, a whole vegetarian *haute cuisine* developed based entirely on bean curd. We sampled some once in a monastery on Taiwan. It featured unusual textures and special effects designed to make the bean curd resemble meat or fish. While none of the dishes were as good as Mrs. Chiang's lusty Szechwanese specialties, they certainly tasted better than the brown rice and mixed grains that American vegetarians consume.

It is possible to make your own bean curd at home, but it is hardly practical. Besides, Mrs. Chiang feels that the commercially prepared varieties available in Chinese and Japanese markets are perfectly good.

There are many types of bean curd. Fresh bean curd is the commonest. It comes in soft, white cakes about 1 inch thick and 3 to 4 inches square. It has the consistency of hard custard, and, though fragile and perishable, it can be kept for a week in the refrigerator if you store it in an uncovered bowl of water and change the water every other day. Both Chinese and Japanese markets usually sell fresh bean curd, the Japanese type being softer and lighter than the kind sold in Chinatown. It is trickier to handle, but has a more delicate taste and finer texture. Japanese stores also sell a powdered "instant" bean curd mix. We have experimented with it and found that when it works, which is only about 50 percent of the time, it makes a very loose and delicate bean curd that is quite hard to cook with. Don't buy it.

Bean curd comes in many other, less common forms. Dry bean curd, or *doufugan*, isn't dry at all. It is just regular bean curd that has been aged and pressed until it becomes dense and turns brown on the outside. It is especially delicious boiled with soy sauce and spices and then sliced and served cold.

Fried bean curd balls, or *youdoufu*, are really dry—light, porous balls that, when soaked, become spongy. Their strange texture and mild taste make them greatly prized in vegetarian *haute cuisine*. Bean curd skin, another form, comes in thin, shiny, brittle sheets. After soaking, it resembles a delicate noodle dough, for which it is generally used as an elegant substitute (see also the recipe for Bean Curd Skin Soup, page 267). There is also "stinking bean curd," which the process of fermentation has transformed into a substance strikingly similar to some of the stronger cheeses.

Finally, there is pickled bean curd, or *doufu lu*. It was popular in Szechwan, and was what Mrs. Chiang's family often ate with rice for breakfast. Chinese groceries occasionally carry jars of the highly spiced Szechwanese version of the stuff. Eaten on top of some plain white rice, it is an amazing gastronomic experience, though not one recommended for the weak in palate. Mrs. Chiang claims that the pickled bean curd her mother made was both hotter and more fragrant.

麻婆豆腐

POCK-MARKED MA'S BEAN CURD (*mapo doufu*)

Eugene Wu, the librarian of the Harvard-Yenching Library, grew up in Chengtu and claims that as a schoolboy he used to eat Pock-Marked Ma's Bean Curd, or *mapo doufu*, at a restaurant run by the original Pock-Marked Ma herself. You ordered by weight, so many grams of bean curd and so many grams of meat, and your serving would be weighed out and cooked as you watched. It arrived at the table fresh, fragrant, and so spicy hot, or *la*, that it actually caused sweat to break out. Dr. Wu says that Mrs. Chiang's version of the dish rivals that of the famous old lady. It is just as rich, fragrant, and hot.

If we had to choose the quintessential Szechwanese dish, this spicy preparation of bean curd and chopped meat would probably be it. Its multiplicity of tastes and textures first stuns, then stimulates, the senses. It assaults the palate with the full spectrum of Szechwanese spices and condiments, from garlic and ginger to hot pepper paste and

Szechwan pepper. It seems to contain almost every taste there is— salty, hot, sweet, and pungent—as well as that uniquely Szechwanese quality, aromatic numbness, or *ma*, which only Szechwan pepper can produce. At the same time, a real *mapo doufu* offers an equally brilliant combination of textures. In each mouthful you can feel the smoothness of bean curd, the crunchiness of water chestnuts, the slipperiness of tree ears, and the graininess of chopped meat. In many ways, the ingredients used in a *mapo doufu*, its appearance, and its actual taste are similar to the classic "in the style of fish," or *yuxiang*, dishes of Szechwan. It is quite possible that the poorly complected lady's masterpiece is just a pseudonymous variation of that traditional style of cooking. Interestingly, Mrs. Chiang's repertoire contains no recipe for fish-flavored bean curd.

As it should be, this is one of the hottest dishes Mrs. Chiang makes. Serve it with plenty of rice to moderate the heat, but don't reduce the amount of hot pepper flakes in oil and hot pepper paste too drastically; the authenticity of this dish depends on its spiciness. You may have trouble locating fresh water chestnuts; leave them out if you can't find them. They, like the tree ears, are primarily texture foods and omitting them won't change the final taste. This recipe produces more food than most of the other recipes in the book—enough, with rice and a light vegetable dish, to provide a meal for four people. For some reason, a *mapo doufu* tastes almost as good the second day as the first, so don't worry if there are leftovers.

PREPARATION

¼ cup dried tree ears 1 cup boiling water	Put the tree ears in a small bowl and pour the boiling water over them. Let them soak for about 15 minutes, until they become soft and gelatinous.
3-inch piece fresh ginger	Peel the ginger, then chop it into tiny pieces, about the size of a match head.
5 scallions	Clean the scallions, then chop them, both the white part and about one-third of the green, into pieces slightly larger than the ginger, about ¼ inch in diameter.
(1 tablespoon of the	Add 1 tablespoon of the chopped ginger

chopped ginger)

(1 scallion's worth of the chopped scallions)

½ pound ground pork or beef

2 tablespoons soy sauce

1 teaspoon sesame oil

1 tablespoon Chinese rice wine or cooking sherry

and 1 scallion's worth of the chopped scallions to the ground pork, along with the soy sauce, sesame oil, and wine. Mix thoroughly, then set aside for about 30 minutes.

8 or more cloves garlic (for a yield of 2 tablespoons chopped garlic)

(the remaining chopped ginger)

Peel the garlic, then chop it coarsely. Combine it with the rest of the chopped ginger and mince them both together until they reach the consistency of a thick paste. (This may take several minutes, but Mrs. Chiang insists that the finer you chop the garlic and ginger the more interesting the finished dish will be.)

6 fresh water chestnuts (optional)

Cut the dark skin off the outside of the water chestnuts, then chop them into pieces about the size of a match head.

2 teaspoons cornstarch

¼ cup water

Combine the cornstarch and water in a small bowl and set aside.

6 squares fresh bean curd

Cut the bean curd into ½-inch cubes.

(tree ears)

Drain the tree ears, then rinse them and pick them over carefully to remove the tiny impurities, like little pieces of wood, that might still be embedded in them. Then mince into little pieces the size of a match head.

1 tablespoon cornstarch

(meat mixture)

Just before you are ready to begin cooking, add the cornstarch to the meat mixture and blend thoroughly.

COOKING

6 *tablespoons peanut oil*	Heat your wok or pan over a moderately high flame for about 15 seconds, then add the oil. It should be hot enough to cook with when the first small bubbles begin to form and a few small wisps of smoke appear.
(garlic and ginger)	When the oil is ready, quickly throw in the garlic and ginger and vigorously stir-fry them over a medium flame for about 30 seconds, using your cooking shovel or spoon to scoop the ingredients from the sides of the pan and then stir them around in the middle, so they won't burn or stick.
❀ 1½ *teaspoons hot pepper flakes in oil* ❀ 1 *tablespoon hot pepper paste* *(water chestnuts and tree ears)*	Continue to stir-fry while you add the hot pepper flakes in oil, hot pepper paste, water chestnuts, and tree ears. Then stir-fry for another 30 seconds.
(meat mixture)	Add the meat mixture and keep stirring it as it cooks, taking special care to break up any large chunks of meat that stick together.
(bean curd) *(scallions)* 1 *teaspoon granu-lated sugar*	After the meat has cooked for about 1 minute and has lost its pinkish color, throw in the bean curd and the chopped scallions and stir-fry everything together for about 45 seconds. Then add the sugar and stir-fry for another 30 seconds.
3 *tablespoons soy sauce* ½ *cup water*	Pour in the soy sauce and the water and wait for the liquid to boil, then let the contents of the pan cook over a moderate flame for 2 more minutes.

1½ teaspoons ground, roasted Szechwan peppercorns	Add the Szechwan peppercorns and stir thoroughly.
(cornstarch and water)	At this point, determine how much sauce there is in the pan. If the dish seems watery, you should get ready to add the cornstarch and water mixture that you have already prepared. But if there does not seem to be much liquid, you won't need the cornstarch.
	Make sure that you stir up the cornstarch mixture before you pour it into the pan, then stir-fry everything over a medium flame until the sauce becomes clear and slightly thickened.
1 teaspoon sesame oil 1 teaspoon salt, or to taste	Add the sesame oil and stir it in thoroughly; then, just before serving, taste the dish for salt. It should taste sharp and clear, with just a hint of sweetness. Stir the salt in and serve.

红 烧 豆 腐

RED-COOKED BEAN CURD (*hongshao doufu*)

Hongshao, or red-cooking, simply means that a dish contains soy sauce; *hongshao* dishes range from stews simmered for hours in rich sauce to simple combinations of stir-fried vegetables. Mrs. Chiang's repertoire of *hongshao* recipes covers a wide range of dishes. Her Red-Cooked Bean Curd is a casual preparation of bean curd and pork in a dark and spicy sauce. The creamy blandness of the bean curd is a marvelous foil for the typically Szechwanese kaleidoscope of flavors in the sauce. You can tone down the pepperiness a bit, but not too much. This is supposed to be a hot dish.

PREPARATION

2 *medium pork chops (for a yield of 8 ounces meat, approximately)*	Cut the bones and fat away from the pork chops, but reserve the fat from one of the chops. Slice the lean sections as thinly as you can, to get wafer-thin slices of meat about 3 inches long by ½ inch wide. (It is always easier to slice meat very thinly if you first put it into the freezer for about 10 minutes, until it becomes slightly stiff but not frozen.) Dice the reserved fat into cubes about ½ inch on each side.
4 *scallions*	Clean the scallions, then cut them, both the white part and about half the green, into 2-inch lengths.
3 *cloves garlic*	Peel the garlic cloves, then chop them rather coarsely into pieces about the size of a grain of rice.
1-*inch piece fresh ginger*	Peel the ginger, then chop it into pieces approximately the size of a match head; you should get about 1 tablespoonful of chopped ginger.
6 *squares fresh bean curd*	Cut each square of bean curd into 12 chunks.
1 *tablespoon cornstarch*	Mix the cornstarch with the water in a small bowl and set aside.
½ *cup water*	

COOKING

¼ *cup peanut oil*	Heat your wok or pan over a high flame for about 15 seconds, then add the oil. The oil should be hot enough to cook with when the first tiny bubbles form and a few small wisps of smoke appear.
(pork fat)	When the oil is ready, throw in the cubes

of pork fat and let them fry until crisp, pressing the cubes gently against the sides of the pan with your cooking shovel or spoon to help them render their fat more rapidly.

(garlic)
(ginger)
❊ *1 tablespoon hot pepper paste*
(pork)

After the fat cubes have become crisp, quickly add the chopped garlic, ginger, hot pepper paste, and pork slices. Stir-fry vigorously for about 30 seconds, using your cooking shovel or spoon to scoop the pork and seasonings from the sides of the pan and then stir them around in the middle, so all are exposed to the hot oil.

(scallions)
5 tablespoons soy sauce
(bean curd)
1 teaspoon salt, or to taste

Add the scallions and soy sauce and continue to stir-fry for another 30 seconds.

Throw in the bean curd, then taste the sauce and add the salt. Bring the liquid to a boil and let the bean curd cook, uncovered, over a moderate flame for about 5 minutes more, stirring occasionally.

(cornstarch and water)

Stir the cornstarch and water to make sure they are well combined, then pour the mixture into the pan. Stir-fry vigorously until the sauce has thickened and become clear, a few seconds at most, then serve.

鍋 溻 豆 腐

BATTER-FRIED BEAN CURD WITH SHRIMP *(guota doufu)*

Not all the good food in China comes from Szechwan. This savory bean curd dish is Pekingese. Said to be the favorite food of Tzu-hsi, the famous Empress Dowager of late nineteenth-century China, it is just the kind of simple, delicate food an experienced gourmet would yearn for after a surfeit of imperial banquets. We first encountered the dish at the most famous Peking Duck restaurant in Taipei. A helpful waiter suggested it—and once we tasted it we were hooked. Mrs. Chiang dug up a recipe in an old Chinese cookbook, experimented with it, and ultimately managed to produce a magnificent *guota doufu*. It is so delicious we decided to include it here despite its alien origin.

Although this type of northern Chinese cooking is far from bland, it does not overwhelm the palate the way a Szechwanese dish does. The sauce is clearer and thinner and the basic flavor more subtle. The bean curd is first marinated in soy sauce and sesame oil and then coated with a thick egg batter before it is fried, giving it a startlingly rich flavor. The shrimps are added as much for textural contrast as for taste.

PREPARATION

3 scallions

Clean the scallions, then smash them, both the white part and green, with the side of the cleaver and cut them into 3-inch lengths. Put the scallions on a large, flat platter.

1-inch piece fresh ginger
¼ teaspoon granulated sugar
¼ teaspoon salt
1 teaspoon sesame oil
¼ cup soy sauce

Peel the ginger, then cut it into slivers about ⅛ inch wide, the width of a wooden matchstick. Put the shredded ginger on the same plate as the scallions. Add the sugar, salt, sesame oil, and soy sauce and mix well.

4 squares fresh bean curd

Gently trim off the outer skin of the bean curd and discard it. (Japanese-style bean curd is softer than Chinese, and doesn't have any tougher outside parts that have to be removed.) Slice each square of bean curd horizontally into 3 thin layers and then cut these into pieces about 1 inch square. Spread the bean curd pieces out on the plate containing the soy sauce mixture and marinate them for 20 minutes. Turn them over at least once during this period, and make sure that every piece has been soaked in the marinade. (Since sliced bean curd is a somewhat fragile substance, handle it gently, using chopsticks or, if you haven't mastered those yet, your fingers.)

½ *pound raw shrimps*
¾ *teaspoon salt*
1 *tablespoon cornstarch*
1 *teaspoon Chinese rice wine or cooking sherry*

Wash the shrimps, then shell and devein them. If the shrimp are large, cut them into 2 or 3 pieces. Put them in a bowl and sprinkle the salt, cornstarch, and wine over them. Stir well and set aside.

1 *tablespoon cornstarch*
3 *tablespoons cold water*

Combine the cornstarch and water in a small bowl and set aside.

¼ *cup all-purpose flour*
2 *eggs*
2 *tablespoons water*

Just before you are ready to begin cooking, mix the flour, eggs, and water together in a shallow bowl.

COOKING

2 *tablespoons peanut oil, approximately*

Use a large, flat frying pan, *not* a wok. Heat it over a low flame, then cover the bottom with a thin film of oil.

(bean curd)
(batter)

Dip the squares of marinated bean curd into the egg batter, then place them gently in the frying pan. (This procedure always reminds me of cooking French toast.) When the bean curd squares have turned a light golden brown on the first side, turn them over and cook them until they are the same color on the other side. Remove them from the pan to a large platter. (You will probably have to cook these bean curd pieces in several batches, so make sure that there is enough oil in the pan to keep the later batches from sticking.)

¾ cup water
(shrimps and their
marinade)

Return the fried bean curd to the pan and add the water and the shrimps and their marinade.

Cover the pan, raise the flame slightly, and boil the bean curd and shrimps gently for 5 minutes.

(cornstarch and water)

Stir the cornstarch and water to make sure they are well combined, then pour the mixture into the pan. Stir the sauce very gently until it comes to a boil again, thickens slightly, and turns clear; this should only take a few seconds. Serve immediately.

两面黄

TWO SIDES YELLOW (FRIED BEAN CURD WITH GARLIC AND SCALLIONS) (*liangmian huang*)

It was no disaster if Mrs. Chiang's mother made more bean curd than she could cook for any one meal. The extra bean curd was put aside for several days (there was, of course, no refrigeration) until it had dried out enough to be turned into the classic Szechwanese dish Two Sides Yellow. Basically, Two Sides Yellow consists of thin slices of bean curd that are first fried in deep fat until they turn a light golden yellow on both sides and then fried a second time in a little oil with some garlic, scallions, and soy sauce. Because this is such a simple, straightforward recipe, it lends itself to innumerable variations. Mrs. Chiang has made it in at least a dozen different ways. Sometimes she adds hot pepper paste, sometimes such vegetables as green peppers or string beans, and sometimes even a few shreds of meat.

PREPARATION

8 scallions

Clean the scallions, then smash the head of each with the side of your cleaver. Cut the scallions, both white part and the green, into 2-inch lengths.

5 *cloves garlic*

Smash the garlic cloves with the flat side of your cleaver, then peel. Chop the garlic into pieces about the size of fresh peas.

5 *squares bean curd (the older and tougher your bean curd is, the better it is for this dish, but only for this dish)*

Rinse off the bean curd, then cut each square crosswise into slices about ¼ of an inch thick, 3 inches long, and 1 inch wide.

COOKING

6 *tablespoons peanut oil, approximately (more if you are using a flat frying pan)*

You can use either a wok or a regular flat frying pan for this step. (Mrs. Chiang prefers a frying pan.) Whichever you choose, heat it over a high flame for 15 seconds before adding the oil. Then heat the oil over the same high flame until you can see a slight haze over it.

(bean curd)

When the oil is ready, put in your first batch of bean curd slices (you don't want them more than one layer deep in the hot oil) and fry them for 5 to 7 minutes, turning them over only about once or twice, *very gently*, to make sure that both sides are golden and lightly speckled. (Mrs. Chiang likes to use a regular flat spatula for handling these delicate slices of bean curd.) Cook all the bean curd slices in this fashion, then set them aside on a serving platter.

Pour out the oil you used for frying the bean curd, reserve it for future deep-fat frying, and clean out your pan with a paper towel if you are going to reuse it. If you have a wok, use it now.

¼ *cup peanut oil*	Heat your wok or frying pan over a high flame for 15 seconds, then pour in the fresh oil.
(garlic)	When the oil is ready, add the chopped garlic. Stir-fry it for 30 seconds, using your cooking shovel or spoon to scoop it off the sides of the pan and stir it around in the bottom, to keep it from burning. Don't panic if the garlic turns brown right away.
✿ 2 *teaspoons hot pepper paste (optional)* *(scallions)* *(bean curd)*	Add the optional hot pepper paste and stir-fry it with the garlic for about 15 seconds, then add the scallions and stir-fry for another 15 seconds. Return the fried bean curd to the pan and stir-fry it with the garlic and other ingredients for 10 seconds.
1 *scant teaspoon salt* 1½ *teaspoons granulated sugar* 3 *tablespoons soy sauce*	Add the salt, sugar, and soy sauce to the pan and stir-fry everything for a final 2 or 3 minutes. Serve immediately.

13 - VEGETABLES

"When I was a child in Szechwan," Mrs. Chiang recalls, "we used to greet the New Year by picking a few young leaves from our neighbors' bean patch. They would also steal some new leaves from our garden. This was *touqing*, 'stealing of the green,' and it guaranteed a prosperous year. Vegetables were the mainstay of our diet, next to rice, and this ritual celebrated the first green vegetable of the year.

"We had fresh or preserved vegetables at every meal, and in between meals they were our favorite snacks. There was always a salted cabbage hanging outside the house to dry, and I remember snatching pieces of it to eat on the way to school. At harvest time we used to pull up the turnips the field hands missed and eat them raw.

"The vegetables on our table changed with the seasons. There were two main harvests, in spring and summer, but there were leafy greens to pick as early as March, and beans didn't ripen until September or October. We grew a lot of different vegetables, so we had fresh produce practically all year. What we couldn't eat, my mother pickled. She sold some at market and put the rest into big earthenware jars for the winter. We grew so many different vegetables, and my mother knew so many ways to preserve them, that we never got bored with them. We always had a much wider selection than I can find at American supermarkets.

"We loved turnips; they were so sweet we ate them raw like fruit. We had green, yellow, and white turnips, long, thin turnips and round ones of all sizes. They were dried, pickled, boiled, steamed, and made in custardlike cakes as well as eaten raw. We grew every kind of bean found in America and many other kinds as well. String beans came in all sizes; there were long beans, a foot long, that were delicious pickled. We grew cauliflowers, cucumbers, eggplants, several different kinds of squash and cabbage, carrots, celery, white and sweet potatoes, green and red peppers, and a lot of other vegetables I don't find in America at all.

"Vegetables were an important staple because they were cheap and nutritious. Vegetables are much better for you than meat; there were no fat people in Szechwan. And because we ate so many vegetables we were famous for our beautiful skin. Strict Buddhists were vegetarian; we peasants weren't very religious, but we followed many of the Buddhist dietary ideas. But the best reason for eating vegetables is that they taste so good, especially in Szechwan cooking. We couldn't afford bird's nest or shark's fins, but anybody could grow a patch of snow peas and feast on *doumiao*, the tender little leaves of the snow pea plant."

One of our favorite restaurants in Taipei specialized in the preparation of *doumiao*; during the few weeks it was in season gourmets would flock there from all over town. Barely braised in a clear sauce with just a few shreds of ginger, *doumiao* was, indeed, everything that a Chinese vegetable should be—crisp, tender, sweet and a brilliant shade of emerald green.

Vegetables are so central to every branch of Chinese cuisine that no elegant banquet would be complete without an elaborate vegetarian dish featuring such delicate or exotic ingredients as mushrooms, cabbage hearts, or baby ears of corn. There is no contradiction between vegetarianism and gastronomy in China, and many dedicated gourmets claim to prefer vegetable dishes to all others. Our own experience bears out their claim. The more familiar John and I became with Szechwanese food, the more we liked vegetables. Just as Mrs. Chiang had predicted, we began to find a steady diet of all-meat dishes too rich and heavy, and vegetables now constitute a large part of our daily food.

The recipes we present here are but a sampling from Mrs. Chiang's repertoire. They range from simple salads to subtle combinations of ingredients that verge on *haute cuisine*. More than anything else, the infinite number of ways in which to cook vegetables attests to their importance in the cuisine of Szechwan. There are recipes containing vegetables in other sections of the cookbook; the ones here are those in which vegetables are the main ingredient. Instead of concentrating on recipes for specifically Chinese vegetables, many of which are seasonal and can be hard to find even in Chinatown, we have emphasized such readily available items as eggplant, cucumbers, spinach, and string beans. They are just as Chinese as snow peas. Freshness is, of course, essential. Under no circumstances should frozen vegetables be used, but reasonable substitutions of fresh ones can be made. Cauliflower and broccoli, for example, are interchangeable, and the spinach recipes could easily be adapted to other leafy greens.

蘆 筍 ˚沙 拉 ˝

ASPARAGUS SALAD (*lusun shala*)

Asparagus reached the Orient only recently; it was unknown in the Szechwanese countryside when Mrs. Chiang was a girl. But, since one of the great strengths of a talented Chinese home cook is her ability to work with new ingredients, Mrs. Chiang managed to devise the perfect combination of condiments for a spicy and refreshing asparagus salad.

Quick and easy to make, this salad can be prepared in advance and refrigerated for several hours before serving. Be forewarned: raw garlic and hot pepper flakes make this a powerful dish whose memory will linger on your breath for hours.

PREPARATION

1 *pound asparagus*	Wash the asparagus carefully, then cut off the tough ends and slice each stalk into 2-inch lengths.
2 *scallions*	Clean the scallions, then chop them, both white part and green, into tiny pieces, about the size of a match head.

6 to 7 cloves garlic

1-inch piece fresh ginger

¼ teaspoon salt

Peel the garlic and ginger and chop them rather coarsely. Put them in a steep-sided bowl or a mortar, then add the salt and, using the handle of your cleaver, a wooden spoon, or a pestle, mash the chopped garlic and ginger together until they become a coarse paste. (The addition of the salt during the process of pulverizing the garlic and ginger not only enhances their flavors, but also ensures your extracting the maximum amount of juice from the raw vegetables.)

COOKING

(asparagus)

1½ to 2 quarts water

Bring the water to a boil in a medium saucepan and drop the asparagus pieces in. When the water boils again, lower the heat and cook the asparagus, uncovered, until it is tender but not mushy; this should only take about 10 minutes. Drain the asparagus and put it in a serving dish.

½ teaspoon granulated sugar

½ teaspoon salt

2½ tablespoons soy sauce

1 teaspoon sesame oil

1 tablespoon rice wine vinegar

❋1½ teaspoons hot pepper flakes in oil

¼ teaspoon ground, roasted Szechwan peppercorns

(garlic and ginger)

Add the sugar, salt, soy sauce, sesame oil, vinegar, hot pepper flakes in oil, and Szechwan peppercorns to the mashed garlic and ginger. Mix thoroughly, then pour over the warm asparagus. Make sure all the asparagus is covered with the sauce, then serve.

Note: Since this dish can be served either

lukewarm or cold, it can be prepared in advance. Whether or not to chill it is purely a matter of personal taste.

The raw garlic in this dish can be quite potent. Mrs. Chiang uses a lot. If you feel somewhat timid, reduce the amount.

炒豆芽

BEAN SPROUTS (*chao douya*)

Mrs. Chiang's family ate many bean sprouts, mainly because they were cheap and easy to grow. But nobody in Szechwan ever thought of them as being a more "Chinese" vegetable than, say, eggplant. Mrs. Chiang finds it amusing that an Oriental mystique surrounds them in this country. Because of that mystique and because health food addicts have taken them up, fresh bean sprouts are often easier to find in America than other Chinese vegetables. You can get them in health food stores and many grocery stores as well as Chinese markets. And, if you are horticulturally inclined, you can get some dried mung beans and sprout them yourself. You cannot, however, open a can. Canned bean sprouts are horrible; they are flabby and have a strong metallic taste.

Bean sprouts are at their best in simple stir-fried dishes where their crispness and fresh flavor don't have to compete with elaborate seasonings or rich sauces. Mrs. Chiang cooks bean sprouts with a light hand, adding only the merest touch of vinegar and soy sauce to cut the blandness. She is equally restrained about the cooking time, and snatches her sprouts away from the flame at that crucial point when they are still crunchy but no longer raw. The result is essence of bean sprout, a crisp, light vegetable dish.

PREPARATION

1 *pound bean sprouts (4 cups, approximately)*

Rinse the bean sprouts several times quite thoroughly, and try to pick out the dark husks that originally covered the beans before they sprouted. (Mrs. Chiang says that some fastidious Chinese cooks also break off the tiny roots from the rest of the sprout and discard them. She doesn't because it's just too much work.)

3 scallions Clean the scallions, then cut them, both green part and white, into 1-inch lengths.

COOKING

¼ cup peanut oil Heat your wok or pan over a fairly high flame for 15 seconds, then add the oil. It will be hot enough to cook with when the first tiny bubbles form and a few small wisps of smoke appear.

(bean sprouts) When the oil is ready, put the bean sprouts in the pan and stir-fry them rather vigorously for 30 seconds, using your cooking shovel or spoon to scoop the sprouts off the sides of the pan and then stir them around in the middle, so each one is exposed to the hot oil.

(scallions) Add the scallions and continue to stir-fry for another 30 seconds.

1¼ teaspoons salt
1 teaspoon soy sauce
2 teaspoons rice wine vinegar Keep stirring while you add the salt and soy sauce, then, after stir-frying for about 45 seconds more, add the vinegar.

Continue to stir-fry the sprouts for about 1 more minute before serving. The cooking time for the beans sprouts shouldn't be more than 3 minutes altogether. They will be cooked when they have reduced in bulk and become much softer. (Do not overcook them or they will lose their delightful crunchy texture and become flaccid and uninteresting.)

炒芥蘭菜

BROCCOLI (*chao jielucai*)

The Chinese word for broccoli, *huacai*, means "flower vegetable." Mrs. Chiang's recipe for it rescues broccoli from sogginess by stir-frying it and from insipidity by adding just enough spiciness to enliven the fresh, clear flavor of the vegetable. The recipe is simple and should not take more than 15 minutes to prepare. Cauliflower, also called *huacai*, can be cooked exactly the same way.

PREPARATION

1 *large bunch broccoli*	Wash the broccoli. Cut the florets off the main stems in fairly good-sized pieces. Cut off the tough bottom part of the stems, then slice the stems in half lengthwise and then into pieces about 2 inches long.
❈ 3 *dried red peppers*	Cut each pepper into 4 pieces.
½-*inch piece fresh ginger*	Peel the ginger, then cut it into shreds about ⅛ inch wide, the width of a wooden matchstick.
1 *tablespoon cornstarch*	Combine the cornstarch and water in a small bowl and set aside.
¼ *cup water*	

COOKING

¼ *cup peanut oil*	Heat your wok or pan over a high flame for 15 seconds, then add the oil. It will be ready to cook with when the first tiny bubbles form and a few small wisps of smoke appear.
(*ginger*) (*red peppers*)	When the oil is ready, throw in the ginger and the red peppers. Use your cooking shovel or spoon to stir them around in the middle of the pan for 5 seconds.

(broccoli)	Now add the broccoli and stir-fry it for 1½ minutes, scooping it off the sides of the pan and stirring it around in the middle so every piece is exposed to the hot oil.
1 teaspoon salt	Add the salt and stir-fry the broccoli for 1 minute longer.
⅔ cup water	Pour in the water, wait for it to come to a boil, then cover the pan and let the broccoli cook over a moderately high flame for 8 minutes.
(cornstarch and water)	Stir the cornstarch and water to make sure they are well combined; then, just before you are ready to serve the broccoli, pour the mixture into the pan. Stir-fry the broccoli for a few seconds over a high flame until the sauce turns thick and clear, then serve.

辣白菜

SPICY CHINESE CABBAGE *(la baicai)*

Here is a simple and most Szechwanese way to prepare that work-horse vegetable of Szechwan, Chinese cabbage. This is a hot dish, and it has to be, for hot pepper paste is just about the only condiment it contains. Even Mrs. Chiang admits that it takes a well-developed palate to appreciate this delightfully crisp and spicy vegetable.

PREPARATION

1 large head Chinese cabbage (1½ to 2 pounds)	Remove the tough outer leaves of the cabbage and discard. Wash the other leaves thoroughly, and then cut them crosswise into pieces about 1 inch wide.
1 tablespoon corn-starch	Combine the cornstarch and water in a small bowl and set aside.
¼ cup water	

COOKING

¼ *cup peanut oil*

Heat your wok or pan over a high flame for 15 seconds, then add the oil. It will be hot enough to cook with when the first tiny bubbles form and a few small wisps of smoke appear.

❀ *1 tablespoon hot
 pepper paste
(cabbage)*

When the oil is ready, add the hot pepper paste and the cabbage. Use your cooking shovel or spoon to stir the cabbage around in the pan so all of it gets some contact with the hot oil. At first there may be so much cabbage in the pan that it will spill over the sides; it will reduce in volume as it cooks. Let the cabbage cook for 5 or 6 minutes, mixing it up gently every once in a while, tumbling it over from the sides into the middle.

*1 tablespoon salt, or
 to taste*
½ cup water
(cornstarch and water)

Add the salt and the water. Cover the pan, without reducing the flame, and let the cabbage boil for almost 15 minutes.

Stir the cornstarch and water to make sure they are well combined, then pour the mixture into the cabbage. Stir-fry the cabbage over the same high flame for about 15 seconds, until the sauce has turned clear and thickened slightly. Serve immediately.

大白菜炒蝦米

CHINESE CABBAGE AND DRIED SHRIMP (*dabaicai shao xiami*)

There was a tradition of rustic elegance in Chinese *haute cuisine*, Gourmets, tired of the contrived artifice of most banquet dishes, would seek variety in the food of peasants, claiming that the honest, earthy flavor of cooked cabbage was more exquisite than that of the most expensive texture food. Of course, these simple peasant dishes were often more sophisticated than their cultivated admirers liked to admit.

According to Mrs. Chiang, this is such a dish. Its unusual character comes from the juxtaposition of cabbage, the most ordinary of vegetables, with dried shrimp, an ingredient noted for its pronounced and complicated salty-pungent flavor. The characteristic flavor of each of the main ingredients comes through, as well as the new and intricate one produced by combining them. Like all banquet dishes, this one also plays upon texture and visual appearance. The cabbage is soft, the shrimps hard, almost leathery. In addition, Mrs. Chiang considers the pale colors of the dish—the light green of the cabbage and the light orange of the shrimps—to be especially beautiful.

Since this dish is simmered for a while after it is stir-fried, it can be made partially in advance—not too much though, or the cabbage will become soggy rather than soft. It is an unusual dish and one that we particularly love.

PREPARATION

⅔ *cup dried shrimps*
1 *cup boiling water,*
approximately

Put the shrimps in a small bowl and pour the boiling water over them. Let soak for at least 30 minutes.

Drain the shrimps and rinse them thoroughly. Pull off the tails or any tiny legs that may still be attached to them. (You can, if you want to, remove the tiny black vein that runs up the back of each shrimp. Mrs. Chiang uses a toothpick to do this. It is tedious work, and is really a question of aesthetics.)

1 *large head Chinese*
cabbage (1½
pounds)

Pull off the tough outer leaves of the cabbage and discard them. Separate the inner leaves and wash them carefully, then drain them well. (If there is too much water clinging to the cabbage leaves when they are cooked, the dish may turn out too watery.) Chop the cabbage into pieces approximately 1 inch wide.

½-inch piece fresh ginger

Peel the ginger, then cut it into 4 or 5 thin slices.

1½ tablespoons corn-starch

3 tablespoons water

Combine the cornstarch and water in a small bowl and set aside.

COOKING

¼ cup peanut oil

Heat your wok or pan over a high flame for 15 seconds, then pour in the oil. It should be hot enough to cook with when the first tiny bubbles form and a few small wisps of smoke appear.

(dried shrimps and ginger)

When the oil is ready, toss in the dried shrimps and the ginger slices. Stir-fry them together for about 30 seconds over a high heat, using your cooking shovel or spoon to scoop the ingredients off the sides of the pan and then stir them around in the middle.

(cabbage)

Now add the Chinese cabbage. This presents a real challenge, for you will probably have more chopped cabbage than the pan can hold. As all cabbage does, it will shrink in volume once it is cooked, so begin by putting in only as much cabbage as the pan will accommodate comfortably and cook it over a high heat, gingerly scooping up the cooked pieces from the bottom and sides of the pan and adding new pieces as the older ones shrink.

1 tablespoon salt

After the cabbage has cooked for about 3 minutes and has reached a manageable volume, add the salt. Continue to cook

	the cabbage over a high flame for another 2 or 3 minutes, stirring occasionally.
⅔ cup water	Pour in the water, wait for it to boil, cover the pan, and let cook over the same high heat for 15 minutes.
(cornstarch and water)	Stir the cornstarch and water to make sure they are well combined, then add the mixture to the boiling cabbage. Stir-fry the cabbage gently for about 2 minutes, until the sauce has turned clear and thickened slightly.
Salt, if necessary *¼ teaspoon freshly* *ground black pepper*	Taste the sauce before you remove the cabbage from the pan (it may need additional salt to bring out the pungent flavor of the dried shrimps), then put the cabbage in a serving dish and sprinkle the pepper on top of it. Although black pepper is not a commonly used spice in Chinese cooking, it is sometimes added to an unusual dish like this one to give piquancy to its special flavor.

凉拌黄瓜

CUCUMBER SALAD (*liangban huanggua*)

It was a tradition in the Szechwanese restaurants of Taipei for the waiters to place several little plates of food on the table while you ordered your dinner. A few pickles or peanuts or a little cucumber salad stimulated the appetite and provided a delicious foretaste of the coming meal.

This cucumber salad is essentially the same as that served in Szechwanese restaurants. Mrs. Chiang usually serves it as a regular vegetable dish instead of as an hors d'oeuvre, but it can also be used as a salad in a Western-style meal. Since it is a cold dish, it can be prepared in advance. Mrs. Chiang recalls that her mother's cucumber salad was so spicy it actually numbed her mouth when she ate it. This version is not so hot and can be made without any peppery condiments at all.

	PREPARATION
2 *cucumbers*	Peel the cucumbers. Cut each one in half crosswise and then again in half lengthwise; scoop out the seedy pulp in the middle. Smash each piece of cucumber with the flat side of your cleaver (this makes the cucumbers more absorbent), then cut the cucumbers into strips about 2 inches long by ½ inch wide.
1 *teaspoon salt*	Put the strips in a bowl, sprinkle the salt over them, and mix thoroughly. Set aside for at least 10 minutes at room temperature.
	Drain the cucumbers and squeeze out all the excess liquid with your hands.
3 *scallions*	Clean the scallions, then smash each one with the flat side of the cleaver. Cut the scallions, both green part and white, into 2-inch lengths and add them to the cucumbers.
4 *cloves garlic*	Smash the garlic cloves with the flat side of your cleaver, then peel. Chop the garlic coarsely, into pieces about the size of grains of uncooked rice. Add the garlic to the cucumbers.
1½ *tablespoons soy sauce* ½ *teaspoon sesame oil* 1 *teaspoon rice wine vinegar* ¼ *teaspoon granulated sugar* ¼ *teaspoon ground roasted Szechwan*	Now add the soy sauce, sesame oil, vinegar, sugar, optional ground roasted Szechwan peppercorns, and optional hot pepper flakes in oil. (If you omit the two optional ingredients, the salad will be considerably less spicy and not at all hot. In that case, you may need to increase the amount of vinegar and sesame oil you use. But taste the cucumbers

peppercorns (op-
tional)

❀1 teaspoon hot pep-
per flakes in oil (op-
tional)

first before you do.) Mix the salad well.

Note: You can serve this salad immediately or you can refrigerate it for several
hours and serve it chilled. In its less
spicy form, it goes well with Western
food.

素拌三鮮

CUCUMBER, CARROT, AND CELLOPHANE NOODLE SALAD
(*suban sansi*)

"Our regular outhouse was next to the pigsty," recalls Mrs. Chiang,
"but we also had an indoor privy just for the women, painted a cheer-
ful vermilion. Nightsoil and manure were our fertilizer; my father
collected the nightsoil and pig manure every night and spread it over
the fields. It was a wonderful fertilizer, but using it meant we rarely
ate raw leafy vegetables; it was too hard to clean them properly. Our
salads were made from cooked vegetables, chilled and dressed with
vinegar and soy sauce, or from raw vegetables with skins that could
be peeled."

This salad, which combines raw carrots, cucumbers and cellophane
noodles in a spicy, garlicky sauce, is a typical raw vegetable salad.
Its contrasting colors and textures are as important as its taste. Note,
however, that despite the fact that no cooking is required, this dish is
not a time saver. Shredding carrots and cucumbers—unless you have
a food processor—is sheer tedium. Fortunately, you can prepare everything in advance and leave it in the refrigerator for hours without any
ill effects.

Mrs. Chiang always serves this salad as the filling of a thin crêpe,
or *baobing* (see the recipe for Pancakes, page 329). Her mother often
served whole meals of *bing* dishes, things that could be eaten as the
filling of a crêpe. Americans who frequent Chinese restaurants specializing in "Mandarin" cooking are probably familiar with one of the

best Pekingese examples of this type of cuisine, Moo Shu Pork. The food of Szechwan abounds in such dishes. Actually, almost any combination of shredded ingredients can be served inside a Chinese pancake, but there are some foods that lend themselves particularly well to such treatment. This salad is one of them. Mrs. Chiang usually serves it with plenty of *baobing* as the main course in a light supper. You can, of course, have the salad without the pancakes as a regular course in a regular meal.

PREPARATION

1 *package (2 ounces) cellophane noodles*
4 *cups boiling water, approximately*

Put the dried cellophane noodles in a bowl and pour the boiling water over them. It should only take 10 minutes of soaking at the most for the noodles to become soft. (If for any reason, the noodles do not seem soft enough after you have soaked them for 10 minutes, put them in a saucepan, cover them with water, and let them boil for about 2 minutes.)

2 *carrots*
1 *teaspoon salt*

Peel the carrots and cut them into very thin strips, 4 inches long and about ⅛ inch wide, the width of a wooden matchstick. (This is not easy; raw carrots are hard to cut, especially with a cleaver. If you have special difficulty try a thinbladed paring knife.)

Put the carrot shreds into a large bowl, sprinkle the salt over them, and mix them very thoroughly.

2 to 3 *cucumbers, depending on their size*
1 *teaspoon salt*

Peel the cucumbers, cut them in half lengthwise and scoop out the seeds in the middle. Then cut the cucumbers into strips the same size as the carrots. Put the cucumber strips in a bowl, sprinkle with the salt, and let stand for 10 minutes.

2 *scallions*

Clean the scallions, then cut them, both

green part and white, into the same size shreds as the other two vegetables. Put in the bowl with the carrots.

6 *cloves garlic*

Smash the garlic cloves with the flat side of your cleaver, then, peel. Chop the garlic into pieces about the size of a match head. Add the chopped garlic to the carrot and scallion shreds.

(cucumber shreds)

Drain the cucumber shreds. Squeeze out as much of their moisture as you can, then add to the shredded vegetable bowl.

(cellophane noodles)

Drain the cellophane noodles and chop them coarsely, the way you would cut spaghetti into smaller pieces for a child to eat. Add the cellophane noodles to the shredded vegetable bowl.

2 *tablespoons soy sauce*

1 *tablespoon sesame oil*

1 *tablespoon rice wine vinegar*

½ *teaspoon ground roasted Szechwan peppercorns*

❧1 *tablespoon hot pepper flakes in oil*

1 *teaspoon salt*

Now add the soy sauce, sesame oil, vinegar, ground roasted Szechwan peppercorns, hot pepper flakes in oil, and salt. Mix very thoroughly so the shredded vegetables and noodles are covered with the sauce.

SERVING

You can serve this salad just as it is. You can also refrigerate it for a while before serving, but the longer it sits the more it will absorb the flavors of the sauce, and it may become overpoweringly spicy.

To serve it the traditional Szechwanese way, as the filling of a pancake, prepare about a dozen plain Pancakes (page 329). Put about a third of a cupful of salad inside each pancake and roll it up like a blintz. You have to eat the filled pancakes with your hands, otherwise they simply fall apart.

凉拌茄子

COLD EGGPLANT WITH SESAME SAUCE (*liangban qiez*)

"Eggplant was a common vegetable in Szechwan. Every spring our front courtyard would be turned into a nursery where my parents grew eggplant seedlings in bamboo trays to sell to our neighbors. We loved eggplant, and ate it nearly every day when it was in season. My mother knew dozens of different ways to prepare it, each one more exciting than the last."

Eggplant naturally lends itself to a variety of treatments; its soft flesh soaks up sauces readily and its rich flavor counterbalances even the most emphatic Szechwanese spices. Only bean curd has as much versatility. This recipe for eggplant, and the two that follow, are each an example of a popular Szechwanese cooking style.

Chinese eggplants are not like American ones. They are much smaller, more the size and shape of a cucumber or zucchini. American eggplants are, however, perfectly acceptable for all Mrs. Chiang's recipes, though she notes they lack the flavor and fragrance of the ones she used to eat in Szechwan. If you ever come across the little Italian eggplants, buy them; they resemble the Oriental ones. In order to avoid overripe eggplants, which are spongy and have too many seeds, check the skin of each before you buy it. Strangely enough, if the skin is shiny and taut, the vegetable has seen better days. The skin of tender, young eggplants is dull.

One of the most amusing things about this dish is the fact that it contains almost exactly the same basic ingredients as one of our favorite Middle Eastern dishes, *baba ghanouj*—eggplant and sesame paste. But what a difference! Instead of a smooth puree, permeated with the rich, nutlike flavor of Middle Eastern sesame paste, or *tahini*, this dish is a highly spiced salad composed of soft eggplant strips in an assertive sauce containing raw garlic, ginger, and hot red peppers, as well as sesame paste.

Although it rarely appears in the dishes of American Chinese restaurants, sesame paste is one of the most important and characteristic of all Szechwanese condiments. It has a much stronger taste and more powerful aroma than the Middle Eastern variety, and appears most frequently as the basic component of this type of highly spiced sauce. It is a sauce that has a remarkable affinity for cold foods, and some of the most famous Szechwanese cold dishes rely on it. This eggplant dish is one of them. Warn your friends before you serve it to them; the hot peppers and raw garlic form a powerful combination.

PREPARATION

1 *large eggplant*	Cut the eggplant into about 6 large pieces; you do not have to peel it.
1-*inch piece fresh ginger*	Peel the ginger, then chop it coarsely. Put it in a small, steep-sided bowl or a mortar.
5 *cloves garlic*	Smash the garlic cloves with the flat side of
⅛ *teaspoon salt*	your cleaver, then peel. Chop the garlic coarsely, too. Add the chopped garlic to the ginger, along with the salt, and, using the handle of your cleaver, a wooden spoon, or a pestle, mash them all together until they become a sticky paste. (The salt aids in the process of pulverizing the other ingredients and helps to bring out their flavor as well.)
1 *scallion*	Clean the scallion, then chop it, both green part and white, into pieces about the size of a match head.

COOKING

(*eggplant*)	Put the eggplant pieces in a saucepan and
1 *to* 2 *quarts water, approximately*	pour in enough water to cover them. Bring the water to a boil, then cover the pan and let the eggplant cook gently

(mashed garlic and
  ginger)
(scallion)
1 tablespoon sesame
  paste
1 teaspoon sesame oil
½ teaspoon
  granulated sugar
2 teaspoons rice wine
  vinegar
1½ tablespoons soy
  sauce
❀ 1 teaspoon hot pep-
  per flakes in oil
¼ teaspoon salt
¼ teaspoon ground
  roasted Szechwan
  peppercorns

until it becomes soft; this may take anywhere from 10 to 25 minutes.

Drain the eggplant thoroughly, then put it
in the refrigerator to chill.

When the eggplant is cold, slice it into
strips about ½ inch wide. Put the strips
in a serving dish and add the mashed
garlic and ginger, the scallion, sesame
paste, sesame oil, sugar, vinegar, soy
sauce, hot pepper flakes in oil, salt, and
ground roasted Szechwan peppercorns.
Mix everything very thoroughly and
serve.

Note: Since this is a cold dish, it can be
prepared in advance and kept in the
refrigerator until you are ready to serve
it. Mrs. Chiang doesn't like to let it sit
for more than a day, however, because
the eggplant gets watery.

魚香茄子

EGGPLANT IN THE STYLE OF FISH (yuxiang qiez)

There is nothing fishy about this dish except its name. Yuxiang is a
classic Szechwanese method of preparing food that employs the condiments and seasoning agents traditionally used in cooking fish. Fish
were scarce in Szechwan, and Mrs. Chiang thinks that it was possible
that yuxiang dishes were created to compensate for that fact. Foods

prepared in the style of fish differ from similarly spicy and reddish colored specialties of Szechwan because they contain sugar and vinegar. These two ingredients give a mildly sweet and sour taste to an already intricate and peppery combination of flavors. Eggplant is the perfect vegetable for such a treatment. Its smooth, absorbent flesh and unctuous flavor complement rather than compete with the sharp tastes and interesting textures of the other ingredients.

Again, this recipe, like others in the book, insists on *fresh* water chestnuts. If you can't get them, forget them.

PREPARATION

3 *dried black mushrooms* ⅓ *cup tree ears* 2 *cups boiling water, approximately*	Put the dried mushrooms and tree ears in a small bowl and cover them with boiling water. Set them aside to soak for at least 15 minutes.
1 *large eggplant*	Peel the eggplant, then cut it into pieces about 3 inches long and ½ inch wide.
6 *fresh water chestnuts (optional)*	Cut off the black outer skin of the water chestnuts. Rinse them, then cut them into shreds about ⅛ inch wide, the width of a wooden matchstick.
4 *scallions*	Clean the scallions, then cut them, both the white part and about half the green, into 1-inch lengths. Slice each piece lengthwise into several shreds.
10 *cloves garlic*	Smash the garlic cloves with the flat side of your cleaver, then peel. Chop the garlic into small pieces, about the size of grains of uncooked rice.
1-inch piece fresh *ginger*	Peel the ginger and cut it into shreds the same size as the water chestnuts.
(mushrooms) *(tree ears)*	Drain the mushrooms and tree ears. Remove the hard stems from the mushrooms and slice the caps into shreds the same size as the water chestnuts. Rinse the tree ears carefully under running

water, making sure you remove all the impurities, like little pieces of wood, that may still be embedded in them. Then slice them into shreds.

COOKING

½ cup peanut oil

Heat your wok or pan over a high flame for 15 seconds, then pour in the oil. It will be hot enough to cook with when the first tiny bubbles form and a few small wisps of smoke appear.

(garlic)
(ginger)

When the oil is ready, quickly toss in the garlic and ginger. Stir them around for 30 seconds in the hot oil with your cooking shovel or spoon. Don't worry if they turn brown very quickly; just don't let them burn.

❀ 1 tablespoon hot pepper paste
(mushrooms)
(tree ears)
(water chestnuts)
(eggplant)
1 tablespoon granulated sugar

Quickly add the hot pepper paste, the shredded mushrooms, and the tree ears. Stir-fry them, together with the garlic and ginger, for about 45 seconds.

Now add the water chestnuts, eggplant, and sugar to the pan. Stir-fry for another 45 seconds, using your cooking shovel or spoon in a continuous scooping motion to spread the eggplant around in the pan.

1 tablespoon rice wine vinegar
1 teaspoon salt, or to taste

Add the vinegar and salt and stir-fry for about 1 minute 45 seconds.

(scallions)
2 tablespoons soy sauce

Add the shredded scallions and the soy sauce and stir-fry everything for another 1½ minutes.

¾ cup water

Finally pour in the water. Wait until it comes to a boil, then cover the pan, without reducing the flame, and cook the eggplant for about 15 minutes more, until it is slightly mushy. Then serve.

紅燒茄子

EGGPLANT WITH CHOPPED MEAT (*hongshao qiez*)

There are some combinations of foods that are so perfect they crop up in many cuisines. Eggplant and chopped meat is such a one. The two have an affinity for each other all around the globe, though the marriage is most brilliantly consummated in Szechwan. Mrs. Chiang's *hongshao* eggplant with meat sauce is, quite simply, the best eggplant dish I've ever eaten. It's also easy to make. It can be prepared in advance and in large quantities, no negligible virtue if you are planning a large dinner party.

The recipe calls for 2 medium eggplants. Don't buy a single large one; according to Mrs. Chiang, smaller eggplants are more tender.

PREPARATION

½ *pound ground pork*	Put the pork in a bowl and add the soy
3 *tablespoons soy sauce*	sauce and sesame oil to it.
1 *tablespoon sesame oil*	
8 *scallions*	Clean the scallions, then chop them, both green part and white, crosswise into tiny pieces, about ⅛ inch wide. Add half of the chopped scallions to the pork and mix thoroughly. Reserve the rest of the scallions for later use.
2 *medium eggplants (1 pound, approximately)*	Peel the eggplants, then cut them into 1-inch cubes.
7 *to 8 cloves garlic*	Smash the garlic cloves with the flat side of your cleaver, then peel. Chop the garlic into little pieces, about the size of grains of uncooked rice.

1-inch piece fresh ginger	Peel the ginger, then chop it into even tinier pieces, the size of a match head.

COOKING

5 tablespoons peanut oil	Heat your wok or pan over a high flame for 15 seconds, then pour in the oil. It will be ready to cook with when the first tiny bubbles form and a few small wisps of smoke appear.
(ginger and garlic)	When the oil is ready, toss in the chopped ginger and garlic and stir-fry for 30 seconds, using your cooking shovel or spoon in a scooping motion to stir them around in the hot oil and keep them from burning.
✿ *2 tablespoons hot pepper paste*	Now add the hot pepper paste and stir-fry it, together with the ginger and garlic, for another 30 seconds.
(chopped pork)	Add the chopped pork and cook for 2 minutes, stirring occasionally to break up any large lumps of meat that are sticking together and to see that all the meat gets exposed to the hot oil.
(eggplant)	After the meat has cooked for 2 minutes, add the eggplant and stir-fry everything over a high flame for about 4 minutes, gently scooping the pieces of eggplant off the sides of the pan and into the middle.
1 tablespoon granulated sugar *1½ teaspoons salt*	Sprinkle the sugar and salt over the eggplant mixture, then continue to stir-fry for 2 minutes more.
⅔ cup water *(scallions)*	Pour in the water and add the reserved scallions. Wait until the water comes to a boil, then cover the pan, without reducing the heat, and let the eggplant cook for another 15 minutes, until it

has become soft and has absorbed the flavors of the meat sauce. It will then be ready to serve.

Note: This dish can be prepared in advance, even several days in advance, and reheated just before serving.

炒油菜

SAUTÉED RAPE (*chao youcai*)

Despite its unfortunate English name, rape is a delicious vegetable. A member of the mustard family, it has dark green leaves and yellow, goldenrod-like flowers. The Chinese name for it, *youcai*, or "oil vegetable," is far more appropriate, for its thick stems contain a considerable amount of oil. When cooked, rape has a slightly bitter, yet buttery, taste.

Rape was such a common vegetable in Szechwan that Mrs. Chiang's family ate it almost every day. They even ate it raw, but mainly they ate it sautéed. This simple recipe exemplifies the kind of plain vegetable dish that was, next to rice, the mainstay of the family's diet.

In this country, rape can be found in the produce section of Chinese grocery stores, tied up in bunches like broccoli. We eat it plain or fry it with noodles in *chaomian* (see the recipe for Fried Noodles, page 283) instead of Chinese cabbage.

PREPARATION

1 bunch rape (for a yield of 6 cups raw, sliced vegetable, approximately)

Wash the rape well, rinsing it at least twice under running water. Tear the leaves, flowers, and thinner stems into pieces approximately 2 inches long. If the stems seem tough, peel off the outer layer of skin. Cut the outer skin off the thicker stalks, and slice them lengthwise into pieces about ½ inch wide. Then cut them into 2-inch lengths.

1½ teaspoons cornstarch ¼ cup water	Mix the cornstarch and water together in a small bowl and set aside.

COOKING

6 tablespoons peanut oil	Heat the pan over a high flame for 15 seconds, then pour in the oil. It will be ready to cook with when the first tiny bubbles form and a few wisps of smoke appear.
(rape)	When the oil is hot, add the rape and stir-fry carefully, using your cooking shovel or spoon in a scooping motion to stir the vegetable up from the bottom of the pan and make sure that it all gets exposed to the hot oil.
1 teaspoon salt ⅓ cup water	After about 1 minute, add the salt, then continue to stir-fry the rape for an additional 30 seconds. Pour in the water. Wait for it to come to a boil, then cover the pan and let the rape cook over the same high heat for 5 or 6 minutes. Don't lift the lid to peek at the vegetable or it will lose its bright green color.
(cornstarch and water)	Stir the cornstarch and water carefully to make sure they are well combined, then pour the mixture into the pan. Stir-fry everything for about 30 seconds longer, until the liquid in the pan turns clear again and thickens slightly. Serve immediately.

炒菠菜

SAUTÉED SPINACH (chao bocai)

Mrs. Chiang's mother knew that spinach was nutritious, but she didn't have to force her children to eat it. She cooked it so well that it was one of the family's favorite foods. It's one of ours as well. In an elaborate multicourse meal, its simplicity, delicate flavor, and color provide a refreshing contrast to heavier, more complicated dishes. It takes about 5 minutes to cook and requires only some shreds of ginger and a few dried red peppers to brighten the final taste.

PREPARATION

1 package (10 ounces) fresh spinach	Wash the spinach and drain it thoroughly, but don't worry if a few drops of water are still clinging to the leaves.
❦ 4 dry red peppers	Cut the dried red peppers crosswise into thirds. If you want the dish to be somewhat milder, remove the seeds from the inside of the peppers, as they are the hottest part.
2-inch piece fresh ginger	Peel the ginger and slice it into small slivers about ⅛ inch wide, the width of a wooden matchstick.
1½ teaspoons cornstarch 1 tablespoon water	Combine the cornstarch and water in a small bowl and set aside.

COOKING

3 tablespoons peanut oil	Heat your wok or pan over a fairly high flame for about 15 seconds, then pour in the oil. It will be hot enough to cook with when the first tiny bubbles form and a few small wisps of smoke appear.
(spinach) (peppers) (ginger)	When the oil is ready, add the spinach, peppers, and ginger and stir-fry them for about 2 minutes, using your cooking shovel or spoon to scoop the ingredients off the sides of the pan and then stir them around in the middle, so that they are all exposed to the hot oil.
½ teaspoon salt, or to taste	After about 2 minutes the spinach will have turned dark green and become

limp. Add the salt, then taste the spinach and, if the flavor is not fresh and bright, add some more salt.

(cornstarch and water)   Stir the cornstarch and water to make sure they are well combined, then pour the mixture into the pan. Continue to stir-fry the spinach for about 20 seconds, until the sauce has thickened and become transparent. Serve immediately.

Note: When you serve the spinach, make sure that everybody gets a bit of the pan sauce on top of their portion so they get the full flavor of the dish. Don't remove the red peppers before serving—they add a nice touch of color—but remember to warn people not to eat them unless they love *very* hot food.

涼拌菠菜

SPINACH SALAD *(liangban bocai)*

"When it got really hot we ate all our meals in the front courtyard," recalls Mrs. Chiang. "It was too hot for meat dishes, and we ate mainly rice, cold dishes, and freshly picked vegetables and fruit. This spinach salad was one of our summer mainstays."

The salad consists of some briefly cooked spinach bathed in a sauce containing ginger, scallions, soy sauce, sesame oil, vinegar, and hot pepper flakes in oil. Because the hot pepper flakes are optional, this can be either a hot cold dish or a mild cold one. The only trick in its preparation is to make sure that the spinach doesn't cook too long; it should be bright green.

PREPARATION AND COOKING

8 *cups water,*
approximately   Bring the water to a rapid boil in a large pot.

1 *scant pound fresh*
spinach   Wash the spinach well and break off and discard the tough stems.

1 *teaspoon peanut oil*

When the water is boiling, add the oil to it and then the spinach. (The oil helps keep the spinach green.) Cook the spinach for 3 minutes only, and without waiting for the water in the pot to return to a full boil. Drain the spinach immediately and put it in a serving bowl to cool.

½-*inch piece fresh ginger*

Peel the ginger, then chop it very fine, until it reaches the consistency of coarse bread crumbs. Add to the spinach.

2 *scallions*

Clean the scallions, then cut them, both green part and white, crosswise into little pieces, about ⅛ inch wide. Add to the spinach.

1 *teaspoon granulated sugar*
¼ *teaspoon salt*
2 *tablespoons soy sauce*

Add the sugar, salt, soy sauce, sesame oil, vinegar, and optional hot pepper flakes in oil to the spinach and mix thoroughly.

Serve the salad either lukewarm or, if you prefer, chilled.

1 *teaspoon sesame oil*
3 *teaspoons rice wine vinegar*
❀ 1 *teaspoon hot pepper flakes in oil (optional)*

乾 煸 四 季 豆

DRY-FRIED STRING BEANS *(ganbian sijidou)*

A gourmet friend introduced us to this famous dish during an expedition to one of Taipei's finest restaurants. We would probably not have ordered such a mundane vegetable, but luckily we took our friend's advice and discovered one of the more unusual and delicious specialties of Szechwan. Had we seen the string beans before we ordered them, our reluctance would have been even stronger; they are limp, shriveled, khaki-colored objects, covered with dry, brown grains of an unidentifiable substance. It takes up to two hours of long, slow cooking for the string beans to reach this unattractive condition, during which time they also absorb the flavors of the chopped dried shrimps and pickled vegetables with which they are fried. The dish that results has an unusual salty and pungent taste that barely hints at the original flavor of the beans.

Like many classic Szechwanese dishes, Dry-Fried String Beans have an unusual texture, which is emphasized when they are eaten in the traditional manner, encased inside a thin pancake, or *baobing* (see the recipe for Pancakes, page 329). The smooth, elastic crêpes highlight the texture of the soft beans and their grainy covering. They also make them easier to eat.

Note that this dish takes a long time to prepare. You have to soak the dried shrimps for 2 hours, after which they are cooked with the string beans for 2 hours more.

PREPARATION

1 *cup dried shrimps* 2 *cups hot water,* *approximately*	Put the shrimps in a small bowl. Cover them with hot water and set them aside to soak for 2 hours. Drain the shrimps and wash them, then, if you wish, with the aid of a pointed instrument, remove the black vein running up the back of each shrimp. Rinse the shrimps well and drain them again, then pound them with the back side of your cleaver until they start to flake. Finally, chop them very fine, until they reach the consistency of coarse bread crumbs.
2 *pieces canned* *Szechwan preserved* *vegetable,* *each the size of a* *Ping-Pong ball*	Rinse the pickled vegetable thoroughly under cold running water to wash off all the salt in which it was packed. Then chop it as fine as you can, until it reaches the same consistency as the dried shrimps.
1-*inch piece fresh* *ginger*	Peel the ginger, then chop it as fine as the other ingredients; you should get about a tablespoonful.

2 *pounds fresh string beans, preferably small and slightly old and wrinkled*

Wash the beans, snap off the ends, and, if the beans are large, break them in half. Rinse them well and set them aside to drain; you should get about 8 cups of raw beans.

COOKING

3 *tablespoons peanut oil*
(beans)

Heat your wok or pan over a high flame for 15 seconds, then add the oil. Wait until the oil is very hot and smoking, then add the beans. Stir-fry the beans over the high flame for about 2 minutes, using your cooking shovel or spoon in a scooping motion to toss the beans around in the pan and expose them all to the hot oil.

After 2 minutes of this, lower the flame and continue to cook the beans, stirring occasionally, for another 6 or 7 minutes. Remove them from the pan.

¼ *cup peanut oil*
(ginger)
(shrimps)

Wipe out the pan with paper towels, then raise the heat again and pour in the fresh oil. It will be ready to cook with when the first tiny bubbles form and a few small wisps of smoke appear.

When the oil is ready, quickly toss in the chopped ginger and shrimps and stir-fry them vigorously for 20 seconds.

(pickled vegetable)
1 *teaspoon sesame oil*
2 *teaspoons gran-ulated sugar*
(beans)

Add the chopped pickled vegetable and stir-fry for 40 seconds longer, then add the sesame oil and the sugar and stir-fry for 1 additional minute.

Return the beans to the pan and lower the heat. Cook the beans for about 10 minutes, stirring them several times, then turn the flame down as far as it will go and let the beans cook, without covering the pan, for about 2 hours; stir the beans around every once in a while. When fully cooked, the beans will be quite shriveled, limp, and dry. The longer and slower they cook, the better they are.

Note: Like most long-cooked dishes, dry-fried string beans can be made several hours in advance and reheated just before serving.

14 - SOUPS

Mrs. Chiang remembers that "soup was for special occasions in Szechwan; my mother would serve a light, clear soup at the end of a feast, after everyone had gorged on her richest and most elegant meat dishes. A delicate soup rinsed out the digestive system and made everyone feel they had eaten gracefully as well as fully.

"Of course, we also had thick soups, like the spicy Hot and Sour Soup that is a famous Szechwan specialty. These would be served as a course in themselves. In the winter a big bowl of Won Ton Soup made a whole dinner for the family. Any time soup came in a small bowl you knew it was soup; in a large bowl it became a main course."

We never serve soup at the beginning of a meal; it is the Chinese tradition to serve it at the end. In addition, it fills you up too fast. In a Chinese restaurant soup will be full of monosodium glutamate; if you have it first your empty stomach will absorb the monosodium glutamate very fast and you are almost certain to get the "Chinese restaurant syndrome," starting with a tight feeling around your temples.

The important thing in Szechwanese soup is the crispness and clear flavor of each ingredient, so most of Mrs. Chiang's soups take only about 15 minutes to make. There is none of the long simmering we are accustomed to in the West. The procedure is very simple, and no special equipment is needed. Canned chicken broth makes an adequate soup base. It contains monosodium glutamate and is rather strongly flavored, but when diluted Mrs. Chiang finds it perfectly satisfactory. Or, if you prefer, you can make your own stock; just simmer some chicken, pork, or beef bones and scraps in a few cups of water for about an hour. A little salt should be the only seasoning; in Szechwan soups are supposed to be bland.

酸 辣 湯

HOT AND SOUR SOUP *(suanla tang)*

You can't make an authentic Hot and Sour Soup in the United States because you can't get coagulated duck's blood. This is a dark brown substance that comes in chunks like bean curd, has the consistency of raw liver, and tastes just as you would expect duck's blood to taste. Even on Taiwan it was hard to find. Mrs. Chiang's recipe is as close to the original as you can get, and produces a delicious soup with an exciting taste and unusual texture. The thick broth teems with so many different kinds of crunchy, chewy, slippery, and soft ingredients that only a connoisseur would quibble about the duck's blood.

The taste of the soup, of course, is famous. It really is both hot *and* sour. It gets its heat from black pepper, instead of the more commonly used red chilies; the sourness comes from vinegar. Though the idea of combining two such powerful and distinctive tastes sounds extreme, the mixture succeeds brilliantly. Its tart pepperiness challenges the taste buds with the kind of extravagance that characterizes the most exciting Szechwanese food.

Hot and Sour Soup is much too thick and highly spiced to be produced at the end of a multicourse meal; it is almost a meal in itself. We usually serve it as the main course in an informal supper, accompanied by a bread or a savory pastry like Oily Scallion Cakes (page 326).

PREPARATION AND COOKING

¼ *cup dried tree ears*
¼ *cup dried lily buds*
5 *dried black mush-*
rooms
2 *cups boiling water,*
approximately
5 *cups water*

Combine the tree ears, lily buds, and dried mushrooms in a small bowl. Pour the boiling water over them and let them soak for 20 minutes.

Bring the 5 cups water to a boil in a medium-sized saucepan.

2 *medium pork chops*
(for a yield of ½
pound meat, ap-
proximately)

Cut the bones and fat away from the pork chops and discard them. Cut the lean meat into slivers about 2 inches long and ⅛ inch wide, the size and shape of a wooden matchstick. (It is always easier to slice meat very fine if you first put it in the freezer for about 10 minutes, until it becomes slightly stiff but not frozen.)

(boiling water)

Put about 2 tablespoonfuls of the shredded pork in the boiling water. Let the meat simmer over a moderate flame for 20 minutes. (This will give both flavor and body to the soup.)

1 *tablespoon soy*
sauce
1 *teaspoon cornstarch*
(tree ears, lily buds,
and mushrooms)

Put the remaining meat shreds in a small bowl. Add the soy sauce and the cornstarch and mix well.

When they are soft, drain the tree ears, lily buds, and mushrooms and rinse them thoroughly. Be particularly careful to pick over the tree ears and remove any impurities, such as little pieces of wood, that might still be embedded in them. Remove the hard stems from the mushrooms and slice the caps into thin shreds, the same width as the pork slivers. Chop the tree ears into shreds as

2 *squares fresh bean*
  curd

(soup)
1 *teaspoon salt*
6 *tablespoons rice*
  wine vinegar
2 *tablespoons soy*
  sauce
2 *scallions*

(meat mixture)

2 *eggs*
2 *tablespoons corn-*
  starch
2 *tablespoons cold*
  water

¼ *to* ½ *teaspoon*
  freshly ground
  black *pepper*

well, then, using your fingers, tear each lily bud into three or four shreds.

Slice each square of bean curd into 4 layers, then cut each layer into slivers about ¼ inch wide.

Add the shredded mushrooms, tree ears, lily buds and bean curd to the soup, along with the salt, vinegar, and soy sauce. Bring the soup to a boil again, then reduce the heat slightly and let it boil gently for 7 minutes.

Meanwhile, clean the scallions and chop them, both white part and green, cross-wise into the thinnest possible pieces.

After the soup has boiled for about 7 minutes, add the scallions and the rest of the meat shreds to it, stirring the soup as you add the meat so the shreds don't stick together. Let the soup boil for 2 more minutes.

While the soup is cooking, beat the eggs in a small bowl. Combine the corn-starch and water in another small bowl and mix well.

After the meat shreds have boiled for 2 minutes, pour the beaten egg and the cornstarch mixture into the soup, stir-ring as you do so the egg will form shreds, not lumps, while it is cooking. As soon as the soup comes to a boil again and has become clear and slightly thickened, remove it from the stove.

Stir the pepper into the soup and serve. (Don't be shy about adding a lot of pepper; this is the ingredient that gives this famous soup its bite.)

Note: We always have extra vinegar and black pepper on the table in case somebody wants to make their own portion a little more hot or sour. This is a good thing to know about when you are dining out. An insufficiently spiced Hot and Sour Soup can often be salvaged by a do-it-yourself job with the pepper and vinegar.

腐 竹 湯

BEAN CURD SKIN SOUP *(fuzhu tang)*

Bean curd skin was a relative luxury in the Szechwanese countryside. It couldn't be produced at home, and its unusual texture lifted it out of the ordinary class of foods. Like most texture foods, bean curd skin has little flavor of its own, and was used by Mrs. Chiang's mother in delicate dishes like this soup, where its interesting resilience could best be appreciated. The soup itself is delightful, its subtle flavor and extraordinary texture accentuated by the slight piquancy of shredded ginger.

Elsewhere in China, bean curd skin plays an important role in vegetarian *haute cuisine.* Clever Buddhist monks have devised many ways to prepare it to approximate ham or chicken or shrimp. Of course it never does, but its pliancy and slightly musty taste do provide for some very intriguing dishes.

Dried bean curd skin comes in thin, shiny, brittle white sheets that have to be soaked before they can be used. They are available at Chinese markets in 8- and 16-ounce packages.

PREPARATION

4 *sheets dried bean curd skin*

3 *cups boiling water, approximately*

After you have separated the sheets of bean curd skin from one another—no easy task—break them into large pieces, roughly 4 inches square. Put them in a bowl and pour boiling water over them. The bean curd will begin to soften and turn white very quickly, but let it stand

	for 10 or 15 minutes to make sure that all of it is soft.
1-inch piece fresh ginger	Peel the ginger, then cut it into 4 thin slices.
2 scallions	Clean the scallions, then cut them, both white part and green, crosswise into little pieces, about ⅛ inch wide.
(bean curd skin)	Drain the pieces of bean curd skin and rinse them under cold running water, then cut them into narrow strips, around ⅛ inch wide.
3 egg whites	Beat the egg whites until frothy and set aside.

COOKING

1 can (10¾ ounces) chicken broth	Bring the chicken broth and water to a boil in a saucepan. Add the bean curd strips and ginger slices, and, when the soup boils again, reduce the heat, cover the pan, and let it simmer for 20 minutes.
3 cups water	
(bean curd skin)	
(ginger)	
(scallions)	Add the chopped scallions to the soup and taste it for salt; add as much as it needs.
2 teaspoons salt, or to taste	
(egg whites)	Give the egg whites another whir with beater, then pour, stirring, into the soup. (The heat of the soup cooks the egg whites immediately, and if you don't stir the soup they will coagulate and form large lumps instead of fine shreds.)
	As soon as all the egg whites are cooked, serve the soup.

冬瓜湯

WINTER MELON SOUP (*dunggua tang*)

Szechwan is famous for its melons. Watermelon, as beloved in China as it is in America, is called *xigua*, or "Western melon," in recognition of its Szechwanese origins. Mrs. Chiang's family grew melonlike squashes and squashlike melons, big ones the size of pumpkins and tiny ones the size of cucumbers. Some were stir-fried with a little meat, some were steamed, and some of the best were used in soups, lovely delicate soups with tender bits of cooked melon floating in them.

Because winter melons are an important ingredient in Cantonese *haute cuisine*, they are one of the few Szechwanese melons that can be bought here. A whole winter melon, hollowed out and filled with a light, clear soup, is the *pièce de résistance* of many a Cantonese banquet. Since winter melons rival the largest pumpkins in size, it is difficult to produce soup on this scale in a home kitchen. Fortunately, Chinese markets sell winter melon by the slice, so you can turn it into a more modest, though no less delicious, soup.

PREPARATION AND COOKING

4 *cups water*	Bring the water to a boil in a medium-sized saucepan.
1 *medium pork chop (for a yield of ¼ pound meat, approximately)*	Cut the meat and fat off the bone; discard the fat and cut the meat into ½ inch cubes. Add the meat to the boiling water. (You can also add the bones—they give the stock more body—but remember to remove them before you serve the soup.)
½-*pound slice winter melon*	Cut the rind off the melon, then cut the flesh into cubes about ¾ inch in diameter. Add these to the soup.
1 *tablespoon salt*	Add the salt to the soup, then let the soup boil gently for 25 minutes.
2 *scallions*	Clean the scallions, then cut them, both

green part and white, crosswise into pieces as fine as possible. A few minutes before you are ready to serve the soup, add the scallions to it.

1 teaspoon sesame oil

Salt, if necessary

Add the sesame oil to the soup, taste for salt, and serve.

紫菜湯

SEAWEED SOUP (*zicai tang*)

Seaweed was an expensive luxury food in Szechwan. Mrs. Chiang's mother used it mainly in mild, delicately seasoned soups that would accentuate its unusual qualities—its salty, sealike flavor and strange, slippery texture.

It is no more expensive here than any comparable imported ingredient, and its faintly pungent flavor can become addictive. Our kids like to munch on it between meals; we prefer it in this subtle, easily prepared soup.

PREPARATION

2 eggs

Beat the eggs and set them aside.

3 scallions

Clean the scallions, then chop them, both white part and green, into tiny pieces, about the size of a match head.

5 sheets seaweed (see p. 33)

Tear the sheets of seaweed into pieces roughly 2 inches square.

COOKING

3 cups water

¾ cup chicken broth, canned or fresh

Bring the water and the chicken broth to a boil in a regular saucepan.

1 to 2 teaspoons salt, approximately

(scallions)

(seaweed)

Add the salt and the chopped scallions to the boiling soup, then add the seaweed and let it boil for 15 seconds.

(eggs)	Pour in the beaten eggs, making sure, as you do, that you stir the soup vigorously so the eggs will form delicate shreds while they cook and not coagulate into a solid mass.
¼ *teaspoon freshly ground* black *pepper*	As soon as the eggs have cooked, which should be almost immediately, add the pepper and serve the soup at once.

肉圓湯

MEATBALL SOUP *(rouyuan tang)*

This hearty soup has a subtle taste, and its combination of savory little meatballs and cellophane noodles is very filling. You could easily serve it as the main course for a light supper, accompanied by some Oily Scallion Cakes (page 326) or an asparagus or cucumber salad (see pages 234 and 243). In that case, it should serve about three or four people; presented as part of a larger meal, it should satisfy six to eight.

PREPARATION

1 *package (2 ounces) cellophane noodles* 3 *cups hot water, approximately*	Put the cellophane noodles in a bowl and cover them with hot water, then set them aside to soak for 10 minutes.
4 *cups water*	Bring the water to a boil in a medium-sized saucepan.
½ *pound ground pork*	Put the ground pork in a small bowl.
2 *large scallions*	Clean the scallions; you will use all the white part and most of the green of both. Chop one of the scallions crosswise into tiny pieces, about ⅛ inch wide, and add to the meat. Cut the other scallion into ½-inch lengths and set aside.
1-inch *piece fresh ginger*	Peel the ginger, then cut it into slivers about ⅛ inch wide, about the width of a

(boiling water) matchstick. Drop half of the ginger shreds into the boiling water and chop the remainder very fine, until it reaches the consistency of coarse bread crumbs. Add this to the ground pork.

½ teaspoon salt
¼ cup cornstarch
1 egg white
2 teaspoons sesame oil
1 tablespoon soy sauce

Add the salt, cornstarch, egg white, sesame oil, and soy sauce to the meat. Beat these ingredients into the meat with a wooden spoon until the mixture is thoroughly blended.

4 ounces fresh spinach or other leafy green vegetable, like Chinese or round cabbage

Wash the spinach carefully and pull off all the tough stalks; you should have about 2 cups of uncooked spinach.

(cellophane noodles) When the cellophane noodles are soft, put them in a colander or strainer. Rinse well and drain, then cut them into 6-inch lengths.

COOKING

(cellophane noodles)
(boiling water)

Add the cellophane noodles to the boiling water.

(meat mixture) Use a wet teaspoon to shape the meat mixture into little meatballs about the size of marbles. (Wet your hands when you do this; it makes it easier to form the meatballs.) Drop the meatballs carefully into the boiling soup; there should be about 40 of them.

1 teaspoon salt Add the salt, then let the meatballs boil gently in the soup for about 4 minutes.

(spinach) Put the spinach in the soup and let it boil for 1 minute more.

½ *teaspoon sesame*
  oil
(remaining chopped
  scallions)
Salt, if necessary

Add the sesame oil and the rest of the chopped scallions and let the soup boil for another 2 minutes, then taste for salt and serve.

榨菜肉絲湯

PICKLE AND MEAT SHRED SOUP (*zhacai rousi tang*)

The pickles of Szechwan are legendary. "Every family made its own pickles, and every kitchen had three or four big earthenware jars full of them," says Mrs. Chiang. "My mother's were particularly good. She made so many that we ate preserved or salted vegetable every day for breakfast, and there were still enough left over to sell at market."

Pickles are one of the few foods Mrs. Chiang is unable to make in America, for many of the vegetables pickled in Szechwan simply aren't grown here. Fortunately, most Chinese grocery stores stock at least one kind of imported Szechwanese pickled vegetable, and since pickles take well to canning, they are reasonably authentic. The best kind is called "Szechwan preserved vegetable."

Szechwan preserved vegetable has an appealing salty-sour flavor that comes across particularly well in soups like this one, otherwise quite bland. Pork shreds add body and cellophane noodles lend their inimitable slippery texture; but it is the pickled vegetable that gives the soup its special character.

PREPARATION AND COOKING

4 *cups water*

Bring the water to a boil in a medium-sized saucepan.

1 *piece canned*
  Szechwan preserved
  vegetable about the
  size of an egg
  (2½ to 3 inches in
  diameter)

Rinse the pickle very thoroughly under cold water to wash it off all the pepper coating it. Slice the pickle into shreds about ⅛ inch wide, the width of a wooden matchstick; you should get slightly less than 1 cup of pickle shreds. Add to the boiling water.

2 *medium pork chops (for a yield of ½ pound meat, approximately)*

Cut the bones and fat away from the pork chop, then cut the lean meat into slivers approximately the same size as the pickle shreds. (It is always easier to slice meat into shreds if you first put it in the freezer for about 10 minutes, until it becomes stiff but not frozen.)

Add the shredded pork to the boiling soup, stirring as you do so that the meat shreds don't stick together. Let the soup boil vigorously over a high flame for 5 minutes, then lower the flame and let the soup simmer for another 25 minutes.

1 *package (2 ounces) dried cellophane noodles*
2 *cups boiling water*

Meanwhile, put the dried cellophane noodles in a medium-sized bowl and pour the boiling water over them. Let them soak for 5 minutes.

When the noodles are soft, drain them, then put them on a chopping block or other flat surface and cut them into segments approximately 3 inches long. Add them to the soup when it has about 15 more minutes of boiling to go.

2 *scallions*

Clean the scallions, then slice them, both white part and green, crosswise, as fine as you can.

½ *teaspoon sesame oil*

Just before you are ready to serve the soup, add the scallions and the sesame oil. Let the soup boil for a few more seconds and then serve.

黄瓜肉片湯

PORK AND CUCUMBER SOUP (*zhurou huanggua tang*)

This delicate soup derives most of its character from the contrasting colors and textures of its main ingredients—pork, cucumbers, and black mushrooms. Its mild, subtle taste is typical of the kind of soup

Mrs. Chiang's mother would serve a special guest. Yet, like most of Mrs. Chiang's soups, it is very easy to make.

PREPARATION AND COOKING

4 *cups water*	Put the water in a medium saucepan and bring to a boil over a high flame.
1 *thick or 2 thin pork chops (for a yield of ⅓ pound meat, approximately)*	Cut the fat and bones away from the pork chop, then cut the lean meat into small cubes, about ½ inch on each side. Add the cubed meat to the boiling water. After the water has come to a second boil and is boiling furiously, reduce the heat. From this point on, the soup is to cook for 45 minutes.
5 *large dried black mushrooms* 1 *cup hot water, approximately*	Put the mushrooms in a small bowl, cover them with the hot water, and let them soak for 5 minutes.
2 *cucumbers, preferably small*	Peel the cucumbers. Cut them in half lengthwise and scoop out all the seedy pulp in the middle. Chop the rest of the cucumber meat into cubes, the same size as the pork cubes. (If your cucumbers are large, you may need to use only half of the second one.)
	If there is any scum on top of the soup, remove as much of it as you can with a spoon. Then add the cubed cucumber.
(mushrooms)	Drain the mushrooms; don't worry if they are not completely soft. Cut them into ½-inch cubes as well, and add them to the soup.
1 *scallion*	Clean the scallion. Then slice it, both white part and green, crosswise into pieces about ¼ inch wide.
1 *teaspoon salt, or to taste*	When the soup has simmered for 45 minutes, and just before you are ready to

¼ *teaspoon sesame*
oil

serve it, add the chopped scallion, salt, and sesame oil. Stir the soup, then raise the heat and let it boil for a few seconds. Serve immediately.

餛 飩 湯

WON TON SOUP (*huntun tang*)

When is a soup not a soup? When it's a dish, of course. Mrs. Chiang's lusty Won Ton Soup is a dish, but it's also a soup and a magnificent one—a soup that makes all other won ton soups seem insipid. Prepare both the won tons and the soup to put them in according to the recipe on pages 318–323; for a soup course just reduce the number of won tons in each bowl.

15 - STARCHES

Like most of China, Szechwan is a rice-eating region, but it lies so near the wheat growing area of North China that many of its farmers cultivate both crops. Mrs. Chiang's father did, and in their home the staple rice was supplemented by noodles, breads, and pastries made with flour of a freshness we Americans can no longer imagine.

"Our wheat was ground nearby right after harvesting; the flour was wonderfully fresh and fragrant, and my mother made noodles and pastries so sweet I can still taste them. Some of the most famous Szechwanese recipes are for noodles, bread, and pastries. We ate them for snacks; the streets of Chengtu were full of noodle stalls and street vendors selling all kinds of sweet and savory pastries. I especially loved the little balls of glutinous rice that came in a sweet soup. When we were very small we were taken into town in a wheelbarrow to visit relatives; it was a long, bone-crunching ride, an hour and a half each way, and only the promise of some sweet pastries made it bearable.

"Noodles and pastries made good meals, too; they were the cheapest and most filling food we ate. Nothing helped fight the chill of a cold, wet winter's day as well as a steaming bowl of noodles."

The breads, noodles, and pastries of Szechwan are little known in this country; we have included a relatively large number of recipes here to give some idea of the wealth and deliciousness of this corner of Szechwan's cuisine.

The range of Szechwan noodle dishes is vast. Noodles can be made with wheat flour, rice flour, or bean flour. They can be boiled or fried, and served dry with a sauce or in a bowl of soup. They can even be eaten cold. Noodles are so adaptable that Mrs. Chiang can prepare them with almost any combination of ingredients. She makes noodle versions of almost every classic Szechwanese recipe. Many of these dishes are hot, but just as many, as well as most of her breads and pastries, are, like the Szechwanese accent, only a slight modification of the standard Pekingese. Mrs. Chiang's Pork Dumplings, or *jiaoz* (page 306) contain the same basic ingredients as Pekingese *jiaoz*, but they are more imaginatively seasoned and come with a hot and garlicky dip sauce. Nor is there anything identifiably "Szechwanese" about her Fried Noodles, or *chaomian* (page 283); they are simply delicious.

"Noodles were what my mother made when she wanted to feed a lot of people fast and cheaply," says Mrs. Chiang. "If she were really pressed and had no time to make her own, she would send one of us to the store for a few packages of dry noodles. She never made cellophane noodles or rice stick noodles; the commercial kind was fine."

Although they may not be in your neighborhood store, Chinese noodles are not hard to find in America. Most of them come dried, and Chinese markets carry a full selection. Recently, many have begun to stock fresh noodles; they come in plastic bags and freeze well. If you can find them, buy them; they are amazingly tender. In a pinch, you can always substitute a pasta. Any long, thin flat noodle like fettucine or linguine will do.

Noodle dishes and such items as Dumpling Knots and Won Tons are basically one-dish meals, the kind of filling and inexpensive dinner you would feed your family on a winter evening. Pork Dumplings, or *jiaoz*, when you make enough of them, can also be a whole meal. Many of the other pastries and breads, however, occupy special places on the menu. Mrs. Chiang always serves a steamed bread like Flower Rolls, or *huajuan*, with Fresh Ham, or *tipan*. She always makes a batch of plain pancakes, or *baobing*, to accompany a dish of Dry-Fried String Beans. She often serves a plate of noodles or fried breads as the final course of a large dinner, in keeping with the Chinese tradition of ending a formal banquet with a starch—a not-very-subtle way for the host to make sure that the guests are thoroughly satiated. Of course, most people are full before the noodle course arrives; its appearance at even the most elegant of occasions testifies to the esteem with which the lowly noodle is treated by everybody in Szechwan.

Mrs. Chiang's breads and filled pastries make superlative party foods. Most of them can be eaten with the fingers, and most of them can also be prepared ahead of time and cooked quickly or reheated just before they are to be served.

饭

RICE *(fan)*

Varied and marvelous as Mrs. Chiang's mother's breads and noodle dishes were, rice was still the family's main source of nourishment; the Chinese word for cooked rice, *fan*, is also the word for meal. Everybody eats *zaofan*, "morning rice," for breakfast, *zhongfan*, "noon rice," at lunch, and *wanfan*, "evening rice," at dinnertime. For Mrs. Chiang's family, rice *was* the meal. Except on the most special of special occasions, New Year's or weddings, every dish was meant to be eaten as an accompaniment to rice. Nobody ever ate, as Americans do in Chinese restaurants, just meat and vegetables. Nor, on the other hand, did anybody eat plain rice all by itself. There was always something to go on top of it, even if it was only a few pickles or a spicy mixture of tiny hot peppers and soy sauce.

When only the family ate together, Mrs. Chiang's mother would prepare rice in an ordinary wok:

"She cooked it until she heard the crackling sound that told her the cooked rice was beginning to stick to the pan. When there were more people, she parboiled the rice in a wok and then transferred it to a steamer that went over a big pot of water with vegetables in it. While the rice steamed and the vegetables cooked, they absorbed each other's flavors. Leftover rice was never thrown away; it was fried or reheated with a little water, or turned into *xifan*, or congee, a souplike cereal made of cooked rice and water. We often ate congee for breakfast with pickles or salted vegetables. We also loved it for snacks, especially late on hot summer nights when nobody could sleep. I always ate it when I was sick, too; congee was food for invalids, small children, and old people."

Rice comes in many shapes and sizes, but the two main types are short- and long-grained. Short-grained rice becomes moist and sticky when cooked; long-grained rice is drier and the individual grains do not stick together as much. There are also differences in taste, so subtle that even experienced gourmets find them hard to describe. Mrs. Chiang remembers the sweet taste of freshly harvested rice. Glutinous rice is a special variety reserved for sweets and pastries; its round, opaque white grains become very sticky when cooked, and it is never served as boiled rice.

Choosing long- or short-grained rice is a matter of taste; both go well with Chinese food. We prefer short-grained rice; we grew accustomed to it on Taiwan. We like its flavor and the way its soft, gluey texture absorbs the complicated sauces of Szechwanese food. Supermarkets often carry both, and Chinese markets always do. If you eat a lot of rice you may want to buy it in 10- or 25-pound sacks in Chinatown, which should also save some money.

Cooking rice used to frighten me. There seemed to be so many ways to do it and so many ways to go wrong. You could use too much water or too little, the rice could turn out too hard or too mushy, it could be undercooked or scorched or both at the same time. However you did it, it was a procedure fraught with danger. Cooking rice Mrs. Chiang's way solves every problem; it's too simple to fail. An even easier way is to use an electric rice cooker (see page 55).

PREPARATION

1 cup raw rice
2 cups water

Measure the rice out into a saucepan and rinse it under cold running water twice. By the second time the rinse water should be fairly clear. Drain the rice thoroughly, then add the 2 cups water to the rice.

COOKING

Cover the saucepan and bring it to a boil over a high flame, then turn the flame down and let the rice simmer for about 20 or 25 minutes. Don't stir the rice while it is cooking.

After you have turned off the flame, let the rice sit, covered, for about 10 minutes before you serve it. Any excess water will be absorbed.

Note: One cup of raw rice yields about 2 cups when cooked; plan your amounts accordingly. And serve the rice directly in individual rice bowls if you have them.

鶏蛋炒飯

FRIED RICE WITH EGGS *(chaofan)*

Real Chinese fried rice is such a simple dish that Mrs. Chiang often serves it instead of boiled rice during the course of a regular meal. Unlike the greasy brown concoctions that pass for fried rice in most American Chinese restaurants, real fried rice is light and delicate; just leftover rice fried together with a few scallions, a little salt, and an egg or two. Such simplicity invites variation, and a creative cook can add almost anything. On Taiwan, many of the local equivalents of short-order restaurants served nothing but dozens of different kinds of fried rice. As a variant on plain boiled rice or as a dish in itself, fried rice is a valuable addition to one's repertoire. With a filling soup or a simple plate of green vegetables, it makes a quick, cheap supper. Besides, what else can you do with leftover rice?

PREPARATION

5 *scallions*

Clean the scallions, then smash each one with the flat side of your cleaver. Slice the scallions, both white part and green, crosswise into tiny pieces, about ⅛ inch wide.

3 eggs   Beat the eggs in a small bowl.

COOKING

5 tablespoons peanut oil   Heat your wok or pan over a high flame for 15 seconds, then pour in the oil. It will be ready to cook with when the first tiny bubbles form and a few small wisps of smoke appear.

(eggs)   When the oil is ready, pour in the beaten eggs and scramble them for 30 seconds, until they are partially cooked. Quickly remove them from the pan.

4 cups cooked rice   Now add the rice to the pan. Stir-fry it for about 10 seconds, using your cooking shovel or spoon to scoop the rice off the sides of the pan and then stir it around in the middle, so every bit is exposed to the hot oil.

(scallions)
1 teaspoon salt   Return the partially cooked eggs to the pan, along with the scallions. Add the salt and stir-fry everything together for about 5 minutes, cutting the eggs into little pieces with your cooking shovel or spoon as you stir up the rice.

Serve immediately.

Note: Traditionally, there are two ways to serve fried rice, either as the starch in a multicourse meal or as a dish in itself. If the former, serve it as you would plain rice, in small bowls. If the latter, heap it on flat dinner plates rather than in bowls.

炒麵

FRIED NOODLES (*chaomian*)

We ate so much and so well on Taiwan that, in retrospect, it is hard to single out any one dish or meal as being particularly memorable. All the fabulous banquets run together into a delicious blur, and, strangely enough, what stands out the most is the simple dish of *chaomian*, or fried noodles, that we ate in a tiny hamlet on the east coast of Taiwan. We had just emerged from a hike through the uninhabited mountains of central Taiwan and had reached the village, which consisted of eight primitive houses strung out along a poorly paved road, about lunchtime. Since we had to kill several hours there before catching the bus to the nearest railroad station, we headed for the only restaurant in town. It was not very promising. It had a few mismatched wooden tables and benches, no menu, and a pig living next to the washroom. Because we have strong constitutions, we are normally fearless about strange food, but even we had qualms about the hygienic standard of the place and so we ordered what we assumed would be the safest item in the house, fried noodles. We were rewarded with one of the most memorable meals of our lives. The noodles were beautifully cooked and had reached that state of perfection for fried noodles where they were crisp but not hard. What made the dish so spectacular was the flecks of strange dark vegetables with which the noodles had been fried. Their unfamiliar smoky taste hinted at rare mountain mushrooms and wild herbs. Such is the glory of Chinese cooking that one can encounter the most sublime food in the meanest of circumstances. Generations of Chinese gourmets have known this, and have always valued such ordinary dishes as *chaomian* as highly as shark's fins.

Chaomian has been desecrated in America. The only thing less authentic than the thick gray glop irreverently called "chow mein" is the crunchy tidbits that are served with it in place of noodles. In Chinese, *chaomian* means, quite simply, "fried noodles." And that is what the dish should be. A real *chaomian* consists of a batch of parboiled noodles stir-fried in a little oil with some vegetables or meat shreds and a few basic condiments. The noodles should be fried only until some of them become crisp, the rest remaining soft. There is no sauce; the noodles absorb the flavors of the ingredients with which they are cooked.

Mrs. Chiang's version of this unpretentious classic relies on dried black mushrooms to give the noodles a smoky flavor. She also adds pork shreds, Chinese cabbage and, when she wants to make the dish more elaborate, shrimp. Actually, almost any combination of meats, seafood, and green vegetables can go into *chaomian*. Among the commonly used ingredients are spinach, liver, rape (a Chinese vegetable known as *youcai*), fresh mushrooms, squid, abalone, and Chinese sausage. The best noodles for a *chaomian* are the fresh ones sold in many Chinese markets. Alternatively, most types of long, thin, flat noodles, Western or Oriental, will produce a decent *chaomian*. I have made some successful ones with Italian fettucine.

PREPARATION

¼ *cup dried tree ears* 6 *dried black mush- rooms* 2 *cups boiling water*	Put the tree ears and dried black mushrooms in a bowl and cover them with boiling water. Set aside to soak for about 20 minutes.
1 *cup raw shrimps* 1 *teaspoon salt*	Remove the shells from the shrimps, then rinse them and devein them, if you want. If the shrimps are large, cut them into pieces about ½ inch long. Add the salt to the shrimps, mix thoroughly, and set aside.
1 *pound noodles, fresh Chinese or fettucine*	The noodles have to be precooked before they are fried; this can be done while you chop the rest of the ingredients. Bring a large pot of water to a rolling boil and add the noodles. Follow the directions on the package for the length of time needed to cook the noodles; fresh Chinese noodles take 5 or 6 minutes. (Don't let any type of noodles boil too long or they will get mushy.) The minute the noodles are done, drain them and set them aside.
1 *small head Chinese*	Pull off the tough outer leaves of the

cabbage (about 1½ pounds)

cabbage and discard them. Wash the other leaves carefully and cut them crosswise into pieces roughly 1 inch wide; you should get approximately 3 cups of shreds.

2 *lean pork chops (for a yield of ½ pound meat, approximately)*

Cut the bone and fat away from the pork chops, then slice the lean meat into shreds about 2 inches long and ¼ inch wide. (The easiest way to slice meat into thin shreds is first to put it into the freezer for about 10 minutes, until it becomes stiff but not frozen.)

3 *scallions*

Clean the scallions, then cut them, both the white part and the green, into 2-inch lengths. Slice these lengthwise into fine shreds.

2 *tablespoons soy sauce*
1 *tablespoon sesame oil*

Add the shredded scallions to the pork, along with the soy sauce and sesame oil. Mix well and set aside.

1-inch piece fresh ginger

Peel the ginger, then slice it into shreds about ⅛ inch wide, the width of a wooden matchstick.

(tree ears and mush-rooms)

Drain the tree ears and mushrooms, then rinse them well under running water. While you are rinsing the tree ears, pick them over carefully to remove any impurities, such as little pieces of wood, that may still be embedded in them. Remove the hard stems from the mushrooms and slice the mushroom heads into slivers ¼ inch wide. Keep the mushrooms separate from the tree ears.

1 *tablespoon Chinese rice wine or cooking sherry*
1 *tablespoon corn-starch*
(shrimps)

Add the wine and the cornstarch to the shrimps and mix well.

COOKING

6 tablespoons peanut oil	Heat your wok or pan over a high flame for 15 seconds, then add the oil. It will be ready to cook with when the first tiny bubbles form and a few small wisps of smoke appear.
(ginger and mushrooms)	When the oil is ready, toss in the ginger and the mushroom shreds. Stir-fry them for 30 seconds, using your cooking shovel or spoon to scoop them off the sides of the pan and then stir them around in the middle.
(meat mixture)	Add the meat mixture and stir-fry for 20 more seconds.
(tree ears)	Now add the tree ears and continue to stir-fry all the ingredients together for another 30 seconds.
(shrimps)	Keep on stir-frying while you add the shrimps. Stir-fry them for 45 seconds, then remove everything from the pan. At this point, the shrimps will only be partially cooked.
3 tablespoons peanut oil	Rinse the pan out thoroughly and dry it with paper towels. Put it back on the stove over a high flame for 15 seconds, then add the fresh oil.
(cabbage) *1 tablespoon salt*	When the oil is hot enough for cooking, put in the sliced cabbage. Stir-fry it for a few seconds, scooping the cabbage shreds off the sides of the pan and tossing them into the center. Then add the salt and continue to stir-fry for about 1 minute.
(noodles)	Now add the drained noodles. (You don't have to stir-fry something like noodles too energetically; just use your cooking

shovel or spoon to spread them around and keep them from sticking to the sides of the pan.)

(meat and shrimp mixture)

After the noodles have cooked for 2½ minutes, return the meat and shrimp mixture to the pan. Stir the ingredients up so they are all evenly distributed throughout the noodles, then let everything cook for 5 minutes more, stirring the noodles occasionally to make sure that they all get fried; longer cooking will produce crispier noodles. Serve immediately.

SERVING

This amount of fried noodles should serve four people as a main dish. The easiest way to serve it is to heap each individual portion on a regular flat dinner plate.

If these fried noodles are but one course in a multicourse meal, they will satisfy a larger number of people. Serve them on a large platter or, as Mrs. Chiang does after an elaborate feast, give each person his portion in a small bowl.

炒米粉

FRIED RICE STICK NOODLES (*chao mifen*)

"During the harvest season we always had extra hands, and my mother would cook for two or three times as many people as usual. Her solution was to fry a huge batch of noodles; they were inexpensive, filling, and very easy to make. She would use rice stick noodles, which we bought; they were one of the few things she didn't make herself."

All Chinese markets carry rice stick noodles or, as they are sometimes called in English, rice vermicelli. They are always dried and come in gaily decorated packages. Dry, they are wire thin, brittle, and opalescent. Cooked, they are stickier than regular wheat-flour noodles, crisper when fried, and have a pleasant smoky taste.

Since fried noodles are traditionally considered as an economy dish, you can, if you wish, use less meat than the recipe calls for.

PREPARATION

1 *pound dried rice stick noodles* 4 *cups boiling water, approximately*	Put the dry noodles in a large bowl and pour the boiling water over them. Let them soak for 15 minutes, then drain them and rinse them twice in cold running water.
½ *cup dried tree ears* 1 *cup boiling water*	Put the tree ears in a small bowl, cover them with boiling water, and let soak for 10 minutes. Drain and rinse them thoroughly, picking them over carefully for any impurities, such as tiny pieces of wood, that might still be embedded in them.
2 *to 3 medium pork chops (for a yield of ½ to ¾ pound meat, approximately)*	Cut the meat into wafer-thin slices, about 3 inches long and ¼ inch wide. (It is always easier to slice meat thin if you first put it into the freezer for about 10 minutes, until it becomes slightly stiff but not frozen.)
3 *tablespoons soy sauce* 1 *teaspoon cornstarch*	Add the soy sauce and cornstarch to the pork shreds and mix thoroughly.
5 *scallions*	Clean the scallions, then cut two of them, both white part and green, in half and slice lengthwise into thin shreds; add these to the meat. Chop the remaining scallions into 2-inch lengths and shred them very fine. Set these shredded scallions aside.

COOKING

6 *tablespoons peanut oil*

Heat your wok or pan over a high flame for 15 seconds, then pour in the oil. It will be ready to cook with when the first tiny bubbles form and a few small wisps of smoke appear.

(pork shreds)

When the oil is ready, add the meat mixture to the pan and stir-fry vigorously for 15 seconds, using your spoon or cooking shovel in a continuous scooping motion to toss the meat shreds around in the pan.

(tree ears)

Add the tree ears and continue to stir-fry for 1 more minute before removing all but a few tablespoons of the pork and tree ears from the pan.

(noodles and shredded scallions)
2 *teaspoons salt*
4 *teaspoons sesame oil*

Add the noodles and shredded scallions to the pan, along with the salt and sesame oil. Stir-fry the noodles, vigorously enough to keep them from sticking to the side of the pan, for 2 minutes.

(pork shreds)
1 *tablespoon soy sauce*

Return the partially cooked meat to the pan and add the soy sauce. Let the noodles cook over a fairly high heat for 10 more minutes (see note below), stirring them regularly to make sure that they don't stick to the pan too much and that all the ingredients are evenly cooked.

Note: The total cooking time for a dish of fried noodles can vary enormously, depending on one's personal tastes. The longer you cook these noodles the crisper they will become. Ten minutes will give you rather soft noodles. If you like really crunchy ones, cook them longer.

This recipe will serve four or five people as a main course, more if part of a larger meal.

妈蟻上樹

ANTS CLIMB A TREE (*mayi shang shu*)

Chinese *haute cuisine* abounds in phoenix and dragon tails; earthier peasant food uses more mundane images, like pock-marked women or, in this case, tree-climbing ants. Even Mrs. Chiang is unsure of the origin of the name for this famous Szechwanese combination of cellophane noodles and chopped meat; perhaps the noodles represent the tree and the tiny pieces of meat the ants. It is a brightly spiced and easily prepared noodle dish with a sharp, clear taste. As the main course in an informal meal, this recipe will serve four or five people, depending on the size of their appetites.

PREPARATION

4 *packages (2 ounces each) dried cellophane noodles*	Put the cellophane noodles in a large bowl and cover them with boiling water. Set them aside to soak for at least 20 minutes.
4 *cups boiling water, approximately*	
1 *pound ground pork or beef*	Put the ground pork in a bowl and add the soy sauce and sesame oil to it.
2 *tablespoons soy sauce*	
1 *tablespoon sesame oil*	
6 *scallions*	Clean the scallions, then slice them, both white part and green, crosswise as fine as you can. Add half of the chopped scallions to the pork and mix well; set the rest of the scallions aside.
6 *cloves garlic*	Peel the garlic cloves, then chop them into tiny pieces, roughly the size of a match head.

½-inch piece fresh ginger	Peel the ginger, then mince it very fine, until it reaches the consistency of coarse bread crumbs.
(cellophane noodles)	When the cellophane noodles have become nice and soft, rinse them several times under cold water and then drain well.

COOKING

5 tablespoons peanut oil	Heat your wok or pan over a high flame for 15 seconds, then pour in the oil. It will be hot enough to cook with when the first tiny bubbles form and a few small wisps of smoke appear.
(ginger and garlic) ❀ 2 tablespoons hot pepper paste	When the oil is ready, toss in the chopped ginger and garlic and the hot pepper paste. Stir-fry these ingredients together for 30 seconds, using your cooking shovel or spoon to keep everything moving around in the hot oil.
(ground meat)	Add the meat and continue to stir-fry for about 1 minute, taking particular care to break up any large chunks of meat.
¼ cup soy sauce	Now pour in the additional soy sauce and stir-fry everything for 30 seconds longer.
(cellophane noodles)	Add the cellophane noodles to the pan and cook for about 1 minute, turning them over occasionally and taking several cuts at them with your shovel or spoon while they cook so that they won't be too long to eat.
⅔ cup water (remaining scallions) 1¼ teaspoons salt, or to taste	After you have fried the noodles for about 1 minute, add the water and the rest of the scallions. Taste for salt and add as much as you need to give a rich, clear taste to the noodles, then cover the pan and let simmer over a moderate flame for 3 or 4 minutes.

| *Freshly ground* black *pepper* | Just before you are ready to serve the noodles, sprinkle some regular black pepper over them. This adds a pleasantly sharp flavor to the dish. |

紅燒牛肉麵

RED-COOKED BEEF WITH NOODLES (*hongshao niuroumian*)

"My father loved beef," recalls Mrs. Chiang. "He thought it was especially nutritious, so although it was scarce he bought it whenever he could. But it came from water buffaloes, so it was tough and had to be cooked for a long time. It had a marvelous flavor that my mother brought out by simmering it for hours in a rich, dark sauce full of hot pepper paste and Szechwan pepper. The result was a gloriously aromatic stew in which the beef was so tender it almost disintegrated."

This is a stew that begs to be combined with noodles. It is too soupy for rice, and, although it can be, and often was, diluted and served as a soup, it is so rich it needs starch as a foil. The resulting combination, beef stew with noodles, is a Szechwanese classic. Mrs. Chiang remembers eating it both as a snack and as a meal in itself.

Fortunately, water buffalo isn't essential; any regular cut of stewing beef will produce essentially the same savory stew. Like all long-simmered Chinese dishes, this can be conveniently made in advance, reheated when necessary, and even frozen. Combined with noodles, it is the kind of filling food we like to serve as the focal point of a winter evening meal or even, since you can double or triple the recipe, an informal dinner party. It is not a particularly hot or spicy dish; the hot pepper paste merely offsets the richness of the sauce.

You can make a similar beef stew by substituting beef for pork in the recipe for *hongshao rou*, or Red-Cooked Meat, on page 92. It will produce a richer, sweeter stew with a pleasant anise flavor.

PREPARATION

| 1½ pounds beef (use whatever cut you generally prefer for stew) | Cut the beef into 2-inch cubes. |

3-inch piece fresh ginger	Peel the ginger, then chop it coarsely into pieces the size of a pea.
8 cloves garlic	Smash the garlic cloves with the flat side of your cleaver, then peel, but *don't* chop.
5 scallions	Clean the scallions, then chop two of them, both the green part and white, into tiny pieces, about the size of a match head; leave the others whole.

COOKING

½ cup peanut oil	Heat your wok or pan over a moderately high flame for 15 seconds, then pour in the oil. It should be hot enough to cook with when the first tiny bubbles form and a few small wisps of smoke appear.
(garlic and ginger) ❀ *2 tablespoons hot pepper paste* *1 teaspoon Szechwan peppercorns* *(the whole scallions)* *(beef)*	When the oil is ready, throw in the garlic, chopped ginger, hot pepper paste, Szechwan peppercorns, whole scallions, and beef. Stir-fry these ingredients over a fairly high flame for 1 minute, using your cooking shovel or spoon to scoop the ingredients from the sides of the pan and then stir them around in the middle, so every piece of meat is exposed to the hot oil.
1 teaspoon granulated sugar *3 tablespoons soy sauce*	Add the sugar and soy sauce and continue stir-frying the contents of the pan for 2 more minutes.
Water	Pour in enough water to cover the meat and bring it to a boil. Then lower the flame, cover the pan, and let the meat simmer for about 1½ hours, or until it has become very soft.
1 pound noodles, fresh Chinese or fettucine	About 15 minutes before you are ready to eat, prepare the noodles according to the directions on the package.

(beef)
*1 teaspoon salt, or to
taste*
(chopped scallions)

When the beef is thoroughly cooked, taste the broth for seasoning. Then add the salt. Sprinkle the beef with the chopped scallions and serve.

SERVING

The best way to serve this dish is to put each person's portion of noodles in a soup bowl and place the beef on top of the noodles, making sure everybody gets a generous helping of the sauce.

Like any long-cooked Chinese dish, this one can be made in advance and reheated just before serving. You can also double the recipe without any serious side effects—and you can even freeze it, as you would any Western-style beef stew.

紹 子 麵

NOODLES WITH MEAT SAUCE (*shaoz mian*)

"My mother always boiled two eggs for a child's birthday," says Mrs. Chiang. "The birthday child ate the eggs and tossed the shells into the canal beside our house. As they floated downstream they carried bad luck away with them. After the eggs came a bowl of very long noodles to ensure a long life. These birthday noodles would usually be boiled and covered with a highly seasoned meat sauce; we loved food cooked this way, and my mother would often cook bean curd, eggplant, and fish the same way."

The most time-consuming part of preparing this dish is boiling the noodles. The sauce itself literally takes only 15 minutes to prepare from scratch and, with the exception of such canned and bottled condiments as sesame oil, soy sauce, and hot pepper paste, every other ingredient in the recipe comes straight off the supermarket shelf. It is the perfect dish for a family which loves the food of Szechwan.

PREPARATION

4 *cloves garlic*	Smash each garlic clove with the flat side of your cleaver, then peel. Mince the garlic as fine as you can, until it almost reaches the consistency of coarse cornmeal.
4 *scallions*	Clean the scallions, then chop them, both green part and white, into small pieces, about the size of a match head.
¾ *pound ground pork* 2 *tablespoons soy sauce* 1 *teaspoon sesame oil* ½ *teaspoon ground roasted Szechwan peppercorns (optional)*	Add 1 tablespoon of the chopped scallions to the pork, along with the soy sauce, sesame oil, and ground roasted Szechwan peppercorns. Mix thoroughly and set aside.

COOKING

1 *pound noodles, fresh Chinese or fettucine*	Prepare the noodles according to the directions on the package. While they are boiling, you should begin to cook the meat sauce. It will only take about 4 minutes to make the sauce, so begin to cook the noodles far enough ahead of time.
3½ *tablespoons peanut oil*	Heat your wok or pan over a high flame for about 15 seconds, then add the oil. It will be hot enough to cook with when the first tiny bubbles form and a few small wisps of smoke appear.
(garlic) *(1 teaspoon of the scallions)* ✿ 1 *tablespoon hot pepper paste*	When the oil is ready, quickly toss in the chopped garlic, 1 teaspoonful of the chopped scallions, and the hot pepper paste. Stir-fry for about 5 seconds, using your cooking shovel or spoon to scoop

(meat mixture)

(the remaining scallions)

3 *tablespoons soy sauce*

1 *teaspoon salt, or to taste*

the ingredients off the sides of the pan and then stir them around in the bottom, to make sure nothing sticks or burns.

Add the meat mixture to the pan and continue to stir-fry for about 1 minute. While you are stirring, try to break the meat up into small pieces.

Throw in the rest of the chopped scallions and continue to stir-fry vigorously for another 30 seconds.

Now add the soy sauce and the salt. Taste the mixture carefully before you add the salt, as the amount you will need can vary quite a bit depending on your personal taste and the saltiness of the soy sauce.

Reduce the heat and let the meat sauce simmer for 1 minute more before you serve it.

SERVING

This dish is served exactly like spaghetti and meat sauce. Each person is given a portion of noodles on his plate. The sauce is ladled out separately and everyone then has to mix the noodles and sauce together for himself.

This recipe will serve three or four people as a main dish.

排骨麵

PORK CHOP NOODLES *(paigu mian)*

"The countryside around Chengtu was full of peddlers. They hauled their wares in carts or carried them in baskets over their shoulders, and each one had his own special noisemaker to tell people he was coming. They usually sold things like buttons or cloth, but some of them sold candy, and we children would wait in the dusty lane in front of the house for the sound of his wooden clacker. In the city, all the vendors sold food; you could get steamed and fried pastries and all kinds of noodles in Chengtu."

Even in Taipei, almost every street corner had its own noodle stand, usually a wooden cart containing several huge vats from which the proprietor would, for a few cents, ladle out a large bowlful of steaming noodles.

This simple noodle recipe produces exactly the kind of dish such a vendor would sell. It consists of a serving of plain boiled noodles in a delicately flavored broth, topped off by a crisp and savory deep-fried pork chop. It sounds like an odd combination, but the crisp and subtly spiced meat and soft noodles complement each other beautifully. This is a good dish for a family supper; it's filling, easy to prepare, and cheap. This recipe serves four.

PREPARATION

4 very thin pork chops (even with bones, they shouldn't weigh more than 1 pound)

Cut off most of the fat from the pork chops, but not the bones. Score the meat lightly on both sides in a tiny diamond pattern with the grids ½ inch apart. Then use the back of your cleaver (not the side) or some other heavy utensil to pound the meat as you would pound and flatten veal scallops. Do this on both sides so that the meat gets really thin. Then put the pork chops on a large platter.

6 scallions

Clean the scallions, then smash 4 of them with the flat side of your cleaver. Cut the scallions, both green part and white, into 2-inch lengths. Sprinkle them over the meat. Slice the remaining scallions crosswise into pieces ¼ inch wide; set these aside.

1-inch piece fresh
  ginger

Peel the ginger, then cut it into thin slivers, about ⅛ inch wide, the width of a wooden matchstick. Add to the meat.

3 tablespoons soy
  sauce
1 teaspoon sesame oil
1 teaspoon granu-
  lated sugar

Sprinkle the soy sauce, sesame oil, and sugar over the pork chops. Turn the chops around in the marinade so the meat is well covered with it, then set aside for 10 minutes.

COOKING

1 pound noodles,
  fresh Chinese or
  fettucine

Bring a large pot of water to a full, rolling boil. Add the noodles and cook them according to the directions on the package, probably 5 to 10 minutes, until they are done.

While the noodles are cooking, get out 4 large bowls for serving them in (ordinary soup bowls probably won't be big enough) and prepare the sauce for the noodles.

(chopped scallions)

Put equal amounts of the chopped scallions into the bottom of each bowl.

½ teaspoon salt, per
  serving
2 teaspoons soy sauce,
  per serving
¼ teaspoon sesame
  oil, per serving

Then put ½ teaspoon salt, 2 teaspoons soy sauce and ¼ teaspoon sesame oil in the bottom of each bowl.

⅓ cup chicken broth,
  fresh or canned, per
  serving
⅔ cup boiling water,
  per serving

Pour ⅓ cup of chicken broth and ⅔ cup of water into each bowl.

(noodles)
1 cup peanut or other
  cooking oil

As soon as the noodles are cooked, drain them and put an equal portion of them in each bowl.

Meanwhile, heat your wok or the pan you normally do your deep-fat frying in over a high flame for 15 seconds. Pour in the oil.

½ cup cornstarch
(pork chops)

While you are waiting for the oil to heat up, a process that will take several minutes at least, pour the cornstarch onto a flat plate. Remove the pieces of scallion and ginger from the pork chops and dip each one into the cornstarch. Make sure that both sides of each pork chop are thoroughly coated with cornstarch; press it in with your hands, if necessary.

When the oil in the pan is hot enough for cooking—when it is smoking lightly—put in the pork chops. They are so thin that they will cook very quickly, so turn them over after just 30 seconds. Fry them for about 1 minute on the second side and then turn them back on the first for a final 15 to 30 seconds. They are done when both sides are a deep golden brown.

Drain the fried pork chops on paper towels for a few seconds and then place each pork chop on top of a bowl of noodles.

Note: Make sure that each person mixes his sauce and noodles together thoroughly before eating.

担担麵

DON DON NOODLES (COLD NOODLES WITH SESAME SAUCE) (dandan mian)

This is the most famous street food of Szechwan. Its name echoes the hollow, clunky sound of the two sticks hit together by the itinerant vendors who hawked it through the streets. They sold a portion of cold, cooked noodles over which they would ladle out each ingredient of the sauce separately—sesame paste, soy sauce, hot peppers, scallions, raw garlic, and ginger. The buyer mixed the noodles and condiments together himself. Nothing could have been simpler, cheaper, or more delicious. Though the most common of street foods, *dandan mian* is a renowned specialty of Szechwan; it is the noodle version of the classic Szechwanese combination of a cold main ingredient with a peppery hot, sesame paste-based sauce. Kidneys, chicken, and eggplant, among other things, are served with this sauce. Noodles, the cheapest of all foods, allows every man to be a gourmet. Such is the glory of the food of Szechwan.

Note that this is an assembled dish; each portion is put together separately. The sauce materials are enough for about four portions.

PREPARATION

12 cloves garlic	Smash the garlic cloves with the flat side of your cleaver, then peel. Chop the garlic coarsely into pieces about the size of a pea.
3-inch piece fresh ginger	Peel the ginger, then chop it into small pieces, about the size of a match head.
¾ teaspoon salt	Put the garlic and ginger into a small steep-sided bowl or mortar. Add the salt and then, using the handle of your cleaver, a wooden spoon, or a pestle, mash everything together until it turns into a coarse paste. The salt helps the pulverization along, as well as bringing out the flavor of the garlic and ginger.
5 tablespoons water	Add the water to the mashed garlic and ginger and stir well, so the water and the juice of the mashed ingredients are thoroughly combined.
6 scallions	Clean the scallions, then chop them, both green part and white, very fine, until they reach the consistency of farina; you should have about 1 tablespoon of chopped scallions for every individual serving of noodles.

COOKING

1 *pound noodles,*
fresh Chinese or
fettucine

Bring a large pot of water to a rapid, rolling boil and cook the noodles according to the directions that are on the package; fresh Chinese noodles take from 5 to 10 minutes. (Test them as they cook to make sure they don't overcook and become mushy.)

Drain the noodles, rinse them in cold water, and then drain them again.

SERVING

1 *tablespoon garlic-*
ginger-water
mixture, per serving
1 *tablespoon chopped*
scallions, per
serving
❀2 *teaspoons hot*
pepper flakes in oil,
per serving
⅛ *teaspoon ground*
roasted Szechwan
peppercorns, per
serving
4 *teaspoons sesame*
paste, per serving
2 *tablespoons soy*
sauce, per serving
½ *teaspoon*
granulated sugar,
per serving

Put each individual serving of noodles on a separate plate or bowl. Then add the following ingredients to each: the garlic-ginger-water mixture, chopped scallions, hot pepper flakes in oil, ground roasted Szechwan peppercorns, sesame paste, soy sauce, and sugar.

Note: Before eating, each diner should mix his sauce ingredients and noodles together very well.

面 疙 瘩

DUMPLING KNOTS (*mian geda*)

This is a dish few Westerners have heard of, much less tasted. Even in China it is never served in restaurants, nor discussed by gourmets. It is a dish eaten by the poorest peasants. In *Fanshen*, his description of life in a northern China village during the Communist revolution, William Hinton says that *geda*, a watery dumpling stew, was the staple food of the villagers.

In Szechwan, a much richer part of the country, *geda* was eaten only by those peasants who were too poor to buy rice. It was the least expensive and most filling food available, a meatless combination of plain flour dumplings and cabbage, the cheapest of vegetables. Although Mrs. Chiang's family could afford to eat rice at every meal, they loved *mian geda*, especially when the dumplings were made with the fragrant flour from the family's own freshly harvested wheat.

Mrs. Chiang's version of this plain peasant dish is comparatively elaborate; it is deftly seasoned and contains sliced pork and tree ears. The pork gives it a richer flavor and the tree ears add a pleasantly crunchy texture. Still, it remains a simple, hearty dumpling stew. The dumplings, which are just like my mother-in-law's Central European spaetzle, and the pronounced flavor of the cabbage give this dish a familiar, almost Western, taste. Mrs. Chiang serves *mian geda* accompanied by a separate bowl of hot pepper flakes in oil so it can be transformed into a properly Szechwanese stew at the table. Each person takes as much of the hot sauce as he wants and stirs it into his own portion of dumplings.

In addition to being cheap, no small virtue in these inflationary times, a *mian geda* is easy to make and can be prepared in advance. The only tricky part of its preparation is the making of the dumplings. If you concentrate on getting them small, you should not have any trouble. This is a great dish for an informal family supper. Our children love it.

PREPARATION

1 *small head cabbage, or ½ large head*

Slice the cabbage into rather coarse shreds, about 1 inch wide.

2 *medium pork chops (for a yield of ½ pound meat, approximately)*

Cut all the bone and fat away from the pork chops, then slice the lean meat as thin as you can, cutting across the grain of the meat; you should get wafer-thin slices of meat about 3 inches long and ½ inch wide. (It is always easier to cut meat into very thin slices if you first put it in the freezer for about 10 minutes, until it is slightly stiff but not frozen.)

¼ *cup dried tree ears*
1 *cup boiling water*

Put the tree ears in a small bowl and pour the boiling water over them. Let them soak for at least 10 minutes. When they have become soft and slightly gelatinous, rinse them off and pick them over carefully to remove any impurities, such as little pieces of wood, that may still be embedded in them.

5 *scallions*

Clean the scallions, then chop them, both the white part and about a third of the green, rather coarsely into pieces about ¼ inch long.

2 *cups all-purpose flour*
¼ *teaspoon salt*
¾ *cup water*

Mix the flour, salt, and water together until the dough is well blended and rather sticky; try to get rid of all the lumps.

COOKING

3 *tablespoons peanut oil*

For this recipe, use a wok or a large pot. Heat the pan over a moderately high flame for 15 or 20 seconds, then add the oil. It will be hot enough to cook with when the first tiny bubbles form and a few small wisps of smoke appear.

(pork slices)
*3 tablespoons soy
sauce*

When the oil is ready, quickly put in the pork slices and the soy sauce. Stir-fry the pork and soy sauce together for about 1 minute, using your cooking shovel or spoon to scoop the pork slices from the sides of the pan and then stir them around in the middle, so every piece is exposed to the hot oil.

(cabbage shreds)

Add the cabbage shreds and continue to stir-fry for about 5 more minutes, using a scooping motion to toss the contents of the pan around so all the cabbage is thoroughly cooked. Start gently, so too much of the cabbage doesn't spill out, then, as the cabbage cooks and reduces in bulk, you can revert to the usual technique of scooping the ingredients into the center and stirring them around there.

*8 cups water,
approximately*

When the cabbage is fairly well cooked and rather limp, pour about 8 cups of water into the pan—or however much is needed to cover the cabbage mixture completely. Wait until the liquid is boiling, then reduce the heat, cover the pan, and let it simmer.

(scallions)
(tree ears)
*1 cup water,
approximately (if
needed)*

After the cabbage has simmered for about 30 minutes, remove the cover and add the scallions and tree ears and enough additional water to cover the mixture, if needed.

When the water is boiling again, you are ready to add the dumplings. Because of the stickiness of the dough, this is a slightly tricky maneuver. The appearance of the finished product is quite unimportant, so don't worry if your dumplings assume weird shapes. You should try to make them all approximately the

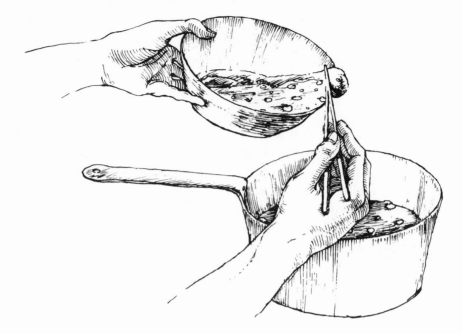

Forming dumpling knots

same size, remembering that they are smaller than American dumplings and should not be more than about 2 inches long. (If you have ever made Central European spaetzle, you have already mastered the technique, which is identical.)

(dough) Take about a teaspoonful of batter in a large spoon and scrape it off into the boiling liquid with another spoon. (It is somewhat easier if both spoons are kept wet by dipping them into the soup before you form each dumpling.) Distribute the dumplings evenly throughout the boiling liquid, but don't stir them for about 2 minutes, or they might fall apart. (There are many other ways of getting the batter into the soup. Mrs. Chiang

picks up a strip of dough between two chopsticks, which she then plunges directly into the boiling liquid and shakes around until the dumpling falls off. It is fun to practice this technique, but its mastery is not essential for the success of the dish.)

1 tablespoon sesame oil

1 tablespoon salt, approximately

¼ teaspoon ground roasted Szechwan peppercorns

After all the batter has been used up, add the sesame oil, salt, and ground roasted Szechwan peppercorns. Taste the mixture after you have added the salt, and add more if it seems necessary.

Regulate the flame so the liquid is boiling steadily but not violently, and let the dumplings cook for at least 10 minutes.

SERVING

❋ *hot pepper flakes in oil*

The traditional method of serving Dumpling Knots is to give each person his own individual portion in a large soup bowl and let him take as much of the hot pepper flakes in oil as he wants and stir it into his dumplings. We think that 1 teaspoonful in a bowl of soup is about right.

The dish can be made several hours in advance and reheated just before you are ready to eat it.

餃 子

PORK DUMPLINGS (*jiaoz*)

Americans know these delicious little meat-filled pastries by so many different titles that we hesitated before giving this recipe an English name. "Peking ravioli," "wraplings," and "crescents" are but a few of the terms restaurateurs and cookbook authors use for these ubiquitous dumplings. *Jiaoz* in Chinese means, quite literally, a "three-cornered, meat filled dumpling," but even in China a *jiaoz* can go by many names, depending on whether it is deep-fried, pan-fried, steamed, or boiled.

Although *jiaoz* are made and eaten all over China, they are traditionally associated with the northern part of the country, where wheat rather than rice is the staple. On Taiwan the best of the classically prepared *jiaoz* were made by people from Shantung, the coastal province that juts out like a thumb into the Yellow Sea somewhat to the south of Peking. Generally the texture of the skins and the composition of the fillings vary according to the prevailing taste of different provinces. Szechwanese chauvinists that we are, we feel that Szechwanese *jiaoz* are the best. They are not too different from the standard Pekingese type, except that they taste better. They are more fragrant and more definitively seasoned. And, while Northerners accompany their dumplings with a sauce composed of soy sauce and vinegar, the natives of Szechwan favor a more potent mixture containing raw garlic and hot red pepper. In any case, in comparison to Mrs. Chiang's, all other *jiaoz* taste bland and uninteresting.

Jiaoz occupy a special place in the cuisine of China. They are eaten both at and between meals. There was a row of open-stall restaurants near the center of Taipei that served nothing but *jiaoz* twenty-four hours a day. They were a temptation we rarely resisted, especially late at night on our way home from an evening on the town. We also ate *jiaoz* for dinner. A mammoth plateful of them accompanied by a bowl of spicy dip sauce was a feast for the whole family. The children competed among themselves to see who could eat the most dumplings; the adults stuffed themselves without counting.

Of course, it takes the better part of an afternoon to make enough of these dumplings to feed a large and hungry gathering, especially for a novice. Mrs. Chiang can roll out a *jiaoz* skin, fill it and pinch it together into a perfect crescent with the speed and dexterity only years of experience can produce. It takes me twice as long and my dumplings are lopsided, but they are fun to make. Children particularly love to wrap their own *jiaoz*.

Some Oriental food stores carry ready-made skins, often called *gyosa* or *choutz* skins. Using them will save you an enormous amount of work. This is the kind of short cut that even experienced Chinese cooks take. Although commercial *jiaoz* skins may not be as fresh as home-made ones, they are perfectly authentic.

Although *jiaoz* can be made in advance and even frozen, handling them requires a few precautions. Uncooked *jiaoz* have the unfortunate habit of sticking to each other and to everything else as well. This is because the moisture from the filling inevitably seeps into the skins and makes the dough sticky. Place the *jiaoz* on a floured surface after you have filled them, don't let them touch each other, and never, never try to keep them nice and moist with a damp towel. If you are planning to freeze them, put them in the freezer on an open plate until they become quite hard, then put them in an airtight container or plastic bag. Don't thaw them before cooking; you can cook them in the same way you cook unfrozen *jiaoz*.

In the following recipes, we give two different fillings for *jiaoz*, one that is mainly pork and a lighter one containing both pork and vegetables. They should each yield about 75 or 80 dumplings. Since a hungry adult will usually eat from 12 to 15 at a sitting, you can plan your guest list accordingly.

PREPARATION

15 scallions	Clean the scallions, then chop them, both white part and green, into tiny pieces, about the size of a match head. (Mrs. Chiang finds it easier to chop so many scallions if she first smashes each one with the side of the cleaver.)
½-inch piece fresh ginger	Peel the ginger, then mince it fine, until it reaches the consistency of coarse bread crumbs.
1 pound ground pork *¼ cup soy sauce* *1½ tablespoons sesame oil* *½ teaspoon ground roasted Szechwan peppercorns* *1 egg*	Put the pork in a mixing bowl and add the chopped ginger and scallions to it, along with the soy sauce, sesame oil, ground roasted Szechwan peppercorns, egg, and salt. Combine very thoroughly, then set the pork mixture aside until the *jiaoz* skins are ready to be filled.

1½ teaspoons salt

3 cups all-purpose flour

¾ cup water

Mix the flour and the water together. (You will probably have to use your hands to work this dough because it is a very stiff one.) The dough should be quite hard and dry and definitely not sticky.

Before you actually begin to roll out the *jiaoz* skins, prepare a platter or tray to hold the *jiaoz* until they are cooked. Flour it heavily or cover it with waxed paper, because filled *jiaoz* have a tendency to stick to an ordinary dry surface.

Knead the dough for 2 minutes on a clean dry surface until it becomes elastic, then divide into 4 roughly equal parts. Take one of the pieces and roll it out into a long snake about 16 inches long and ¾ inch in diameter. Cut the snake into about 20 pieces, each one about the size of the bubblegum balls that come from penny candy machines.

Prepare a floured surface for rolling out the *jiaoz* skins. Then take one of the little dough balls and roll it out with a rolling pin until it is a flat circle about 3 inches in diameter. (Mrs. Chiang rolls out and fills about 5 skins at a time, rather than monotonously rolling all of them out at once.)

(meat mixture)

Take about 1½ teaspoons of the meat mixture and put it in the middle of a *jiaoz* skin. Fold the dough over the filling and then use your fingers to make 4 or 5 little pleats on one side of the *jiaoz* skin. As you make each pleat, pinch it together with the dough on the other side of the *jiaoz* skin. The finished product should be a little crescent-shaped pouch of **dough.**

Place each *jiaoz* on a floured surface as you finish it, and be sure the dumplings don't touch each other.

COOKING

Bring a very large pot of water to a full, rolling boil. Gently put about 15 or 20 *jiaoz* into the pot and wait for the water to boil again. (Don't try to cook all the *jiaoz* together at one time; 20 is about all that even the largest pot can hold.)

When the water is boiling heavily again, pour in enough cold water to stop the boiling. Let the *jiaoz* come to a boil again and repeat this step twice more. After the *jiaoz* have come to a boil for the fourth time, remove them from the pot. Drain them well in a strainer or colander and then serve.

SERVING

Jiaoz can be eaten in many ways. I am a purist of sorts and usually eat mine plain. John prefers to dip his into a sauce. The easiest to make is a simple mixture of equal parts of soy sauce and rice wine vinegar.

Mrs. Chiang creates a more potent Szechwanese version, peppery hot and permeated with raw garlic.

Filling and shaping a pork dumpling

DIP SAUCE

4 *cloves garlic*

¼ *teaspoon salt*

Smash the garlic cloves with the flat side of your cleaver, then peel. Put them in a small, steep-sided bowl or mortar with the salt; then, using the wooden handle

1 teaspoon rice wine
  vinegar
❀ 1 teaspoon hot
  pepper flakes in oil
¼ teaspoon sesame
  oil
3 tablespoons soy
  sauce

of your cleaver or a wooden spoon or pestle, mash the garlic and salt together into a thick paste.

Add the vinegar, hot pepper flakes in oil, sesame oil, and soy sauce to the garlic paste. Stir the resulting sauce well, then pour it into small bowls or saucers for everybody to dip their *jiaoz* into.

餃 子

DUMPLINGS WITH VEGETABLE AND MEAT FILLING (*jiaoz*)

PREPARATION

1 medium head
  Chinese cabbage
1 teaspoon salt

Separate the leaves of the cabbage and rinse them well, then chop them into little pieces, about the size of grains of uncooked rice; you should get about 2 cups of chopped cabbage. Put the cabbage in a bowl, sprinkle the salt over it, and stir well. Let sit for 15 to 30 minutes.

4 scallions

Clean the scallions, then cut them, both white part and green, crosswise as fine as you can.

1-inch piece fresh
  ginger
¾ pound ground
  pork, the fattier the
  better
(scallions and ginger)
¼ cup soy sauce
1½ tablespoons
  sesame oil
1½ teaspoons salt

Peel the ginger, then chop it into tiny pieces, about the size of a match head.

Put the ground pork in a bowl and add the chopped scallions and ginger, then the soy sauce, sesame oil, and salt.

(cabbage)	Using your hands, squeeze the excess moisture out of the cabbage; add it to the meat.
2 *tablespoons peanut oil*	Heat the peanut oil in a small saucepan over a moderately high flame. When the oil starts to smoke, add it to the meat mixture and mix very thoroughly.
	You are now ready to stuff and cook your *jiaoz*. Follow the directions for making the *jiaoz* skins and cooking the stuffed *jiaoz* in the preceding recipe.

VARIATION

1 *pound string beans, or 1 small head regular round cabbage, or 1 pound fresh spinach*	Chinese cabbage, though the most commonly used vegetable for stuffing *jiaoz*, is not the only one. String beans, regular cabbage, or spinach can also be used.
	If you use string beans, you must parboil them first for about 7 minutes before you chop them up. You do not, however, have to salt them and let them sit after you chop them, but can add them directly to the meat mixture.
	If you use regular cabbage, follow the directions for Chinese cabbage in the recipe.
	Spinach does not need to be salted and set aside. Just chop it and add it to the meat.

春捲

SPRING ROLLS (*chunjuan*)

What a travesty most American egg rolls are! They have the drab, sour taste of overcooked celery; any other ingredients are anonymous, flavorless, and mushy. Authentic Chinese spring rolls like Mrs.

Filling and rolling a spring roll

Chiang's, with their crisp skins and savory filling, seem like a completely different order of food.

Most spring rolls made in America are wrapped in skins made from a relatively heavy egg noodle dough; the Chinese variety uses real spring roll skins, delicate, paper-thin pancakes. Chinese spring roll wrappers are made from the skin that forms when a ball of dough is touched to a hot pan. When they are filled and deep-fried, they become crisp and shiny. Because making spring roll skins is such a delicate business, most Chinese cooks, including Mrs. Chiang, prefer to buy them. This presents a problem for although genuine spring roll skins, sometimes called "Shanghai spring roll skins," are produced commercially in America, they are not always available even in Chinese markets. They usually come in plastic bags containing about 30 skins. Since they are so hard to find, we usually buy several bags at a time; they freeze well. If all else fails, use egg roll skins; they are much easier to find.

The filling is equally important. Mrs. Chiang's spring roll filling includes roughly equal amounts of shredded pork, eggs, and cabbage, with some tree ears thrown in for contrast. It resembles that all-American Chinese favorite, Moo Shu Pork, although, since it is Szechwanese rather than Pekingese, it is richer and more fragrant.

If you can't locate the right kind of spring roll skins, make the filling separately and serve it as if it were Moo Shu Pork with some Pancakes, or *baobing*. But don't give up the search for the skins; this recipe makes the best spring rolls in the world. Eaten in the Szechwanese fashion, with a dip sauce redolent with raw garlic and hot peppers, they are a gourmet's delight.

Because it involves so many separate steps, making spring rolls is a time-consuming, though not very difficult, process. Although spring rolls lose their crispness if they are not eaten immediately after they are fried, all the other steps in their preparation can be taken ahead of time. It is not, however, advisable to freeze them; the cabbage in the filling gets limp.

Spring rolls are snacks in China; they are rarely included in a regular meal, except as the final starchy course in a large banquet. And they are marvelous party food, since the final stage of frying them is easy and they can be eaten with the fingers. This recipe will produce about 15 or 16 spring rolls.

PREPARATION (FILLING)

¼ *cup dried tree ears* 1 *cup boiling water*	Put the dried tree ears in a small bowl and pour the boiling water over them. Let them soak for at least 15 minutes.
4 *medium pork chops (for a yield of 1 pound meat, approximately)*	Cut the bones and fat away from the pork chops, then slice the lean meat into very thin slivers, about 2 inches long and ⅛ inch wide, the size and shape of a wooden matchstick. (It is always easier to slice meat into very thin shreds if you first put it into the freezer for about 10 minutes, until it becomes slightly stiff but not frozen.) Put the pork in a bowl.
8 *scallions*	Clean the scallions, then cut them, both the white part and most of the green,

into 2-inch lengths. Slice these lengthwise into shreds, about the same width
as the pork shreds.

2 *tablespoons soy
  sauce*
1 *teaspoon sesame oil*
1 *tablespoon corn-
  starch*

Add one-third of the scallions to the pork,
along with the soy sauce, sesame oil,
and cornstarch. Mix thoroughly and set
aside.

¼ *head cabbage (for
  a yield of 2 cups
  shreds, approxi-
  mately)*

Cut the cabbage into very fine shreds, approximately the same size as the meat
shreds.

(tree ears)

Drain the tree ears and rinse them under
cold water, carefully picking them over
to make sure they don't contain any
impurities, such as little pieces of wood,
that might still be embedded in them.
Chop the tree ears into shreds the same
size as all the other shreds.

3 *eggs*

Beat the eggs in a small bowl.

COOKING (FILLING)

1 *teaspoon peanut oil*

Heat a regular flat frying pan over a moderate flame and pour in the peanut oil.

(eggs)

When the oil is hot, pour in the beaten
eggs. Let them cook, without stirring,
until they are almost firm, then turn
them over and cook for about 10 seconds on the other side. (You don't have
to be fastidious about turning the eggs
over, since you are going to chop the
omelet into shreds as soon as it is
cooked.)

Remove the omelet from the frying pan to
the chopping block and slice it into
shreds just like the meat and cabbage.

¼ cup peanut oil	Now heat the pan you usually use for Chinese cooking over a high flame for about 15 seconds, then add the oil. It will be ready to cook with when the first tiny bubbles form and a few small wisps of smoke appear.
(meat mixture)	When the oil is ready, add the meat shreds. Stir-fry them for 10 seconds, using your cooking shovel or spoon to scoop the pork shreds off the sides of the pan and then stir them around in the middle. Remove the meat from the pan after about 10 seconds of frying, even though it will still be pink.
(cabbage) *(tree ears and remaining scallions)*	Now add the shredded cabbage to the pan and stir-fry for 15 seconds before adding the shredded tree ears and the rest of the scallions. Cook these vegetables together for another minute, stirring occasionally to make sure that all of the cabbage gets cooked.
(meat shreds) *(egg shreds)*	Return the meat shreds to the pan and stir-fry for about 15 seconds. Then add the egg shreds and cook everything together for 1 minute more, stirring several times.
1 teaspoon salt *1 tablespoon soy sauce* *½ teaspoon ground roasted Szechwan peppercorns* *½ teaspoon sesame oil*	Finally add the salt, soy sauce, ground roasted Szechwan peppercorns, and sesame oil. Stir-fry the mixture for 1 more minute, then remove it from the pan. Let it cool for a few minutes before you try to stuff the spring roll skins with it.

PREPARATION (SPRING ROLLS)

1 egg
15 or 16 spring roll
skins
(meat, cabbage and
egg mixture)

Beat the egg. Separate the spring roll skins and lay one of them on a flat surface. Take about 2½ tablespoons of the cooked meat mixture and put it at one end of the spring roll skin. Roll it up as tightly as you can, folding the sides over to make sure the filling doesn't spill out. Paint the top edge of the spring roll skin with the beaten egg and seal shut. A perfectly rolled spring roll bears a strong resemblance to a blintz.

Before you begin to fry the spring rolls, prepare the dip sauce (see below) for serving with them. (This sauce is quite hot and permeated by the powerful taste of raw garlic, so be forewarned.)

COOKING (SPRING ROLLS)

2 cups peanut or any
other cooking oil,
approximately

You can use either a wok or a regular frying pan for frying spring rolls. (A wok will require about 2 cups of oil; a flat frying pan, about 2 inches' worth.) Pour the oil into the pan and heat it over a moderate flame; there is so much oil in the pan that it will take quite a while for it to get hot enough to cook with.

You will probably have to fry the spring rolls in several batches because a wok can efficiently fry only about 7 or 8 at one time. When the oil is hot (test it by frying a trial roll), put a batch of 7 or 8 spring rolls into the pan. Turn them occasionally while they are frying to make sure that every side is cooked.

After the spring rolls have cooked for about

3 or 4 minutes and have turned a rich golden brown, remove them from the pan. Drain them on some paper toweling for a few seconds and then serve, along with the peppery hot garlic sauce (see below).

DIP SAUCE

4 *cloves garlic*
¼ *teaspoon salt*

Smash the garlic cloves with the flat side of your cleaver; then peel. Put the garlic in a small, steep-sided bowl or mortar with the salt; then, using the wooden handle of your cleaver, or a wooden spoon or pestle, mash the garlic and salt together into a thick paste.

1 *teaspoon rice wine vinegar*
❀ 1 *teaspoon hot pepper flakes in oil*
¼ *teaspoon sesame oil*
3 *tablespoons soy sauce*

Now add the vinegar, hot pepper flakes in oil, sesame oil, and soy sauce to the garlic paste. Stir the resulting sauce well, then pour it into individual small bowls.

Note: One warning: Freshly cooked spring rolls are burning hot; be careful when you first bite into one.

餛 飩

WON TONS (*huntun*)

Szechwanese Won Ton Soup bears no resemblance to the pallid affair found in Chinese-American restaurants. Mrs. Chiang remembers that "at home it was a whole meal. On dark winter evenings, when I was cold and tired from playing too long in the snow, I loved coming home to a big bowlful of steaming broth filled with won tons. My mother stuffed her won tons with a highly seasoned mixture of ground pork, preserved vegetables, and dried shrimp. The same ingredients went into the soup, as well as a colorful helping of spinach and scallions."

About fifteen of these little noodle pouches in a large soup bowl makes a hearty supper. A smaller portion can be served as a regular soup. And plain won tons, fried in deep fat, make a delightfully crunchy appetizer or snack. They freeze well, too.

Ready-made won ton skins are usually available in Chinese grocery stores. They vary greatly in quality, the thinner and fresher the better, but one rarely has many options.

PREPARATION

⅓ *cup dried shrimps*
1 *cup hot water, approximately*

Put the shrimps into a small bowl and cover them with hot water, then set aside to soak for at least 30 minutes.

3 *pork chop bones (optional)*
4 *cups water (optional)*
¼ *teaspoon salt, approximately (optional)*

This step is optional; it is the preparation of the broth in which the cooked won tons are finally served. You may easily— and Mrs. Chiang usually does—substitute any delicately flavored clear soup, such as canned chicken broth, for a homemade stock. If you do want to make your own, simply boil the pork bones, or any other suitable soup bones, in about a quart of water for about 30 minutes. Skim off the fat, remove the bones, and add a little salt to taste.

2 *ounces fresh spinach, approximately*

Count out about 6 large leaves of spinach for each individual serving of won tons. Wash the spinach carefully and break off the tough stalks.

1 *piece Szechwan preserved vegetable, roughly the size of a Ping-Pong ball*

Rinse the Szechwan preserved vegetable very carefully under cold running water to wash off all the spices and red pepper in which it was preserved. Then slice it into shreds ⅛ inch wide, about the width of a wooden matchstick; you should get about ¼ cup of shredded vegetable.

Measure out about 1 tablespoon of the shreds and put the rest aside. Chop the tablespoon of preserved vegetable very fine, until it reaches the consistency of coarse bread crumbs.

Scant ½ pound ground pork
(chopped preserved vegetable)

Put the ground pork in a small bowl and add the chopped preserved vegetable to it.

½-inch piece fresh ginger

Peel the ginger, then chop it until it, too, reaches the consistency of coarse bread crumbs. Add the chopped ginger to the pork.

(dried shrimps)

Remove and drain 10 of the dried shrimps, then chop them very fine, until they reach the same consistency as the ginger and preserved vegetable. Add them to the pork. Let the rest of the shrimps continue to soak.

3 scallions

Clean the scallions, then chop one of them, both the white part and about half of the green, into tiny pieces, about the size of a match head. Add to the ground pork. Slice the remaining scallions, both the white part and *most* of the green, crosswise as fine as possible; set aside.

½ teaspoon ground roasted Szechwan peppercorns
¼ teaspoon salt
1½ teaspoons cornstarch
1 tablespoon soy sauce
1 teaspoon sesame oil
1 egg white

Add the ground roasted Szechwan peppercorns, salt, cornstarch, soy sauce, sesame oil and egg white to the pork. Mix well.

1 egg

Crack the egg into another small bowl. Beat it and set it aside.

You are now ready to begin wrapping the won tons.

WRAPPING

1 package ready-made won ton skins
(beaten egg)

Place about ¾ teaspoon of the meat mixture in the corner of one of the won ton skins. Roll the won ton skin diagonally over the filling until you reach the center of the skin. Then take up the two rolled ends of the skin and twist them around until they cross each other on top of the filled part of the won ton. Moisten the place where the two ends meet with a little of the beaten egg and pinch the ends together.

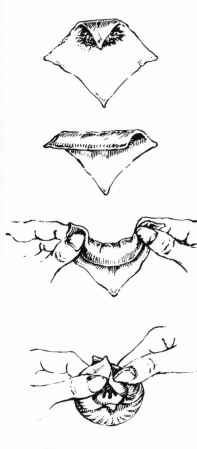

(There is another method of filling won tons that is easier to master, though less classical in form. Put the meat mixture squarely in the center of the won ton skin and gather up all the edges to form a little pouch. Pinch the won ton skin very tightly together at the top of the pouch.)

You should end up with about 50 won tons; they are now ready to be cooked. (At this point, they can keep for several days in the refrigerator. They can also be frozen. The only problem is that the won ton skins are very delicate, and I have never managed to store any filled won tons without having their brittle edges break off.)

Wrapping a won ton

COOKING

(won tons)

Bring a large pot of water to a rapid boil.

Don't try to cook too many won tons at one time; drop about 20 gently into the pot. Wait a few seconds, then use a slotted spoon or Chinese strainer to stir them very gently, in order to loosen any that have stuck to the bottom of the pot.

½ to 1 cup cold water, approximately

When the water boils again and the won tons have risen to the top of the pot, let them boil for 2 or 3 minutes, then pour in enough cold water to stop the boiling. Wait until the water comes to a second boil and let the won tons cook for 2 minutes longer.

Remove the won tons gently with a slotted spoon or strainer. Drain them slightly, then place them in large soup bowls for serving. Fifteen won tons usually comprise an individual portion.

Repeat the steps above until you have cooked as many won tons as you need. When you are finished boiling the won tons, do not pour the water out of the large pot; you will need it for cooking the spinach.

While the won tons are boiling, you should begin assembling the rest of the dish.

ASSEMBLING AND SERVING

(4 cups broth or canned soup stock)

Bring the broth to a boil in a saucepan.

(dried shrimps)

Drain the dried shrimp and wash them off carefully, then chop them into tiny pieces, about the size of a match head.

(spinach)

When all the won tons have been boiled, add the spinach to the large pot of boiling water. Let the spinach boil for 1 minute, then remove it from the pot, drain it, and put about 6 leaves in every bowl of won tons.

(broth)
(preserved vegetable
  shreds)
(remaining scallions)
(dried shrimps)
1 *tablespoon soy*
  sauce, per serving
❀ ¼ *teaspoon hot*
  pepper flakes in oil
  (optional), per
  serving

Pour enough of the boiling broth into each bowl to cover the won tons, then add 1 tablespoon each of the preserved vegetable shreds, remaining scallions, dried shrimps, and soy sauce to each bowlful of won ton soup. If you would like a spicier soup, add ¼ teaspoon hot pepper flakes in oil to each portion.

¼ *teaspoon salt per*
  serving, or to taste
  (optional)

Stir the soup gently, taste for salt, and, if necessary, add a little to each bowl. (You will probably only need to add salt if you have made your own soup stock; commercial broths are usually salty enough.)

蘿 蔔 絲 餅

FLAKY TURNIP CAKES (*luobosi bing*)

A visit to downtown Taipei was never complete without a fried turnip cake, bought from a sidewalk vendor who cooked his wares in the open on a charcoal brazier. The filling was steaming and juicy and the flaky crust was coated with sesame seeds, some of which always stuck to my chin. The mess was part of the pleasure; these little pastries are *the* Chinese street food, bought on the run to eat as you go about your errands.

Mrs. Chiang's turnip cakes are even better than those we remember from Taiwan. They are crisper on the outside and less greasy. They aren't hard to make, and can be served as a snack or as the final course in a more elaborate meal, especially since they can be prepared in advance and reheated in the oven. Make a lot; they're irresistible.

PREPARATION

1 small or ½ large turnip
¾ teaspoon salt

Peel the turnip and cut it into very thin slices, then cut it again into shreds, about 1 inch long and ⅛ inch wide, the width of a wooden matchstick; you should get about 1½ cups turnip shreds. Put the shredded turnip in a bowl and sprinkle the salt over it. Mix well and set aside for 15 minutes.

2 cups all-purpose flour
1 teaspoon salt
⅓ cup boiling water
⅓ cup peanut oil

Mix the flour and the salt together, then add the boiling water and peanut oil. As soon as you have blended the liquids into the flour, put the dough on a large, flat surface and knead it with your hands for 2 minutes, then set it aside to sit for a few minutes. (There is so much oil in this dough that you won't need to flour the surface you are working it on. It is a very short dough, one that closely resembles that used for pie crust.)

3 scallions

Clean the scallions, then chop them, both white part and green, into tiny pieces, about the size of a match head.

(turnips)
2 teaspoons soy sauce
2 teaspoons sesame oil

Drain the turnips and squeeze out as much excess moisture as you can with your hands. Add the chopped scallions to the turnips, along with the soy sauce and sesame oil, and mix well.

Salt, if necessary

Taste the turnip mixture for salt, adding more if necessary.

(dough)

Now, back to the dough. Knead it again for another 2 minutes. Then, using your hands, roll it out into a long snake, about 16 inches in length. Divide the roll into 10 pieces, each about the size of a golf ball. Flatten each ball of dough slightly with the palm of your hand, then roll it out with a rolling pin into a rough circle, about 4 inches in diameter.

(turnips)

Place 1 heaping tablespoonful of the turnip mixture in the center of the circle of dough. Bring up all sides of the dough and pinch them together on top to make a little pouch. Then flatten the round turnip cake slightly with the palm of your hand.

Next, take a rolling pin and roll out the filled turnip cake into a circle about 3 inches in diameter. Do this very gently, taking special pains to keep the skin from breaking and the filling from bursting out. Repeat the steps above with the remaining circles of dough.

½ cup sesame seeds
1 egg

Put the sesame seeds on a small flat plate. Beat the egg. Take up one of the turnip cakes and dip it first into the beaten egg and then into the sesame seeds. (This procedure always reminds me of breading a veal cutlet!) Press the sesame seeds into the turnip cake with the palm of your hand so they don't fall off when you fry it.

COOKING

3 tablespoons peanut oil, approximately

Preheat the oven to 400°.

Fill a regular flat frying pan with ¼ inch of oil and heat it over a medium flame.

Put the turnip cakes in the hot oil and fry them for 4 minutes on one side, or until they turn a light gold. Then turn them over and fry them for about 3 minutes more, until the second side is golden. Place the fried turnip cakes on a cookie sheet and put it in the preheated oven. After the turnip cakes have baked for 10 minutes, reduce the heat to 250°. Bake the turnip cakes for another 15 minutes, then serve.

葱 油餅

OILY SCALLION CAKES (*congyou bing*)

Around the corner from our first house in Taipei there was a tiny open-air restaurant, really no more than a covered shed with a few rough tables. In front of the restaurant stood a teen-aged boy who did nothing but make Oily Scallion Cakes all day long. He worked up the dough, kneaded it, sprinkled it with scallions and oil, twisted it into snail-shaped rolls, flattened them, and then fried each individual cake on a primitive iron grill. The sureness and economy of his motions marked him as a true virtuoso. The only thing better than his performance was his cakes—crisp, salty, and delicious.

Mrs. Chiang says nothing can rival the Oily Scallion Cakes her mother made with the fragrant flour from the family's own freshly harvested wheat, but those she made for us with regular American flour are magnificent. They are crisper and more delicious than the Oily Scallion Cakes we recall from Taiwan, and we have found our passion for them is universally shared. When we bring them out at the end of a big Szechwanese banquet our already overfed guests are inspired to eat still more; the pestering of our friends for Mrs. Chiang's recipe induced us to begin this cookbook. And our editor's enthusiasm for Oily Scallion Cakes enabled her to put up with all our subsequent delays.

Since Oily Scallion Cakes were originally a street food, they have no special place in a Szechwanese meal. We serve them either as the final, devastating course of a larger meal or else separately with drinks. They aren't hard to make, and require no special Oriental ingredients. Leftover scallion cakes tend to become soggy; luckily, a few minutes in a moderate oven is all that is needed to resuscitate them.

PREPARATION

3 *cups all-purpose flour*

1 *cup water*

10 *to* 15 *scallions (depending on their size)*

1½ *teaspoons sesame oil, approximately*

Mix the flour and the water together very well; you should get a very stiff dough. Set it aside for at least 30 minutes.

Trim the scallions, then chop them, both white part and green, into very fine pieces, about the size of a match head.

Since the dough for the scallion cakes has to be rolled out, you will need the same kind of a large flat surface that you use for making any other kind of pastry, a large wooden board or tabletop. Prepare the surface on which you are going to roll out the scallion cakes by sprinkling it with the sesame oil. (This serves the same purpose as flour in keeping the dough from sticking.)

Knead the dough for about a minute until it is easy to work with, then separate it into two balls.

Take one ball and roll it out into a rectangle about 8 by 10 inches. (If you are using a rolling pin, make sure to rub it with some sesame oil so that the dough doesn't stick to it. You can also use your hands instead of a rolling pin to press the dough out.)

1 *teaspoon salt*

Sprinkle 1 teaspoonful of the salt over the rectangle of dough. Press the salt into the dough with your fingers.

1½ *tablespoons lard, at room temperature, or peanut oil (if you fear cholesterol)*

(*half the scallions*)

Spread the lard generously over the dough. (Although you can use a knife to spread the lard, it is easier, though less aesthetic, to do it with your fingers.)

Sprinkle half of the chopped scallions over

the rolled-out dough, then roll the dough up like a jelly roll. Pinch the ends of the roll together so the scallions don't fall out, then divide the roll into three sections, twisting the ends of each segment to keep the filling from falling out. Each piece should be roughly the size of a tennis ball.

1 teaspoon salt
1½ tablespoons lard
(remaining scallions)

Using more salt, lard, and the remaining scallions, do the same thing to the other half of the dough.

Just before you are ready to begin cooking the scallion cakes, take one of the balls and gently flatten it out into a circle about 8 inches in diameter. This is the trickiest part of making the scallion cakes, for it is very hard to keep them from breaking open slightly while you are flattening them and letting the scallions escape. (Even Mrs. Chiang has trouble keeping the scallion cakes from bursting while she is pressing them out.) Luckily, it doesn't make too much difference if the cakes split slightly at this point. Make sure that the surface on which you are working is still well oiled.

While the first cake is cooking, you can press out the next. (You can't really flatten them all out in advance, because it is not a good idea to handle them very much before you cook them.)

COOKING

3 tablespoons peanut
oil, approximately

Heat a regular flat frying pan over a moderate flame and fill it with ¼ inch of oil. When the oil is quite hot and has just be-

gun to smoke, put in the first scallion
cake. Let the cake fry for about 3 minutes on each side, until it has turned
golden brown and become quite crisp.
Remove the fried cake from the hot oil
and let it drain on some paper towels.
Fry all the other scallion cakes in the same
way.
Serve each scallion cake cut into 8 wedge-
shaped pieces. (Since the cake is so
crisp, it may be easier to cut with a
cleaver than with a regular knife.)
Note: Although there is plenty of salt inside the scallion cakes, they are especially delicious if you salt them after
they have been fried.

薄 餅

PANCAKES (*baobing*)

Right after the wheat harvest, when there was plenty of fresh, sweet
flour, Mrs. Chiang's mother would often make a *bing* meal, in which
everything was eaten rolled up inside pancakes. Moo Shu Pork, a
popular specialty of America's "mandarin" restaurants, is a *bing* dish.
Szechwan was famous for them, and Mrs. Chiang's mother made dozens of different kinds. Many of the recipes in this cookbook can be
made as pancake fillings: Cucumber, Carrot, and Cellophane Noodle
Salad; Pork, Cucumber, and Cellophane Noodle Salad; Dry-Fried String
Beans; Bean Sprouts; and the filling for Spring Rolls which produces
an extraordinary Szechwanese version of Moo Shu Pork. Almost any
dish consisting of shredded ingredients can be eaten inside a pancake.

The pancakes themselves are easy to make. Mrs. Chiang's are
neither too fragile nor too coarse. You can make them in advance, but,
if you do, keep them covered so they don't dry out. Reheat them in a
steamer or low oven just before serving.

3 cups all-purpose
flour
¾ cup water

Mix the flour and the water together. (Don't hesitate to plunge right into the dough with your hands to get it really well blended.) The dough should be very stiff and dry. Set it aside for at least 30 minutes.

Knead the dough for 2 minutes. Then divide it into three sections. Roll one of the sections into a long snakelike shape and cut it into 8 small pieces, each piece about the size of a walnut. Do the same thing with the other two pieces of dough.

Flour as needed

Prepare a large floured surface for rolling out the dough.

Roll one of the walnut-sized balls of dough into a thin circle, roughly 7 inches in diameter. Roll out a second circle of dough the same size.

Sesame oil

Sprinkle a few drops of sesame oil (¼ teaspoon should be plenty) on the surface of one of the pancakes and cover it with the other pancake.

These pancakes are so thin that it is easier —and quicker—to cook two of them together.

You are now ready to fry the pancakes. (Since it takes a few minutes to cook each pancake, it is easier to roll out each set of pancakes right before you cook them rather than try to prepare them all ahead of time.)

spoon dry yeast
lespoon granula-
d sugar
p lukewarm water
ups all-purpose
lour

lour for kneading

4 scallions

½ teaspoon salt
1 tablespoon lard
(half the scallions)

PREPARATION

Mix the yeast, sugar, and water together in a small bowl. Set it aside for 3 or 4 minutes, until the yeast begins to bubble.

Sift the flour into a large bowl. Slowly pour in the yeast and water mixture and stir it with a wooden spoon until it is thoroughly blended. (You may have to use your hands toward the end.)

Sprinkle some flour over a large wooden surface, set the dough on it, and knead for 5 minutes.

Put the dough back in the bowl, cover it with a barely damp cloth, and set it aside to rise in a warm, draft-free place for 1½ to 2 hours.

After that time, when the dough has just about doubled in bulk, put it back on the floured surface and knead it for another minute.

Put the dough back in the bowl to rise again, this time for only about 30 minutes, until it has again doubled in bulk.

Meanwhile, clean the scallions, and cut off their roots, then chop them, both the white part and about half the green, into tiny pieces, about the size of a match head. Set the chopped scallions aside.

As soon as the dough has risen enough, separate it into two equal parts. Roll out one of the pieces into a large rectangle, roughly 10 by 12 inches.

Sprinkle the salt evenly over the dough and press it in with your hands. Spread the lard over the dough, as if you were

COOKING

1 to 2 teaspoons pea-
nut oil, enough to
coat the bottom of
the pan with a thin
film of oil

Heat the oil in a s
(*not* a wok) over a l
oil is ready for cool
pancake into the pan
about 2 minutes. Then
fry it for another minute
side. Later pancakes will
less time to cook.)

Because they have a tendency
these pancakes do not brov
Fully cooked ones are mainly w
some brownish spots.

Pull the two pancakes apart befc
serve them.

1 tea
1 tal
te
1 c
3 c

花捲

FLOWER ROLLS (*huajuan*)

Mrs. Chiang remembers, "My aunt lived in a nearby market town, and we loved to visit her. On market days the town swarmed with people. Peasants came in from the countryside to sell their extra eggs or vegetables, and men like my father came looking for special cuts of meat or fresh fish. Peddlers came to sell candy or big steamed buns that we ate plain or filled with meat and vegetables. Steamed buns were the staple food in the north of China, but in Szechwan they were eaten for snacks. My mother made them for banquets, to go with Fragrant, Crispy Duck or a Fresh Ham. She twisted her steamed buns into fancy shapes, so they were much more elegant than the ones the street vendors sold. This recipe is for the rolls she made to go with a fresh ham; they are twisted to look like flowers. In elegant restaurants you can get steamed buns in the form of ducks and all manner of flowers, fans, and spirals."

Because they are yeast breads, Flower Rolls take several hours to prepare. They can be made in advance and reheated in a steamer just before serving. Left-over *huajuan* are magnificent deep-fried.

buttering a piece of bread. Finally, sprinkle half of the chopped scallions over the dough, then roll the dough up, jelly-roll fashion, into a long cylinder.

½ teaspoon salt
1 tablespoon lard
(remaining scallions)

Using more salt and lard and the remaining scallions, repeat the steps above with the other piece of dough.

Cut each cylinder of dough crosswise into segments, roughly one inch wide. Then take a chopstick and press it down across the middle of each piece so the inside layers flare out, sort of like a fan. (Make sure that you press the dough hard enough so that the middle of each piece sticks together and the layers don't fall out.)

You should get about 2 dozen of these fan- or flower-shaped rolls.

Put the rolls on a flat plate and set them aside to rise for a final hour before you steam them.

COOKING

Set up your steamer. If you are using a Chinese one, line the bottom with a dish towel or piece of cheesecloth; you will then set the rolls directly on it. If you don't have a Chinese steamer, construct a substitute according to the directions on page 54, and place the rolls on a lightly oiled plate instead of using a piece of cloth.

Fill the bottom of your steamer with water and bring it to a boil over a high flame. Place the *huajuan* in the steamer, cover it, and let the rolls steam for 15 minutes.

Note: You can, if you want, make the *hua-juan* ahead of time and reheat them just before serving by steaming them for a few minutes. They do tend to get hard if they sit around for any length of time.

Leftover *huajuan* are particularly good if they are fried in deep fat until they turn golden. Many restaurants in Taipei served them this way, and they were magnificent—crisp on the outside and soft on the inside.

16 - PICKLES, APPETIZERS, AND GARNISHES

No Szechwanese cookbook would be complete without recipes for some of the delicious tidbits served as appetizers, garnish, or simply for nibbling.

Mrs. Chiang recalls: "We ate a lot of things like pickles, preserved eggs, salted vegetables, boiled nuts, and fermented bean curd. Salted vegetables were sprinkled on congee for breakfast. When my father and his friends sat around the kitchen table playing cards and drinking warm rice wine, they would nibble on nuts, melon seeds, or boiled soybeans. We Chinese never drink anything alcoholic without eating something, and these little snacks were the only thing my father ever tried to cook himself. He wasn't very successful, since he was usually in his cups before he gave it a try."

Pickling and salting meats and vegetables are complicated methods of preserving food that refrigeration has made unnecessary. The recipes that follow provide only a small sampling of easily prepared Szechwan nibbling foods. They can all be made in advance, and serve beautifully as snacks or appetizers.

八角花生米

ANISE BOILED PEANUTS (bajiao huashengmi)

The true test for a chopstick virtuoso is to pick up a boiled peanut with a pair of smooth ivory chopsticks. Many Szechwanese restaurants on Taiwan give you ample opportunity to try your skill by putting tiny plates of boiled peanuts on your table the minute you sit down. Mrs. Chiang's recipe for this traditional hors d'oeuvre uses soy sauce, star anise, and Szechwan peppercorns to produce fragrant, anise-flavored peanuts that are slippery enough to give any chopstick expert a good workout. We serve them as a cold appetizer before a large meal, but they make a good snack at any time. They are also very easy to prepare, and can be cooked in advance and stored for days in the refrigerator.

You must use fresh raw peanuts for this dish. They are available at health food stores as well as at Chinese markets.

COOKING

2 cups raw peanuts

You do not have to remove the dark red skins from the peanuts.

3½ cups water

5 whole star anise, or the equivalent in pieces

4 teaspoons Szechwan peppercorns

3 tablespoons soy sauce

1 teaspoon salt

1 teaspoon sesame oil

Put the peanuts in a medium-sized saucepan and pour the water over them. Add the star anise, Szechwan peppercorns, soy sauce, salt, and sesame oil.

2-inch piece fresh ginger

Do not peel the ginger; just cut it into 3 or 4 chunks and add them to the pot.

Bring the peanuts to a boil, then turn down the flame and let them simmer for about 1 hour and 15 minutes, until they have absorbed most of the cooking liquid.

	Stir them several times while they are cooking.
Salt, if necessary	Taste the peanuts for seasoning after they have cooked for an hour or so (they may need a little more salt), then remove from the heat and refrigerate until ready to serve.

糖酥核桃

SWEET FRIED NUTS *(tianzha hetao)*

"On rainy days we children liked nothing better than to pick nuts from our nut trees and fry them. We would crowd around the biggest wok and toss sugared nuts into the hot oil. As soon as they were brown and crisp we'd fish them out with wire scoops and wait impatiently for them to cool. They were better than candy."

We first encountered fried nuts at an elegant Hunanese restaurant in Taipei, where they were definitely *haute cuisine*, one of the required cold appetizers preceding a banquet. We felt a little inhibited about eating a sweet before dinner, but we quickly got over it; the nuts were too delicious to let our dinner companions have them all.

In America we serve fried nuts in the traditional manner, as an introduction to a multicourse meal; they are delicious for cocktail parties as well, and can be made in advance.

Restaurants on Taiwan made this dish with black walnuts. We haven't found any here, and have substituted pecans instead. They're just as good.

PREPARATION

2 *cups shelled pecan halves*	Put the nuts in a pot or heatproof bowl and cover them with the boiling water. Let soak for 3 minutes.
3 *to 4 cups boiling water, approximately*	
½ *cup granulated sugar*	Put the sugar on a flat plate.
1 *teaspoon water,*	Drain the nuts and put them on the plate

approximately
(optional)

with the sugar. Stir them very thoroughly, until all the nuts are completely coated with the sugar, which should be practically dissolved. (You may want to add a little extra water if you find the sugar not sticking to the nuts enough.)

Transfer the sugared nuts to a dry plate and set them aside to dry overnight or, preferably, for 24 hours.

COOKING

3 cups peanut or other
cooking oil,
approximately
(nuts)

Heat the oil in a wok or regular saucepan. When it is hot enough, add the sugared nuts and fry them until they turn a rich, golden brown and their sugar coating is crisp and candylike; this should take about 8 to 10 minutes. Don't burn the nuts, or let them turn very dark, but make sure the sugar melts.

Remove the nuts from the oil with a slotted spoon. Spread them out on a plate to dry and cool off. Before you serve them, break them into individual nuts.

糖醋豆子

SOYBEANS (*tangcu douz*)

Whenever Mrs. Chiang's father invited a group of cronies or relatives over, her mother would make up a large batch of soybeans to serve with the wine. These crunchy, spicy beans are the traditional accompaniment of a Szechwanese drinking session, just as salted peanuts are in America. Mrs. Chiang's soybeans are bathed in sauce and can't be eaten with the fingers, which makes them poor candidates for a cocktail party. They are, however, the perfect introduction to a multi-course Chinese meal, and we often place a few bowls full on the table for nibbling before the serious eating begins. These beans are easy to prepare, and will keep for days in the refrigerator.

PREPARATION

6 *cloves garlic*

Smash the garlic cloves with the side of your cleaver, but don't peel them. Put them in a large bowl.

½-*inch piece fresh
ginger*

Peel the ginger, then chop it coarsely, into pieces the size of grains of uncooked rice. Put them in the bowl with the garlic.

3 *scallions*

Clean the scallions, then chop them, both the white part and about half of the green, into pieces about the same size as the ginger. Put the chopped scallions into the bowl.

2 *teaspoons
granulated sugar*
1 *teaspoon salt*
1 *teaspoon sesame oil*
1 *tablespoon rice wine
vinegar*
¼ *cup soy sauce*
❀ 1 *to 2 teaspoons hot
pepper flakes in oil
(optional)*
⅔ *cup water*

Then add the sugar, salt, sesame oil, vinegar, soy sauce, optional hot pepper flakes in oil, and water to the bowl. Mix thoroughly and set aside.

1½ *cups dried
soybeans*

Rinse the soybeans well.

COOKING

(soybeans)

Heat your wok or pan over a medium flame for about 15 seconds, then add the soybeans directly to the dry pan.

Cook them carefully for 10 minutes, stirring them occasionally to keep them from sticking to the pan or burning. Then, when they are slightly brown and no longer inedibly hard but still crunchy, remove them from the fire.

(sauce) Quickly dump them in the bowl of sauce. The hot soybeans will absorb the liquid, and in about 5 minutes they will be ready to eat.

Note: You can serve the soybeans right away or keep them for days in a covered container in the refrigerator. They are best eaten at room temperature.

泡 菜

PICKLED VEGETABLES (*paocai*)

"My mother knew dozens of ways to salt, dry, or pickle the fresh vegetables we grew," recalls Mrs. Chiang. "In the summer she festooned our house with strings of drying cabbages and turnips; whatever other vegetables we couldn't eat fresh were laid down in big earthenware jars with brine and aromatic spices. In the winter the jars would be opened and we ate pickled vegetables every day. For breakfast we had rice or congee [rice gruel] sprinkled with dried, pickled, or salted vegetables, and pickled vegetables were often served at lunch and dinner as well. We ate pickles for snacks, and my mother added them to some dishes, like soups, for pungent flavoring."

This recipe produces the most easily made as well as the most common Szechwanese pickled vegetable. Every traditional Szechwanese restaurant in Taiwan had huge bowls of the stuff, from which the waiters would fill little plates to bring to your table when they came for your order. As Szechwanese pickles go, these are mild. Western pickle connoisseurs would probably call them "half-sour." They consist of a variety of such vegetables as cabbage, carrots, cucumbers, turnips, and string beans in a brine containing vinegar, wine, Szechwan peppercorns, and red peppers. Once you have prepared the brine and made a batch of pickles, you can continue to use the brine over and over again, adding new vegetables to replace the ones you eat. Mrs. Chiang serves these pickles either as an appetizer or as a regular vegetable dish. Either way they are a convenient method for stretching a menu without making extra work for yourself.

For this recipe, you will need a large, widemouthed jar or crock with a lid. The one we use for making pickles holds about 2 quarts of ingredients, but you can use a larger one if you want. Mrs. Chiang remembers that, when she was a child, her mother used to put up pickles in vats that were considerably larger than she was.

PREPARATION

3-inch piece fresh ginger

Don't peel the ginger. Cut it lengthwise into slices about ¼ inch thick. Put the ginger slices into your pickling jar.

❀ *10 dried red peppers*
1½ tablespoons Szechwan peppercorns
1½ tablespoons rice wine vinegar
2 tablespoons Chinese rice wine or cooking sherry
1 tablespoon granulated sugar
2 tablespoons salt
3 cups water

Break five of the dried red peppers in half and add them and the whole red peppers to the jar, along with the Szechwan peppercorns, vinegar, wine, sugar, salt, and water. Stir this mixture very well, until most of the salt and sugar is dissolved.

Now you are ready to add whatever vegetables you want to pickle. Cabbage, carrots, and cucumbers are classic, but turnips, string beans, and Chinese cabbage are equally good. (In fact, according to Mrs. Chiang, almost any vegetable can be pickled successfully, with the exception of eggplant, which turns black and ruins all the other pickles.) You can use as much or as little of any vegetable you like. No rules apply and you can experiment with various combinations of colors and textures.

Cabbage, regular or Chinese

If you are going to use cabbage or Chinese cabbage, discard the outer leaves and cut the inner ones into pieces that are about 2 inches square. Half a small head of round cabbage should give you enough for 2 quarts of pickles, if you are planning to use other vegetables as well.

Carrots

Prepare carrots by peeling them and cutting them crosswise into segments about 3 inches long. Then cut each piece lengthwise into slices about ¼ inch thick.

Turnips

Other root vegetables, like turnips, should also be peeled and sliced, though the slices should be slightly thicker.

Cucumbers

Cucumbers don't have to be peeled (unless, of course, they've been waxed); their dark green skins provide a nice touch of color. They do, however, have to be seeded. Cut the cucumbers in half lengthwise and scoop out all the soft, seedy part in the middle. Slice the firm outer meat into strips about 2 inches long and ½ inch wide.

String beans

Remove the tips from the string beans and, if they are long, break them in half.

1 tablespoon salt

Fill your jar up to the top with the vegetables that you have prepared. Sprinkle the additional salt over the top layer of vegetables, then close the jar tightly and let it sit at room temperature for 2 or 3 days.

After a few days, put the jar in the refrigerator, where it will keep indefinitely.

Although the first batch of vegetables has to begin pickling at room temperature, later ones don't and you can continually replenish your pickle supply merely by adding new vegetables to the jar of brine.

1 tablespoon Chinese rice wine or cooking sherry
1 teaspoon salt
½ teaspoon granulated sugar

Whenever you add any substantial amount of new ingredients to the pickle jar, add some more wine, salt and sugar as well, to revivify the brine. It improves with age, and later batches of pickles tend to be tastier than the initial ones.

17 - DESSERTS

Although the children sometimes made their own candies and sweet fried nuts, Mrs. Chiang's mother cooked very few sweets herself. Desserts were not her forte, nor are they the strong point of any Chinese cook. Chinese desserts do not appeal to us. Part of the reason may be that Chinese cooking has never used chocolate or dairy products, and has no tradition of fine baking. Fruit was the dessert of Mrs. Chiang's childhood; almost every kind of fruit flourishes in the varied Szechwan climate. The family grew melons and cultivated fruit trees. They produced peaches, oranges, pomelos (a yellow fruit halfway between an orange and a grapefruit), pomegranates, grapes, and Chinese fruits like the green, nectarinelike *lis*, little white *pibas*, and loquats, used as cough medicine. A big plate of cubed watermelon was welcome fare on a hot summer evening or after a fiery dinner.

Even on Taiwan, we rarely encountered any interesting sweet dishes. Our favorite was a concoction of bite-sized pieces of apple coated with batter, deep-fried, and covered with a thick syrup that hardened into candy when you dipped them into a bowl of cold water. The gossamer-like threads of candy that form as each piece of syrup-covered fruit is lifted off the plate give the dish its name—*basi pingguo,* or, literally, "pulled silk apples." Unfortunately, we can't include a recipe for it. It is a Pekingese dish and Mrs. Chiang's mother never made it. It was part of the curriculum at the cooking school I attended during our first stay on Taiwan, but, when it came time to prepare the crucial syrup, the teacher turned her back to the class and wouldn't let us watch her make it. She was a traditional Chinese cook, and believed in guarding her professional secrets.

We have, however, included one spectacular recipe for a spectacular dessert—Eight Treasure Rice, or *babaofan.* Mrs. Chiang's is the best one I've ever tasted. It's so rich and complicated we don't normally serve it at the end of a dinner party; we prefer fruit, which is refreshing, easy, and completely authentic.

八 寶 飯

EIGHT TREASURE RICE (*babaofan*)

Probably the most famous Chinese dessert of all is a *babaofan,* or Eight Treasure Rice. It is a sticky, sweet pudding made of glutinous rice, sweet bean paste, with such other "treasures" as dried red dates and sweet potatoes arranged in decorative patterns on top of the rice. Mrs. Chiang's version of this famous dish is unusual because it contains fresh bacon (a *must* in the recipe, even though this super-fatty cut of meat is difficult to obtain outside of Chinese grocery stores; a leaner cut won't do). Putting pork into the pudding sounds strange, but it works. The fatty meat goes beautifully with the sticky rice and sweet bean paste. The result is an obscenely rich and heavy concoction, oozing with lard. It illustrates with unctuous clarity why Chinese gourmets prize fat—it's marvelous.

Such a heavy dose of cholesterol is not for daily consumption. Because a *babaofan* takes a long time to prepare and an even longer time to recover from, it was served only on the most festive occasions in rural Szechwan where it was, in fact, the equivalent of a wedding cake. Mrs. Chiang's exceptional Eight Treasure Rice became famous on Taiwan, and her talents were in great demand for weddings.

Though you don't need to get married to enjoy this magnificent pudding, it really is too rich to treat as a regular dessert. Nor does it tempt all palates. Few Americans find the idea of eating pure pork fat, even sweetened pure pork fat, immediately appealing. But it is an easily acquired taste, and it would be a good idea to experiment with this pudding if only to experience one of the greatest achievements of Chinese gastronomy. Although its preparation does take a long time, none of the individual steps required are difficult. The preparation will require at least 6 hours from start to finish. It will not, however, be 6 hours of concentrated labor, since much of the time is spent soaking, simmering, and steaming.

PREPARATION

1½ cups dried Chinese red beans
2 cups water, approximately

Put the beans in a bowl, cover them with water, and let them soak for at least 1 hour. Then rinse them thoroughly.

4 cups water

Put the beans in a medium saucepan, cover them with the 4 cups water, and bring them to a boil over a high flame. Let them cook for about 10 minutes before you reduce the flame, then cover the pan and let the beans simmer for 2 hours.

1 cup glutinous rice
2 cups water, approximately

While the beans are cooking, put the glutinous rice in a bowl and cover it with water. Set it aside to soak for at least 1 hour.

(beans)

After the beans have simmered for 2 hours and are nice and soft, remove them from the heat and, without draining them, let them cool off. Then puree them, liquid and all. (Mrs. Chiang discovered that the easiest way to do this using Western implements was to force the beans through a strainer with a wooden spoon.) The pureed beans will probably be rather runny.

1½ tablespoons lard (beans)
½ cup granulated sugar

Heat the lard in a flat frying pan over a medium flame. When the lard is melted, add the pureed beans and the sugar. Cook, stirring constantly, and if the beans are particularly watery, turn up the flame while you cook them. When they reach the consistency of mashed potatoes, remove them from the heat and let them cool off.

2 tablespoons peanut oil
1½ tablespoons granulated sugar

Heat the peanut oil in a wok or flat frying pan over a medium flame for about 15 seconds, then add the sugar and stir it continuously until it melts and turns dark brown. Be very careful that it doesn't turn too dark a brown and burn.

1½ pounds fresh bacon

Cut the fresh bacon into 3 large chunks. Add these to the caramelized sugar in the pan and fry them gently for 4 or 5 minutes. Turn the meat often, so it gets brown and slightly caramelized on all sides. Remove from the pan and let cool.

20 dried red dates
2 cups water, approximately

While you are waiting for the pork to cool off enough for you to handle, wash the dates well under cold running water, then put them in a small bowl and cover them with water. Let soak for at least 20 minutes.

(meat)

When the meat is cool enough to handle, slice it in the following way:

First, cut the meat across the grain into a piece about ⅛ inch thick, but do not cut the meat completely through. Then cut a second slice of the same thickness, but this time cut all the way through the meat. This will give you a slice of meat that you can open like a book. Cut all the meat into the same kind of slices.

(sweet bean paste)

Stuff the cavity of each piece of meat with

about 1 tablespoonful of the sweet bean paste.

1 large sweet potato

Peel the sweet potato and cut it into 1 inch cubes; you should get about 2 cups of cubed sweet potato.

You are now ready to assemble the dish. Before you begin, it is a good idea to assemble your steamer. You will have to steam the Eight Treasure Rice in a large round bowl and you may find that such a bowl will not fit into a regular Chinese steamer. You may be able to devise one out of a wok and its top, or, if necessary, you can always make a serviceable one out of a large pot. (See page 54 for more detailed instructions on constructing a steamer.)

(glutinous rice)
(dates)
(filled meat slices)

Drain the glutinous rice and the dates. Arrange the bean paste-filled meat slices in a regular pattern around the sides and bottom of the bowl. The meat slices should be slightly overlapping.

(dates)

Arrange the dates decoratively in the spaces between the meat slices.

(sweet potatoes)

Cover the meat with the sweet potato cubes.

(glutinous rice)
1 cup granulated sugar

Finally, heap the glutinous rice on top of everything and sprinkle the sugar evenly over the rice.

COOKING

Make sure that there are several inches of water in the bottom of your steamer. Place the bowl of Eight Treasure Rice on a rack over the water, then turn the heat to moderate.

When the water is boiling, cover the

steamer and steam for 2 or 3 hours, or until the rice is completely cooked, checking the steamer repeatedly to make sure there is enough water in the bottom and adding more if necessary.

¼ *cup water, approximately*

If the rice seems to be drying out slightly while it is steaming, sprinkle several tablespoons of water over it; repeat this process whenever you feel it is necessary.

SERVING

When the rice is thoroughly cooked, moist, and sticky, remove the bowl from the steamer. Let it cool enough to handle and then unmold it by inverting the bowl gently over a large, decorative platter. Since the inside of the bowl should be swimming in fresh pork fat, you shouldn't have any trouble unmolding the rice. If it doesn't slip right out, loosen the rice gently from the sides of the bowl with a knife.

You can eat the Eight Treasure Rice while it is still hot or you can wait until it cools down to room temperature. Don't serve it cold; the liquid fat that is such a special feature of this dish is not very appetizing when it congeals.

INDEX